LEAVING MARXISM

Leaving Marxism

STUDIES IN THE DISSOLUTION
OF AN IDEOLOGY

Stanley Pierson

STANFORD UNIVERSITY PRESS

STANFORD, CALIFORNIA   2001

Stanford University Press
Stanford, California
© 2001 by the Board of Trustees of the
Leland Stanford Junior University
Printed in the United States of America

Library of Congress Cataloging-in-Publication Data

Pierson, Stanley.
    Leaving Marxism: studies in the dissolution of an ideology / Stanley
Pierson.
        p.   cm.
    Includes bibliographical references and index.
    ISBN 0-8047-4404-1 (alk. paper)
        1. Communism and intellectuals—Case studies.   2. Man, Hendrik
de, 1885–1953.   3. Horkheimer, Max, 1895–1973.   4. Kolakowski,
Leszek.   I. Title.

HX528.P54   2001
335.4'092'2—dc21   2001049128

This book is printed on acid-free, archival-quality paper.

Original printing 2001

Last figure below indicates year of this printing:
10   09   08   07   06   05   04   03   02   01

Typeset at Stanford University Press in 10/13 Galliard

For Mike, Kit, and Paul and their
wonderfully spirited wives,
Caroline, Rachel, and Tracey

Acknowledgments

This book completes a long intellectual journey. It began in the struggles of my working-class family during the Great Depression. My interest in socialism, as an alternative social system, grew during World War II when, as a combat infantryman, I witnessed the devastation in Europe at first hand. And so, four books — examinations of the efforts of European intellectuals and politicians to advance the socialist cause. Now the socialist challenge to the dominant institutions of Europe may have ended. It is too soon to say. But the socialist adventure, particularly in its Marxist form, is an essential part of the story of Europe in the twentieth century.

In the course of my study I have incurred many debts. Most of these have been acknowledged in the earlier books. Here I want to thank the institutions that have made my journey possible, especially the libraries at Harvard, Stanford, the University of California, and the University of Oregon. It is to the latter that I owe most, for the University of Oregon has been my academic home, first as an undergraduate and then as a faculty member.

Special thanks to Paul Robinson for a generous and helpful reading of an earlier version of the manuscript; to Cathie Filip for her skill in moving the manuscript onto a computer; to a weekly luncheon group for continuing stimulation. I owe more to Randy McGowan, Dick Stein, Dan Pope, Julie Hessler, Alex Dracobly, David Luebke, and John McCole than they might imagine. Thanks as well to Ray Birn for our frequent talks.

I am pleased to dedicate this book to our three sons and to the women who share their lives. My greatest debt is to my wife, Joan, not only for her critical reading of the manuscript, but for her wisdom in the matters that make scholarship possible. For better or for worse she is very much a part of this book.

Contents

LEAVING MARXISM

Introduction

Karl Marx was a creature of the bourgeois world he would seek to destroy. From that world he drew his view of the human condition, centered on the value of work. And like a number of his contemporaries he drew from his bourgeois background an exhilarating sense of new human possibilities. Fed by the Enlightenment faith in reason and by romantic notions of the creative personality, this new sense found expression in the utopian projects planted across the European landscape during the 1830s and 1840s.

In his student years Marx fixed on the mythical figure of Prometheus, "the most eminent saint and martyr," as the symbol for his hope that human beings were on the threshold of radically new ways of living.[1] The Greek hero's defiance of the ancient gods provided a model for those who were casting off the old authorities and proclaiming the absolute freedom and "absolute autonomy" of the individual.[2] Prometheus became, for Marx, a "guidepost for mankind" and a "prefiguration of the proletariat."[3]

Marx's early writings envisioned a new man, self-creating and shaper of the world around him through his labor. In the light of this ideal, existing human beings could only be seen as alienated, unable to fulfill their potentialities. Here Marx challenged the Judeo-Christian understanding of human self-division and limitation, expressed in the myth of the fall. What in the religious tradition was viewed as the inescapable human condition Marx saw as historically contingent and hence subject to human control and correction.

To Marx's vision of dealienated human beings, living and working in harmony with each other, one can trace what has been variously described as the mythic, the messianic, or the utopian component in the Marxist ideology.[4] The remarkable power of that ideology to move men and women derived from its promise of a radical transformation of human existence. No wonder Marxism has often been likened to a religious movement.[5]

The radical humanism in Marx's earliest writings faded from view as he developed his analysis of capitalism and his interpretation of history. And the proletariat became the bearer of the new human possibilities promised in the rise of the bourgeoisie and then thwarted, according to Marx, by its own economic and social institutions. In time Friedrich Engels, influenced by the materialistic and deterministic outlook of contemporary science, gave Marxism its modern orthodox form.

When, in the closing decades of the nineteenth century, Marxism began to attract a following, its recruits included idealistic young men and women from the middle classes. Like Marx himself, they drew from their bourgeois backgrounds ethical and cultural aspirations that found little scope in the world of their parents. And after joining the working-class movements the bourgeois recruits dedicated themselves to the task of making the movements worthy vehicles for the Marxist vision.

The present study grows out of my long-term interest in the efforts of Marxist intellectuals to guide the workers into a socialist society. The previous studies, dealing with the British and German movements, were, in large part, stories of political failure.[6] For the working classes in the two societies tended, in the end, to resist ideological appeals in favor of the material gains offered by representative political systems.

What concerns me here is the other side of that external failure—the internal dissolution of the Marxist ideology in the lives of those who were its strongest advocates. Signs of the dissolution were evident even before World War I. My opening essay explores the beginnings of the breakup of the ideology by examining the curious appeal of Friedrich Nietzsche to intellectuals in each of the main European movements around the turn of the century. As they lost confidence in the liberating role of the proletariat, these intellectuals looked to Nietzsche's idea of the superman as a substitute agent of historical redemption.

The opening essay also offers a preview of several of the main themes in the study. For the intellectuals who turned to Nietzsche were confronting dilemmas that would face their Marxist successors in the years after World War I. They struggled, in particular, with the deficiencies—ethical, psychological, and sociological—that they discovered in the orthodox form of Marxism. They were responding as well to the failure of the proletariat to develop the revolutionary consciousness forecast by Marx. In dealing with these dilemmas the prewar Marxist intellectuals also attempted to reconcile their aspirations, essentially bourgeois, with the realities of working-class development.

The main part of this study explores the process of dissolution in the lives of three intellectuals. Each of the figures I study brought to the Marxist cause a critical and independent spirit. Each set out to make the Marxist ideology fit his private convictions as well as his perceptions of a changing world. Following the collapse of his Marxist faith, each went on to develop alternative meanings—personal, social, and historical—out of his experience of disenchantment.

Henri De Man (1885–1953) was the most adventuresome of the three intellectuals. Not only did he move most easily across the national boundaries in European socialism, but he expressed most clearly the bourgeois sensibility that the intellectuals brought to the movement. His break with Marxism, evident in his pioneering study of its orthodox form, *The Psychology of Socialism*, led to an attempt to reconstruct socialism on new, mainly ethical, foundations. He also set out, amid the economic difficulties of his native Belgium, to apply his conception of socialism in the realm of practical politics. The frustrations resulting from this effort, which moved him to collaborate briefly with the German Nazis, found expression at the end of his life in a remarkable confession of ideological disenchantment.

The intellectual journey of Max Horkheimer (1895–1973) was shaped in large part by the Nazi defeat of the Marxist cause in Germany. Driven into exile, he, together with a remarkable group of expatriate intellectuals, attempted to reconstruct a Marxism more relevant to the economic, political, and cultural changes taking place in Europe. The effort served, however, to convince him of the inadequacies of Marxism and, indeed, its complicity in a development that was leading inexorably toward authoritarian systems in all Western societies. Horkheimer's post-Marxist reflections present another version of ideological disenchantment.

Leszek Kolakowski (1927–) encountered Marxism in the institutional form that Stalin had imposed on his native Poland. And while he shared, as a young philosopher, the dream of social transformation still present in the ideology, he was soon forced to confront the ways in which the dream had been translated into a new form of tyranny and exploitation. Following an abortive effort to recover the humanistic values in Marxism, long buried in its orthodox version, Kolakowski reconsidered the sources of those values in the Western tradition. He also undertook a systematic inquiry into the origins, the development, and the perverse uses of Marxism. His three-volume study of Marxism constituted an epitaph for the ideology.

The three intellectuals traveled different roads. They faced different challenges in their efforts to advance the Marxist cause. And they drew different lessons from their journeys. Together they illuminate the process through which Marxism lost its hold on European life in the twentieth century.

PART I

Anticipations

CHAPTER I

The Nietzschean Presence in the European Socialist Movements

I

Writing in 1900, a young socialist intellectual in Germany, Ernst Gystrow, declared that Nietzsche "is our prophet even though he didn't know it."[1] It was a strange statement for a socialist to make. For in Germany, as in much of Europe at the turn of the century, the socialist cause was dominated by a Marxism that seemed to have little in common with the philosophy of Nietzsche. While the Marxists explained the social conflicts of the period in terms of a capitalist system caught up in insoluble contradictions, Nietzsche's diagnosis centered on a profound cultural crisis resulting from the exhaustion of the religious tradition. Marxists looked to the proletariat as the agent of social regeneration; Nietzsche's disciples envisioned the emergence of *Übermenschen,* heroic individuals who would create new values and political forms capable of rescuing European societies from nihilism and social chaos. The two perspectives were, on the surface at least, poles apart. And yet, to explore Nietzsche's attraction for young Marxist intellectuals in the 1890s and beyond is to lay bare dilemmas within not only the German movement but also the wider development of European Marxism.[2] For the intellectuals were responding to problems within Marxism that would continue to trouble its most important theorists in the twentieth century and help to explain its ultimate failure to maintain its hold on European intellectual life.

It is not surprising that the difficulties presented by Marxist theory and the resort to Nietzschean solutions should have been most evident in Germany. Not only was the influence of the two thinkers strongest in their homeland, but in Germany Marxism had found, in the Social Democratic Party, its most powerful political organization. By 1890, moreover, the Marxist ideology in Germany had taken on the orthodox form it would maintain for most of its European adherents up until World War I and after. Formulated by Engels, and represented in the German Social Democratic Party by Karl Kautsky, orthodox Marxism was based on a strict economic determinism. Social relationships, political institutions, and cultural life were shaped decisively by the modes of production. Capitalism was moving inexorably, through the deepening conflicts between the modes and the relations of production, toward a social upheaval out of which the proletariat would create a radically new kind of society.

In their efforts to apply Marxism to conditions in Germany, however, the Social Democrats soon faced dilemmas that divided their followers. The conflict became acute in 1890 when the legal disabilities imposed by Bismarck were removed and the party entered a new stage in its development. Although the party's Erfurt conference of that year established Marxism as its official ideology, its parliamentary leaders soon softened its revolutionary rhetoric in favor of a broader appeal to the immediate interests of the working class. The contradiction between the revolutionary goals of Marxism and its increasingly pragmatic course generated sharp protests within the party.

The protests came mainly from a group of young intellectuals. Their outlook clashed sharply with that of the Social Democratic leaders. To explore the social background of the dissenters as well as the moral and cultural aspirations they carried into the party is to encounter a sensibility that would continue to collide with the orthodox Marxist doctrines.

The dissenting Marxist intellectuals came, with few exceptions, out of the German bourgeois world. It was a highly differentiated social world, encompassing an upper-middle class of affluent propertied groups, and reaching down through the professions to a lower-middle class made up of artisans, shopkeepers, and small farmers that was being augmented during the second half of the nineteenth century by a new *mittelstand* composed of white-collar workers.[3] The lower-middle class contributed disproportionately to the group of young intellectuals who made their way into the socialist movement. They had grown up in provincial towns and cities during the sixties and seventies and were exposed most fully to the dislocations as well as the opportunities resulting from rapid industrialization in Germany.[4] While customary paths of livelihood had been closed off, other avenues were opening. Many of the sons of lower-middle-class families were being sent to the universities, which were undergoing rapid expansion in these years, to prepare for careers in the professions—law, teaching, medicine, the clergy, or the civil service. By the late 1880s, however, candidates for those positions exceeded the places available.[5] No wonder there was growing frustration and anger among those who had hoped to enter one of the professions. Some turned to journalism or to creative writing, others found themselves in jobs that fell far beneath their expectations; they constituted, to use the terms widely employed by social observers of the time, an "intellectual proletariat."

These young men were especially sensitive to the deepening cultural and spiritual uncertainties of the age. Raised for the most part in pious homes, they had, as university students, entered into the German cultural inheritance summed up in the concept of *Bildung*: the forming, deepening, and perfecting of one's own personality.[6] At the same time they confronted the challenge that scientific ideas presented to both the religious and humanistic traditions. Along with their strong sense of social estrangement, the intellectual proletarians were often struggling with existential questions.

By the late 1880s Berlin had become the main gathering place for the intellectual proletarians. They were drawn to the German capital and its increasingly vital cultural life, some to continue their educations, others to work as journalists. They discovered, in the discussion circles that soon sprang up, mutual stimulation and support.[7] It was in Berlin that the new Naturalist movement in German literature found its most vigorous expression. The fiction of the Naturalists, frequently autobiographical, often dealt with the vicissitudes of educated young men who were adrift in a world that had ceased to provide satisfactory institutional ties or moral guidelines. To understand this troubled sensibility, and the competing appeals of Marx and Nietzsche, we can turn to one of the most influential of the Naturalistic novels in these years, Hermann Conradi's *Adam Mensch*, published in 1888. It ran, so a writer in the Social Democratic paper, *Neue Zeit*, observed, "like a gospel" among those circles from which the party drew its educated recruits.[8]

Conradi's novel described the psychological and social condition of the "proletarians of the spirit."[9] His leading character, Adam Mensch, after gaining a doctorate in philology, had failed to "find a sphere within which ... I can work."[10] He was disgusted with the monotonous lives of the lower middle class—"the same duties, the same concerns, the same words, the same ideas." Even to participate in ordinary social life, to "speak the jargon of the day," reinforced his sense of estrangement.[11] Unable to connect in any meaningful way with the outer world, or what he called the "Not I," his eyes remained focused "too much on the inner life."[12]

The introspective bent of "Adam Mensch" only demonstrated, however, that his social alienation was accompanied by the loss of a stable sense of self. His inner consciousness was a battlefield of conflicting values and impulses. He confessed to a feeling of extreme fragmentation, of the presence of "a thousand small separate interests."[13] They included mystical and metaphysical yearnings along with strong aesthetic aspirations. But his sense of "unused forces" was overwhelmed at times by a perception of the darker aspects of life, indeed, by the lure of Thanatos and thoughts of suicide. And while many of the traditional religious and moral sentiments remained, they were countered by the thought that all of "our ideas are illusions."[14] He was, in fact, morbidly intellectual; the rationalism developed by nineteenth-century science deprived him of any confidence in the significance of his will or his capacity to act.

Adam Mensch yearned, however, to escape from the condition in which he found himself. He spoke of the need for a "new Bible," or a modern New Testament, to provide guidance in a world that had lost its old moorings.[15] Convinced that he lived between two worlds, that he was an *Übergangsmensch*, a man of transition, he looked for signs that a new way of life was being born. He acknowledged his "messianic disposition."[16] At times he saw the working class as the hope of the future. He was attracted to the "great Marx" and considered the possibility of becoming a Social Democratic leader.[17] But he concluded that the working-class movement would produce at best people who were "healthy and sober" and yet narrow minded and incapable of great passion. In looking beyond the "great convulsions" that lay ahead, he turned to Nietzsche. The influence of Nietzsche pervades the novel. The future, "Adam Mensch" declared at one point, would belong to the few who, like himself, had been emptied of the old values, who could transcend the Christian or Semitic moral code, with its disgusting concealments and repressions, and undergo the "spiritual deepening" necessary for a "freer, clearer, more objective set of values."[18] We are, "Adam Mensch" declared, "the aristocrats of the future."

For Conradi, the contemporary cultural and spiritual crisis was comparable to that during the breakup of the Roman empire and the emergence of Christianity. Hence his concept of the Übergangsmensch, the "candidate for the future," who would be capable of representing the "still, un-differentiated, unintellectual will" hidden in the present.[19] A few months before his death at the age of twenty-eight in the spring of 1890, Conradi claimed that he embodied "what the modern really means"—that he was a "pedagogue for the future."[20]

To this belief that one historical era was ending and a new one was beginning both Nietzsche and Marx appealed. Indeed, despite their different diagnoses of European social and cultural development, the two thinkers had much in common. The thought of both was rooted in the Enlightenment; they carried forward its rationalistic critique of traditional beliefs and its naturalistic view of the human condition.[21] Both thinkers, moreover, owed much to the romantic outlook, renewing its Promethean bent and its emphasis on human freedom and creativity.[22] In their reinterpretations of the human condition Marx and Nietzsche both offered secular versions of the older "theological model," according to which humanity had fallen out of a state of initial harmony and embarked on a historical journey, characterized by personal and social discord but moving toward higher forms of integration.[23] While they viewed the human journey very differently, Marx and Nietzsche provided answers to the question that troubled many young intellectuals in Germany, and Europe in general, during the closing years of the century—what gives meaning to life in a post-Christian world?

For a number of the intellectual proletarians in Germany in those years, the Marxism of the Social Democratic Party offered new meaning and, indeed, the promise of a transformed world. Hence their violent reaction in 1890 when the party, having been freed of its political disabilities, began to soften its revolutionary claims in order to reach a wider electorate.[24]

This was the background for the *Jungen* rebellion, the challenge that a group of the young Marxist intellectuals presented to the party's leadership during 1890 and 1891.[25] The individual who initiated their protest, Bruno Wille, had become a leader in those circles in Berlin where young intellectuals—journalists, students, creative writers, and social activists—came together. His Marxism was little more than a veneer for aspirations that were ethical, religious, and aesthetic.[26] But he accepted Marx's claim that the working class would regenerate society and culture and inaugurate a radically new way of life. He was dismayed, therefore, at the seeming abandonment by the Social Democratic politicians of the Marxist vision of social transformation in favor of electoral policies that, through an appeal to the immediate interests of the workers, would simply reinforce existing attitudes and values. A number of the young Marxist intellectuals quickly rallied behind Wille on behalf of the imperiled Marxist vision.

Party policy was not the only threat, in the eyes of the young Marxist intellectuals, to socialist goals in the summer of 1890. Several had begun to question the adequacy of Marxist theory, particularly the doctrine of economic determinism. It collided directly with their own heightened sense of activism. Thus one of the ablest of the party's young journalists, Paul Ernst, contended that economic determinism encouraged a passive outlook and failed to account for the actual psychology of the Social Democrats.[27] It denied, for example, the significance of fantasy and its capacity to generate enthusiasm.

Similar doubts about economic determinism were raised by two young Marxists in Königsberg, Conrad Schmidt and Joseph Bloch. They expressed their doubts in separate letters to Engels in the summer of 1890. Schmidt had been persuaded, as he wrote Engels, by Paul Barth's study of the materialist conception of history and his claim that "the economic does not determine the political in a one sided way but that the political also determines the economic."[28] Bloch's skepticism was evident in the question he put to Engels: could "economic conditions overall, directly, alone and completely independent of persons, unalterably and irrevocably work as natural laws?"[29] Nor did Engels's well-known concessions to the play of noneconomic forces satisfy Ernst, Schmidt, or Bloch. In time each would break with orthodox Marxism.

The Jungen challenge was soon defeated by the Social Democratic leadership. When, before a large, mainly working-class audience in Berlin late in August 1890, Wille debated the issues with the party chairman, August Bebel, he found scant support.[30] What is of interest here, however, was Wille's turn to Nietzsche to rescue the hope for radical change that he could no longer find in the Social Democrats. He had concluded that the workers were, in terms he drew from Nietzsche, being left in a "herd-like condition" by their leaders. They were losing sight of the new individuality that was, for the educated recruits, a central feature of the Marxist promise.[31]

Following the defeat of the Jungen, several of the young intellectuals concluded that the Marxist vision of a radically new way of life could be realized only by a new party. In drawing up a Manifesto for an "Independent" socialist party, they again emphasized their commitment to "individuality."[32] "We oppositional socialists," they declared, "place great value on the individuality of the worker. ... We want him to form his own opinions. ... The more the individuality of the worker develops ... the more revolutionary he is." No wonder Nietzschean ideas assumed a prominent place in the outlook of those who had broken with the Social Democrats. In the philosopher's idea of the Übermensch they could see the fulfillment of the bourgeois ideal of the autonomous personality as well as the ethical and aesthetic interests that had moved them to adopt Marxism.

The dissenting intellectuals had hoped to make the Social Democratic Party, and its working-class following, a vehicle for their own bourgeois values. But their central value of individuality had little relevance to the immediate interests and desires of the workers. Through their selective reading of Marxism, the intellectuals had, in fact, cut themselves off from the proletariat. As Ernst concluded, the educated recruits discovered that they were still "part of another class."[33]

The Jungen episode confirmed the orthodox Marxist view that Nietzsche was an apologist for capitalism. Within the Social Democratic Party, Franz Mehring developed this view. Even before joining the party in 1891 and assuming the task of writing leaders for the *Neue Zeit*, he had described Nietzsche as the philosophical spokesman for the later state of capitalism.[34] The vision of Übermenschen, according to Mehring, sanctioned the efforts of the new capitalists to break free from traditional moral restraints and the "petty bourgeois respectability" of the previous generation. Nietzsche defended a new "brutal and mindless" morality and "crowned with laurels" those who were exploiting the workers. He demonstrated, Mehring observed, "how much capitalism has destroyed our spiritual life."

In subsequent writings Mehring continued to argue that Nietzsche's philosophy, particularly his concept of the will to power, expressed the new economic era of "large capital."[35] He conceded that Nietzsche was "too intelligent to settle for a shallow liberalism," but he had been unable to "find his way to socialism as the living force of historical development."[36] This failure, and Nietzsche's indifference to the movement of the working class, disqualified him as a serious thinker. Lacking insight into the real forces of history, he had, in effect, glorified such leading German capitalists as "Krupp, Stumm, and Rothschild" and accepted these "shabby figures of bourgeois decadence" as signs of the "dawning of a new world." It was a very selective reading of Nietzsche, one that largely ignored his penetrating criticism of many features of the capitalistic and bourgeois order.

Nietzsche continued to influence a number of the young intellectuals who were entering the socialist movement. Hence the testimony of Wolfgang Heine, a young lawyer who would become a leading Social Democratic politician. "What a feeling of redemption and liberation, a new penetrating joy in life," he recalled, had come from the writings of Nietzsche.[37] Although Heine rejected the philosopher as an adequate guide, he welcomed his bold search, "against the background of a dead liberalism," for new values. So too, for a young aristocratic woman, Lily von Kretschmann, who set out to develop the feminist implications of Marxism. Her reading of Nietzsche had been her "first call to personal freedom."[38]

The "dangerous and seductive attraction" that Nietzsche exercised over "many enthusiastic socialists" during the early 1890s led Kurt Eisner to address the problem in two articles published in 1891.[39] Eisner's acceptance of Marxism was qualified by doubts about historical materialism, but his articles were designed to demonstrate the superiority of Marx over Nietzsche. He conceded, however, that Nietzsche's critique of existing society was largely correct. The philosopher had touched, moreover, in his emphasis on the "individual factor," a crucial and neglected element in Marxism. It was hardly surprising that the Jungen had been "led astray by Nietzsche."[40] Had Nietzsche not "mistaken the essence of socialism," what Eisner described as its "soul," or religious element, he might have helped to show the way ahead. But lacking any feeling for the ways in which the socialist movement combined altruistic and egoistic motives, or what Eisner called the "robust naturalism of the masses," Nietzsche had turned reactionary. He was, Eisner concluded, the "philosopher of capitalism," the spokesman for the "aristocracy of money." Yet Eisner continued to view Nietzsche as a social "diagnostician of genius."[41]

The suggestion, implicit in Eisner's discussion, that Marx and Nietzsche were complementary rather than adversarial, was developed by Frank Servaes in two articles published during 1892.[42] His point of departure was Wille's fear that the development of the Social Democrats threatened the "subjectivity" or "independence of spirit" of their followers. Wille brought to expression, according to Servaes, "that which separates me from the party." Servaes went on to show the "identity of pathos and mood" in the disciples of Marx and Nietzsche. No wonder Nietzsche continued to have "many followers among the younger Social Democrats." While the goals of the two thinkers seemed "wholly different," Servaes argued, their specific aims were less important than their common effort to "go toward new undiscovered territory," into "gardens which no eye has yet seen."[43] Their parallel aspirations opened, therefore, the possibility for mutual criticism.

Servaes hoped for a synthesis of the two thinkers. Each supplied what was lacking in the other. Nietzsche's affirmation of the individual countered the danger that the Marxist emphasis on equality and material happiness presented to the human personality, while Marxism corrected Nietzsche's tendency toward megalomania and loss of "contact with the living."[44] The coming of a "new golden age" would require both the "ethical revolution" guided by Nietzsche and the "economic revolution" forecast by Marx. Hence the need for the "two streams" of thought to "come together."

The hope that Nietzsche might correct the deficiencies of orthodox Marxism was also taken up in 1897 by Hermann Duncker, a young Marxist intellectual working on a doctorate at the University of Leipzig. Engels, he argued, had provided only fragments of a philosophy. Socialists needed, therefore, "a new philosophical grounding."[45] Duncker looked to Nietzsche for ways to express the new "self-feeling of the masses" being awakened by capitalism.

Nietzsche also appealed to the "revisionist" Marxists who, at the turn of the century, were calling into question the orthodox doctrines. Led by Eduard Bernstein, they were setting aside revolutionary goals in favor of the immediate possibilities for social reform. Socialists, according to the "revisionists," should focus not on the distant future but on the day-to-day struggle of the workers. Here, according to Gystrow, cited earlier, "the ideal which Nietzsche had outlined" was especially relevant.[46] His forecast of a "social aristocracy" challenged socialists to "raise humankind to a new level." When socialists became fully aware of the new "I feeling" among the workers they would recognize Nietzsche as their prophet.

Marxist intellectuals who looked to Nietzsche to correct the deficiencies of orthodox Marxism might conclude, however, like Wille earlier, that it was necessary to choose between the two thinkers. This was the outcome of Ernst's struggle to reconcile Marx and Nietzsche. By the late 1890s he had decided that orthodox Marxist doctrines prevented any understanding of the inner life, of an "unexplainable 'x' in human nature."[47] What distinguished human existence, according to Ernst, was the inner moral struggle of the individual. Having lost sight of that struggle and the "call for a new man," the Social Democrats had dismissed Nietzsche's counter vision of social transformation and the "progressive ennoblement of the human race."[48] Ernst soon left the Social Democrats and turned in later years to the extreme right in his continuing hope for a new form of human existence.[49]

After 1900 Nietzsche continued to appeal to those socialist intellectuals who were seeking fresh content for the Marxist vision of the future. Efforts to blend the ideas of the two thinkers were now most evident among Social Democrats who were committed to the revision of orthodox Marxism—the intellectuals gathered around the *Sozialistische Monatshefte*, edited by Joseph Bloch, and those who took part in Heinrich Braun's attempt to reorient the party by means of his journal, the *Neue Gesellschaft*.[50] One of these was Max Maurenbrecher, a clergyman and former leader in Friedrich Naumann's Christian Social Union. Shortly after joining the Social Democrats in the summer of 1903 he declared that the socialist quest for a "new type of man" would require the "deepening of personality" inspired by Nietzsche.[51] Despite the fact that Nietzsche saw himself as a passionate enemy of socialism, he was, Maurenbrecher declared, "flesh of our flesh and bone of our bone." Indeed, Maurenbrecher saw in the development of the proletariat the qualities—a "manly firmness" together with a capacity for "judgment and decisiveness"—that Nietzsche had described in his Übermensch. Nietzsche had brought "to expression what the working class really is."[52]

Maurenbrecher's later use of Nietzsche mirrored the changing fortunes of the Social Democrats in Germany. After the party suffered a major setback in the parliamentary elections of 1907, when its representation was cut in half, it became more difficult to believe in the imminent arrival of socialism and a radical transformation of life. The new generation of socialists recognized, according to Maurenbrecher, that they would not "receive the whole prize of the struggle," that the "refashioning of society" would be a "long and possible reversible process."[53] Nietzsche, so Maurenbrecher now argued, could help socialists overcome their tendency to devalue the present struggle in favor of the future triumph. Nietzsche's claim that joy and meaning in life stemmed from the struggle itself, from the exercise of the will to power, would fortify those socialists who would "not experience the end of suffering."

It was a deeper reading of Nietzsche than that evident in earlier socialist intellectuals. But the ideas of Nietzsche were now directing socialists away from the revolutionary goal of Marx. They were being employed to justify the immediate economic and political struggles of the workers and indeed, the efforts of the "revisionists" to reintegrate them into German society. Maurenbrecher's hopes, in fact, shifted from the working class back to the nation. The heroic virtues celebrated by Nietzsche could now be enlisted on behalf of the new German nationalism expressed in the concept of *Weltpolitik*. It is not surprising that Maurenbrecher left the Social Democratic Party and moved to the political right.[54]

Meanwhile Nietzsche's ideas had been taken up by Marxist intellectuals outside of Germany. In the wider movement as well, Nietzsche seemed to offer to disappointed Marxists ways of recovering the radical hopes that the socialist political parties, driven more and more by the immediate interests of the workers, were abandoning.

II

In the British socialist movement Nietzsche's presence indicated that even where the Marxist doctrines had been altered in fundamental ways the educated recruits from the middle class confronted dilemmas much like those with which their German counterparts struggled.[55] The Social Democratic Federation, which had attempted to inculcate the orthodox doctrines into the working class, had, apart from a few industrial areas in the North, gained little following.[56] But two indigenous forms of socialism, more suited to British traditions, had developed out of an initial Marxist inspiration. Fabianism, a rationalist, gradualist, and reformist version of socialism, was indebted to the British utilitarian tradition while carrying over much of the economic determinism in Marxism. The second, more popular form of socialism in Britain, "Ethical socialism," drew together elements from Marxism, the Nonconformist religious past, and a current of social romanticism shaped by the ideas of Thomas Carlyle, John Ruskin, and William Morris. When in Britain, as in Germany, the party that carried the socialist hope began to concentrate on the immediate interests of the workers, leading intellectuals in both of the main wings of the movement turned to Nietzsche.

Within the Fabian Society, George Bernard Shaw was the clearest example. Although he had become, by the turn of the century, the chief spokesman for Fabianism, he had never given up the hope, expressed in his early Marxism, that socialism would mean a radical break with bourgeois institutions.[57] That hope continued to inform Shaw's work as a dramatist and cultural critic even as he advocated the economic collectivism and pragmatic policies of the Fabians. But he had become convinced that the Fabians, in concentrating on the economic and political sides of the social question, had ignored its ethical and psychological implications. Shaw still

saw himself as a "moral revolutionary," concerned with the "struggle between human vitality" and the present "artificial system of morality."[58] And
he recognized that Nietzsche, along with such contemporary figures as
Tolstoy, Ibsen, and Wagner, was developing new visions of human possibilities. Shaw welcomed, in fact, the proposal to form a Nietzschean society. It might, he wrote, bring "individualism around again on a higher
plane." Unless a "new race of men" could be bred, he declared, mankind
could make no serious progress toward a new society.[59]

Shaw's plays in the early years of the century reflected his continuing
effort, with the help of Nietzsche, to renew the radical socialist vision.
Thus in the "Revolutionary Handbook," appended to his play *Man and Superman*, Shaw declared that no movement could rescue humanity from "its
idols and cupidities" until "human nature was changed."[60] There he presented his own version of the "superman" as the goal of socialism. In employing the Nietzschean image, however, Shaw diverged sharply from the
German thinker. For in viewing his superman as the servant of a cosmic
"life force," Shaw adopted a transcendental and optimistic myth that
Nietzsche would have repudiated.

Nietzsche not only helped Shaw to rehabilitate the ideal of a new socialist man but he challenged the economic determinism that was nearly as
strong in Fabianism as it was in orthodox Marxism. In Nietzsche's notion
of the will to power Shaw found, as one commentator observed, fresh inspiration for "a socialist doctrine endangered by inertia."[61] Like orthodox
Marxists across Europe in these years, Shaw was increasingly occupied
with the problem of social energy—the need to tap the nonrational levels
of human motivation.

Shaw addressed that problem in *Major Barbara*, written in 1905. Here
he employed the Greek god "Dionysus" as a symbol for the upsurge of passion that destroyed stultifying conventions and released creative energies.
The debt to Nietzsche was less direct than in *Man and Superman*, for Shaw
derived his understanding of the Dionysian from Gilbert Murray's recent
translation of the *Bacchae*. Indeed, in the preface to *Major Barbara* Shaw
denied that Nietzsche had influenced his attempt to outline a new morality.[62] Shaw's divergence from Nietzsche was apparent both in his continuing adherence to the myth of the "life force" and in his search for a new religious foundation for socialism.[63] Nietzsche soon ceased to be a recogniz-
able influence on Shaw's development, but his periodic disillusionment
with the socialist movement in Britain would find expression through his

ongoing interest in heroic individuals in his dramatic work and in his later praise for Mussolini and Stalin.

Several of the Ethical Socialists in Britain also turned to Nietzsche in the hope of saving their dream of a radical transformation of life. Like the Jungen in Germany they recognized that the socialist politicians were setting that dream aside in order to pursue the material interests of the working class. Their disaffection was expressed most clearly by A. R. Orage, editor of the chief vehicle for the Ethical Socialists, the *New Age*. Orage's interpretation of Nietzsche's thought was quixotic; he regarded the philosopher as essentially a mystic.[64] But he found in Nietzsche the qualities that had appealed to Shaw—the heroic values characteristic of the new socialist man, and the energies, "elemental, irreligious, immoral, barbaric, and anarchic," that would transform bourgeois society.[65]

But Nietzsche could only provide, as one of the Ethical Socialists confessed, "a last desperate foothold on a dying dream of the future."[66] For they could not find a way of introducing the Nietzschean values and a new will into the popular movement. This problem was addressed more directly by socialist intellectuals in France. They also discovered new political possibilities in the meeting of Marxist and Nietzschean ideas.

III

Nietzsche's influence on French socialist intellectuals before World War I was less direct than his influence in Germany or Britain. For much of the space that would have been open for a Nietzschean presence had been occupied by a figure who played a major role in introducing Marxist ideas into France—Georges Sorel. As Sorel attempted to deal with the problems presented by orthodox Marxism, however, he turned to Nietzsche as a kindred spirit and ally.

Sorel's diagnosis of modern European development was strikingly similar to that of Nietzsche. He, too, had concluded that bourgeois society, indeed, European civilization as a whole, was hopelessly decadent.[67] Sorel also had looked to the ancient world for heroic values against which he could measure contemporary moral decline. Both thinkers, moreover, saw in the rationalism of Socrates—renewed in modern science—a force that undermined traditional culture and social solidarity. For Sorel, as for a number of European intellectuals at this time, the cultural renewal inspired by Christianity amid the declining Roman empire represented a paradigm for the modern crisis. What was needed was a new faith, capable of providing the personal and social integration no longer derived from Christianity.

In Marxism Sorel found a compelling answer to that need. Not only had Marx provided a convincing analysis of the economic and social process; he had envisioned, in the development of the proletariat, the qualities required for a new civilization. From the outset, however, the moral promise in Marxism was central for Sorel. To describe the mission of the proletariat he used Nietzsche's "celebrated phrase—a new evaluation of values."[68]

By the late 1890s Sorel had become convinced that the socialist movement in France was losing its revolutionary drive. Its political leaders were, through their efforts to secure material gains for the workers, making their peace with parliamentary institutions and becoming hopelessly entangled in the corrupt bourgeois world. To free the workers from that process, he set out to identify those aspects of Marxism to which it owed its power to move its followers. He discovered the source of the movement's energy in what he called the "social poetry" in Marxism—the ethical, religious, and aesthetic features beneath its rational exterior.[69] Sorel was determined to recover what Edward Shils described as the Marxist vision of an "apocalyptic transformation in which everything is totally changed."[70]

Sorel found in the French syndicalist movement workers who seemed to have the potential for such a change. Through their rejection of the political system and their creation of autonomous economic associations, the syndicalists were developing, he believed, a distinctive proletarian way of life. Sorel attempted, in his *Reflections on Violence*, to connect his conception of syndicalism with his reinterpretation of Marxism. What he had defined earlier as "social poetry" now became the "myth." It found tangible form in the syndicalist tactic of the general strike. Out of the energies generated by class warfare—expressed most clearly in the strike—would come a new social order. In Nietzsche's "master morality," Sorel now recognized heroic values similar to those he saw emerging within the workers.[71] The syndicalists were creating, in fact, a new individuality, a morality "without masters," and thus making possible the "transition from one world to another."

But if *Reflections on Violence* showed a certain convergence of the ideas of Sorel and Nietzsche, the book also indicated profound differences. For Sorel blended the Nietzschean outlook—heroic, pessimistic, and tragic—with the traditional ascetic values of the bourgeoisie that the German philosopher had repudiated.[72] Sorel's new European man would be hard working, self-denying, dedicated to family, and disciplined in ways that served a society marked by advancing technology and increasing efficiency in production. The syndicalist workers were charged with the task of re-covering, through their practices and institutions, values that the bour-geoisie had discarded.

In reaffirming those values Sorel revealed his continuing ties to his bourgeois origins. But his conception of the myth also separated him from the working class. For the effectiveness of the myth of the general strike presupposed the absence of the kind of awareness possessed by Sorel him-self. Only if the myth evoked "instinctively all of the sentiments ... which correspond ... to the war waged by socialism against modern society" could it generate mass energies.[73] Intellectuals like Sorel, by virtue of their understanding of the instrumental nature of the myth, continued to stand outside.[74]

In fixing on the mythic as the key to social and cultural regeneration, Sorel had come close to Nietzsche's claim that the human imagination was the source of the meanings that moved individuals and societies. But the difficulty of translating the mythic into social action became evident during the period following the publication of the *Reflections*. For the syndicalist workers did not fulfill Sorel's hopes. Not only did they fail to preserve the autonomy necessary to develop unique social practices and institutions, but the syndicalist leaders, like the socialist politicians before them, soon set aside their revolutionary goals in favor of the material concessions of-fered in the parliamentary process.[75]

It was not Sorel, however, but his "most faithful disciple and trusted friend," Edourd Berth, who responded to the failure of the myth of the general strike to renew the revolutionary energies of the proletariat.[76] At the same time Berth brought the ideas of Sorel and Nietzsche closer to-gether. As the hopes of Sorel and his disciples "decomposed in the swampy ambiance of democracy," Berth adopted Nietzsche's view of the Dionysian to rescue the myth of the general strike.[77] The syndicalists, he declared, were the "new incarnation of Dionysus," creators of a "new collective soul."[78] Their tactic of the general strike announced the "end of the old world and the opening of a new era." Berth now conceded that the workers acting alone could not bring about the desired transformation. Additional energies were needed to continue the movement toward social regenera-tion.

During 1909 Berth turned to the "Action Francaise," the right-wing movement led by Charles Maurras, as a force capable of supplementing the revolutionary drive of the workers. The monarchist ideal, and the classical values advanced by Maurras, provided, according to Berth, an Apollonian balance to the Dionysian energies of the proletariat.[79] In the passionate nationalism of the Action Francaise Berth saw a mythic force which would complement that of the general strike in calling forth mass action. Working together the syndicalists and the Action Francaise would "give birth to a new great century."

For a time Sorel joined Berth in viewing the Action Francaise as a possible ally and shifted his hopes for the future from the working class to the nation. His disappointment with the proletariat also led him to look to elites as embodiments of the myth and as agents of change, and to place a new emphasis on leadership.[80] Thus Sorel loosened the tie between myth and the proletariat and indicated its availability to other social groups. He also pointed to a common ground on which the disillusioned followers of Marx and the disciples of Nietzsche could meet.

Sorel himself revealed the common ground when, at the end of World War I, he identified Mussolini and Lenin as figures who, having emerged from creative minorities within their respective socialist movements, offered the kind of leadership necessary for radical change.[81] In the Bolshevik revolution Sorel now saw a confirmation of the power of myth and, indeed, the syndicalist ideal he had abandoned earlier. The Russian revolution renewed the Marxist vision that had faded from the movements in the West.[82] But while Sorel partly reaffirmed the Marxist faith in the proletariat, he entrusted the hope for a radical transformation of life to a heroic leader.[83] This was the new element in his thought—the charismatic, heroic leader whose qualities "set him apart from the masses."[84] Thus a Nietzschean ideal stood at the end of Sorel's intellectual trajectory.

The decomposition of orthodox Marxism—the rejection of economic determinism, the declining faith in the proletariat, together with the emphasis on the role of the leader—can also be followed in the developments of Mussolini and Lenin. Conditions in Italy and Russia were much more favorable to the triumph of resolute minorities and the rise of heroic leaders. In these relatively backward societies the aspirations that had led disappointed Marxist intellectuals elsewhere to turn to Nietzsche were translated into new ideological terms and popular political appeals.

IV

Mussolini, according to Ernst Nolte, "brought Nietzsche and Marx into a paradoxical yet not impossible dialogue."[85] Marx remained, for some time, the dominant figure in that dialogue. Nietzsche served Mussolini, as he served Sorel, to support an interpretation of Marxism that emphasized volitional and heroic values. Where Sorel's revolutionary revisionism remained abstract, distant from the working-class struggle, however, Mussolini engaged directly in political agitation. In his reworking of Marxism and his discovery of the "terrain on which Marx and Nietzsche came together," Mussolini demonstrated new potentialities in that meeting.[86]

Mussolini's place in the Marxist-Nietzschean dialogue was, in part, an expression of his own temperament, in part a consequence of the historical situation in which the Italian socialist party found itself during the first decade of the century. That Mussolini was an uncommonly aggressive personality has been remarked by all of his biographers.[87] As early as 1904, at the age of twenty-one, he discovered in the writings of Nietzsche a rationale for his highly developed ego.[88] In Nietzsche's "superman" he also found an ideal that answered the needs of a Europe that was passing through a profound cultural crisis. But here, as at other points in his life, ideas functioned mainly not to build up a solid core of conviction but to rationalize Mussolini's own will to power and to serve the tactical changes required to fulfill it.

That will went hand in hand, however, with Mussolini's fierce commitment to the apocalyptic vision in Marxism.[89] It was the threat to that vision—the readiness of many of the socialist leaders in Italy to follow a reformist course—that occupied Mussolini as a journalist and a political agitator. In his reassertion of the revolutionary drive in Marxism he drew on Sorel's notion of violence as creative action and his insights into the function of myth in mobilizing mass energies.[90] But Mussolini, like a number of contemporary intellectuals in Italy and elsewhere, was troubled by the spiritual vacuum resulting from the decline of Christianity.[91] To fill that vacuum he turned not to Marx but to the wider European current of "life philosophy," and its emphasis on the nonrational and willful elements in human nature, within which Nietzsche had been a major influence.[92] Without discarding the orthodox Marxist doctrines—economic determinism, the inevitable triumph of the proletariat, and the coming of a classless society—Mussolini made room in his socialism for the values affirmed by Nietzsche. The resulting theoretical inconsistencies mattered little to a Mussolini who was primarily concerned with action and whose outlook had been from the beginning strongly elitist. His contradictory blend of Marx and Nietzsche served, in fact, a concept of leadership that was favored by the condition of the socialist party in Italy.

The proletarian basis of the Italian party was weak—a reflection of a society that was still mainly agrarian and marked by a high degree of illiteracy.[93] Moreover, the socialist leaders could not count on strong trade unions to discipline and unify the workers. The absence of well-developed structures within the Italian labor movement helps to explain the instability of the party, as control in the years before World War I shifted back and forth between its revolutionary and the reformist wings. Nor did the Italian political system encourage the growth of parties with broad appeals. Italian parliamentary leaders had failed to anchor the political process firmly in the economic and social development of the nation. By 1910 the system was, as several historians have argued, drifting toward a crisis.[94]

This was the context for the victory of the revolutionary left, led by Mussolini,[95] at the socialist party conference in 1912. When, a short time later, Mussolini was appointed editor of the party's chief paper, *Avanti*, he was well placed to translate his version of Marxism, and his Nietzschean conception of leadership, into practice. Yet even at this moment of triumph he confessed that his "personal and spiritual situation" made him feel "homeless" amid his fellow revolutionaries.[96] His "religious conception of socialism" separated him from those who were still fixed within the scientific and deterministic categories of orthodox Marxism. Although he had not reconciled his intransigent Marxism with the volitional and heroic values he had drawn from Nietzsche and the syndicalists, Mussolini gave new life to the party over the next two years.[97] His ability to revitalize the hopes for revolutionary change was evident in the readiness of a number of young intellectuals, including Antonio Gramsci and Palmiro Togliatti, to follow his lead. But when, in the summer of 1914, the attempt of the socialists to call forth a revolutionary uprising proved to be a fiasco, Mussolini reached a crossroad. The failure of "Red Week" demonstrated that the condition for the classical Marxist conception of revolution—through an uprising by the workers—did not exist in Italy. The proletariat, Mussolini concluded, was "deaf, confused, and remote."[98]

The process through which Mussolini discovered, in nationalistic feeling, a force capable of reinvigorating his vision of social and cultural transformation has been described by several historians.[99] That process again demonstrated the way in which Mussolini's ideological and tactical flexibility served his will to power. It also indicated how the myth of a new man and a new Italy could be disengaged from the proletariat and come to be centered on the leader himself.[100] Indeed, even as Mussolini exploited the economic, social, and political malaise of postwar Italy and established his fascist regime, the hope for cultural and spiritual regeneration derived from revolutionary socialism continued to move many of his followers. As the "cult of the 'duce' displaced Fascism," young intellectuals in the movement protested that Mussolini had betrayed the dream of a "new fascist man."[101] Mussolini had completed, however, the process through which the Nietzschean presence had triumphed over the socialist vision.

If fascism can be seen as "an attempt to give concrete form" to a revolutionary hope that had been "preached vainly" by the socialists, the course of Mussolini provides striking parallels, as a number of historians have pointed out, with that of Lenin.[102] For the Russian socialist movement presented its intellectuals with the problem faced by other orthodox Marxists—the failure of the proletariat to develop the consciousness necessary for it to play its historical role. Lenin's resolution of that difficulty would exemplify the features though not the terminology of a Nietzschean presence.

V

In Russia, as in Italy, economic and social backwardness contributed to the rise of the heroic leader, first within the socialist movement and then in political life. Here, too, the socialists lacked a strong proletarian base. And given the highly repressive political system in tsarist Russia, the Marxists were forced to adopt a conspiratorial tactic and an elitist conception of organization. That conception was developed by Lenin in his essay "What Is To Be Done?" But Lenin was also responding to the threat that working-class desires for immediate material gains posed to the revolutionary vision of Marx.

The readiness of intellectuals in Russia to adopt that vision reflected the extraordinary force of the apocalyptic dispositions within that society. Here, as elsewhere in Europe, many of the younger generation suffered from a profound sense of social alienation. Hence the appeal of Marxism, as one of its early converts, Nicolas Berdyaev, recalled:

> The Marxist movement of the late nineties was born of a new vision: it brought with it ... a purpose and a new conception of man. ... Marxism at that juncture was in fact a signal for the spiritual as well as social liberation of man.[103]

It seemed clear to Berdyaev that the proletariat had a "messianic calling," for it was "free from the sin of exploitation, and its social and psychological condition enables it to receive and bear witness to truth."[104] Berdyaev soon broke with Marxism to take part in the development of the "new religious consciousness" that was a striking feature of the time.[105] But the spiritual ferment in Russia during the early years of the century provided another meeting place for the ideas of Marx and Nietzsche.

The meeting took place among Marxist intellectuals who, like the revisionists in the West, were dissatisfied with historical materialism. They were troubled, in particular, by the Marxist neglect of ethical issues and the role of the individual. Hence the appearance of a small group of "Nietzschean Marxists," who were seeking to overcome the limitations of orthodox Marxism and develop the new values and the culture appropriate to a socialist society.[106] For Anatoly Lunacharsky, a leader of the group, Nietzsche's notion of the Übermensch provided the basis for a new atheistic socialist religion. The "true Marxist socialist," he declared, was the "most deeply religious of men."[107] The "freedom, creativity, power, and passion" of the future socialist man would make "the most creative efforts of mere men today" seem "awkward, weak, and foolish." The "Nietzschean Marxists" included several of the leading Bolsheviks—Lunacharsky, A. A. Bogdanov, and Maxim Gorky.[108] Like their counterparts in the West, they were seeking to revitalize Marxism by generating the kind of enthusiasms that in the past had come from religion. They described themselves as "god-builders," dedicated to the deification of man.

The "Nietzschean Marxists" assumed greater significance after 1905, when the failure of the first Russian revolution forced the Social Democrats to reconsider questions of theory and tactics. The self-examination that followed brought the "god-builders" into new prominence. And they attempted in the years just ahead to develop, under Gorky's leadership, a training school for their program on the island of Capri.[109] For Lenin, firmly committed to the orthodox Marxism, which he had taken over uncritically from Engels, the challenge of the "god-builders" could no longer be ignored.[110] The philosophical foundation of Bolshevism was threatened. In his book *Materialism and Empirocriticism*, published early in 1909 after months of intensive study in the libraries of Geneva and the British Museum, Lenin attempted to seal all cracks in the solid edifice of historical materialism.

Lenin's book was not aimed directly at Nietzsche; the philosopher was not even mentioned. Lenin was concerned, rather, with what he described as the "Machist epidemic among a section of the Social Democrats."[111] In the

Austrian physicist and philosopher of science, Ernst Mach, the "Nietzschean Marxists" had found a criticism of mechanistic materialism—and dialectical materialism as well—that made room for their ideas. For Lenin, however, Mach's denial of the objective and self-sufficient truth of the material entities of classical physics had opened the door for "voluntaristic idealism" and a disgusting "flirtation with religion."[112] He was determined to eliminate the heretics from the party or, at least, reduce them to silence.

He succeeded.[113] But having triumphed over the "Nietzschean Marxists" and disposed of other threats to the integrity of the Marxist doctrines, as well as threats to his own leadership of the Bolsheviks, Lenin proceeded to exemplify willful and heroic qualities that had no basis in orthodox Marxism. The contradiction between Lenin's style of leadership and the economic determinism of Marxism has often been noted. Thus one historian claimed that "Lenin's own superhuman will, his discipline, and his 'will to power' approach to politics" constituted an example, "intentional or not, of Nietzsche's concept of self-overcoming."[114] With that form of leadership went Lenin's conviction, expressed in "What Is To Be Done," that workers could not achieve liberation on their own.

As Lenin attempted to lead the proletariat into the promised land, the ironies multiplied. In the chaotic situation in which Russia found itself after three years of war and, amid the collapse of so many of the old institutional restraints, the Bolsheviks were able to impose their will on a demoralized and structureless society. In the process Lenin's own personality, elevated by his followers to mythic dimensions, occupied the place "left vacant" in the rationalistic and deterministic version of Marxism.[115] The charismatic leader became the repository of the millennial hopes that had been disengaged from the immanent development of the proletariat.

The climax came with Lenin's death and entombment. For it presented an opportunity for the "god builders," Lunacharsky and another leader of that group, Nicholas Krasin, to complete the process of deifying the leader.[116] The two men assumed major roles in creating a cult around the mummified remains of Lenin. And while the cult was, in part, a result of political needs—the search for political legitimacy at a time when the old authorities had fallen—the consecration of Lenin can also be seen as a solution to the failure of the proletariat to fulfill its appointed role in the Marxist scenario.

The outcome would have horrified Marx as well as Nietzsche. But the forms of leadership exercised by Mussolini and Lenin, as well as the idiosyncratic paths of a number of the Marxist intellectuals in Germany, Britain, and France, were expressions of the frustrations resulting from the radical hopes aroused by Marxism. The frustrations were felt most deeply by alienated young men whose aspirations had been formed in the bourgeois world. Convinced that the institutions and conventions of that world thwarted its professed values of social justice, equality, and freedom, as well as its ideal of individuality, they had discovered in Marxism the promise of realizing those values.

This discussion of the "Nietzschean presence" has introduced two central problems confronting Marxist intellectuals in Europe after World War I. First, how to reconcile the ethical and cultural aspirations they brought to the movement with the orthodox Marxist doctrines? Second, how to connect those aspirations with the actual development of the working class? The early intellectual journeys of De Man, Horkheimer, and Kolakowski, and the ways in which they left Marxism, can be understood in terms of their responses to these problems.

PART II

Three Case Studies

CHAPTER 2

Henri De Man

I

When Henri De Man, a Belgian, published *The Psychology of Socialism* in 1926, he joined a growing number of socialist intellectuals in Europe for whom orthodox Marxism had ceased to provide a satisfactory understanding of working-class development.[1] De Man, like his contemporaries—George Lukács, Karl Korsch, and Antonio Gramsci—was struggling with a problem that the earlier generation of Marxists had not been able to solve—the failure of proletarian class consciousness to evolve into a genuine socialist mentality. The collapse of international socialist solidarity at the outbreak of World War I had dramatized that failure. But the fate of the socialist revolution was still tied, so these intellectuals believed, to the capacity of the workers to embody a radically new consciousness.

De Man's *Psychology* was his response to the problem. It was also the centerpiece of his remarkable career as a socialist thinker and politician. Because of its ending—his condemnation by a Belgian court for collaboration with the Nazis—De Man's career has been the subject of ongoing debate.[2] But his life presents a unique and illuminating commentary on the development of European socialism between the wars. No socialist thinker matched the boldness with which he challenged the Marxism still dominant in the wider movement. None of the leading socialists moved so easily across national boundaries; fluent in German, French, and English, as well as his native Flemish, he identified himself fully with the international mission of socialism. De Man was unique, too, among the major socialist theorists of the period in having attempted to apply his ideas to the realm of practical politics.

Any exploration of De Man's life will depend in large part on his own accounts. His autobiographies—he wrote four versions—are rich, both in terms of personal experiences and in observations about the European socialist movement in general.[3] De Man was, in fact, a figure of extraordinary ability, personal force, and self-confidence. Caught up in his autobiographies, one easily becomes captive to his own interpretation of his life as a socialist. To view his life, as the titles of two of his autobiographies suggest, as that of an "errant knight," or one who constantly went "against the stream," is to recognize important features in his makeup. But the autobiographies were also exercises in self-justification. As such they challenge the historian to view these accounts critically, to question De Man's judgments about the development of socialism and his own relationship to the movement—in short, to reinterpret his life.

De Man's life provides a case study of a central problem in the development of modern socialism—the troubled relationship between intellectuals of bourgeois origin and the working-class movement. He exemplified the paradoxical nature of that relationship. For he remained, throughout a career devoted to the displacement of what he denounced as bourgeois culture, a bourgeois man.[4] This paradox, the way in which it shaped and in the end undermined De Man's conception of socialism, provides the main argument of this essay.[5]

The paradox begins with his account of his conversion to socialism:

> In brief, if I became a socialist at the age of seventeen, it was not in spite of but because of a particularly happy childhood. My family milieu, that of the patriarchal household, formed in me the scale of values which led me to revolt against the reality … of the outside world I learned to know.[6]

The conflict arose out of De Man's family background. Born into a prominent Flemish family in Antwerp in 1885, his early life was shaped by the rich and diverse traditions out of which the modern bourgeoisie in Belgium developed. His mother belonged to a family that reached back to the burgher class of the fourteenth century and continued to be part of the social and political establishment in Antwerp. With that inheritance came academic and artistic values, embodied most fully in the grandfather, Jan van Beers, a Flemish poet with a deep love of the popular culture of the countryside. The extended family included two uncles—one an amateur scientist, the other a printer of art books—both of whom influenced the young De Man.

His father's origin was modest in comparison, though it held, in addition to entrepreneurial values, aristocratic ambitions. Having been barred by an injury from the military career to which he aspired, the elder De Man became an executive in a shipping company. A vigorous, practical man, he imparted to his son an intense joy in physical activity and a love of nature, which he retained throughout his life. The influence of the father was most evident, however, in the strongly ethical outlook of the son. It was a strictly secular ethic, long removed from its Protestant origins and nurtured in the older De Man by the Masonic lodges that contributed much to the development of liberalism in Belgium.[7] The ethic combined the traditional Christian virtues of charity and self-sacrifice, the humanistic virtues of civility and service to the community, and an aristocratic sense of obligation toward the weak.

De Man's inheritance was, therefore, complex.[8] Along with the ascetic values commonly associated with the bourgeois tradition was a well-developed aesthetic sensibility, a delight in art and music and the beauties of nature. There was an obvious tension between those two sides of bourgeois development, and it had already produced in Belgium, as elsewhere in Europe, the adversarial culture that was such a marked feature of European society in the nineteenth century.[9] But the bourgeois way of life also found expression in an ethical idealism that acknowledged few if any limitations on the capacity of human beings to realize their finer possibilities. So it was with De Man. From his prosperous and secure middle-class home he derived an ideal that had become central to the bourgeois sensibility—the ideal of autonomy. Individuals were capable, according to this ideal, of giving satisfactory shape to their lives, and to society as well, by means of their natural resources of conscience, reason, and will.[10]

Looking back on his bourgeois home, De Man described it as a "perfect communism."[11] And while the phrase was hyperbolic given the essentially patriarchal nature of this family, it expressed his sense of a household marked by harmony and tolerance for individual differences. Here was the social microcosm in terms of which he judged the outer world. But the harshness of that judgment, when it came, presupposed a fierce sense of independence. Several episodes in his childhood testified to De Man's willfulness and his determination to realize the bourgeois ideal of self-reliance. He paid a price, however, for he never lost, so he claimed, a sense of being an outsider.

Given his outlook and his temperament, the shock that he experienced when he encountered the "outer world" was predictable. It came at the age of fifteen, when the workers in his uncle's printing business went on strike. De Man now recognized that the social and economic world was "governed by quite different norms" than those he had known within the family.[12] What impressed him most at the time, and this would become a key to his understanding of class conflict, was not the economic interests at stake in the contest but its psychological features. He was struck by the feelings of resentment on the part of the workers, their sense that their self-respect had been violated. His uncle and the other employers, on the other hand, were filled with moral indignation, convinced that their workers had ceased to honor the qualities that enabled them to conduct their business. Two years later a strike by the dock workers in Antwerp, followed by a general strike in Belgium, drew De Man into the working-class struggle. On May Day, 1902, he joined the socialist "Red Guard," the youthful auxiliary of the Belgian Labor Party.

The Belgium Labor Party had been founded in 1885, the outcome of an attempt to bring together a variety of groups—trade unions, cooperatives, and socialists—for the purpose of common political action.[13] Although the party contained Marxist and anarchist currents of thought, it remained pragmatic, concentrating during its early years on the goal of universal manhood suffrage. In 1894, following a general strike, it achieved that goal, though provisions for plural voting, which favored the educated and the propertied, weakened the democratic nature of the new system. By permitting the growth of socialist representatives in parliament, numbering twenty after the election of 1894, the reform significantly reduced the power of the Liberal Party and consolidated Catholic control over Belgian political life.[14]

Within this context the Labor Party, though led by two Marxist intellectuals of bourgeois background, Emile Vandervelde and Julius Destres, followed a reformist course, combining demands for revisions of the electoral law with a program designed to improve the lives of the workers. Pressures from the party contributed to the passage of a series of measures that gave the working class greater security and strengthened its bargaining power.[15] During the first decade of the new century Belgium developed a social security system comparable to those being created in Germany and Britain. Although revolutionary aims continued to be part of the party's

ideology and rhetoric, they ceased to bear any close relationship to its political practice.

When De Man entered the movement in 1902, he adopted a form of socialism that followed naturally from the values he carried over from his
bourgeois family. He was attracted in particular to the anarchist ideal
found in the writings of Proudhon and contemporary thinkers—the
Frenchman Jean Grave and the Dutchman Domela Nieuwenhuis—that
each individual should govern himself by a "moral imperative." It seemed
to De Man the "logical outcome of that liberalism," with its emphasis on
the free individual, that he had absorbed in his home.[16]

De Man soon recognized that anarchism did not provide any "bridge
between the personal ethical command" and the "real impulses" in the
working-class movement.[17] At the same time, however, he realized that
those impulses—the pursuit of material interests and the drive for political
power—would not be sufficient to bring about a new society. Already he
saw in the parliamentary activity of the Belgium Labor Party a tendency
toward opportunism. He thus confronted early what he would identify as
the "cardinal problem in the socialist movement," that of countering the
tendency within the working class toward "embourgeoisement."[18] How
could the workers be prevented from "being infected by their bourgeois
surroundings?"

Marxism, which De Man discovered in 1904, solved the problem of
connecting his ethical idealism with the immediate struggles of the workers. But Marxism provided much more.

> I found at one stroke a substitute religion, a philosophy of history, a scientific
> method, a social ethic, a political strategy, and all that drawn together in a
> comprehensible logical system. And with that came such a feeling of security
> and personal force that it functioned ... like a constant state of intoxication.[19]

No wonder De Man likened his conversion to the experience of the early
Christians.

Marxism explained the rift that had opened within De Man's world. It
confirmed his discovery that the "world outside the microcosm of the family was ruled by material interests" and marked by class conflict.[20] But
Marxism also showed how the proletariat, shaped by the inner contradictions of capitalism, had become the agent of social transformation. At the
same time Marxist theory posed a dilemma for De Man. If, as Marx
claimed, social being determined consciousness, the workers would, by
virtue of their social situation, naturally achieve an understanding of their

role in history. What then was the function of estranged intellectuals from the bourgeois class?

Initially De Man drew the logical conclusion. Only by shedding his bourgeois identity could he take part in the redemptive movement of the proletariat. He considered becoming a worker, or at least a newspaper vendor in a working-class district, in order to share or learn at first hand the "life conditions" of the proletariat.[21] Soon, however, he realized that the workers needed to be educated, that intellectuals like himself could play a distinct role in the movement. Putting aside the strict logic of economic determinism, he set out to teach the workers the Marxist meaning of their struggles.

Yet, as De Man recalled, the cultural interests that had been nurtured in his bourgeois home had not been completely devalued by his Marxism. In the Dutch socialists to whom he looked for guidance in understanding Marxism—Richard and Henriette Rolland Holst, Hermann Gorter, and Frank Van de Goes—he found not only an appreciation of art and literature but also an assurance that the socialist movement would save the best part of the cultural inheritance from bourgeois decadence.[22]

The clash between De Man's residual bourgeois identity and his Marxist convictions was, nonetheless, increasingly evident. His dedication to the cause of the workers led to the neglect of his studies, first at the University of Brussels, and then at a polytechnic institute at Ghent. He realized that a bourgeois career was out of the question. His conviction that his Marxism required a "complete break with my class and my family" was also expressed in his attachment, later marriage, to a working-class woman.[23] She seemed "to embody the virtues of the redemptive class." This union would also teach him that it was not "as easy to change his class identity" as he had imagined.

In 1905 De Man informed his family that he was determined to be economically independent. His father, according to the son's account, was remarkably tolerant, assuring him that financial help would be available should he need it. An assignment from the Belgian party paper to cover the annual conference of the German Social Democratic Party enabled De Man to start his new life. After reporting on the conference in Jena, he traveled to Leipzig, "the mecca of the new religion," and secured a position on the most radical of the German socialist newspapers, the *Leipziger Volkszeitung*.[24] But even as he deepened his commitment to orthodox Marxism through contact with several of its leading representatives, including Franz Mehring and Rosa Luxemburg, De Man continued to develop the cultural interests of earlier years. Indeed, one of the editors of the Leipzig paper, Gustav Morgenstern, recognized, in De Man's words, that his "soul still contained a corner which had not been invaded" by the "desert of Marxism."[25] Morgenstern not only provided tickets to concerts, operas, and the theater but also placed his personal library at De Man's disposal and guided his reading in contemporary literature.

The influence of De Man's bourgeois past was suggested too by his decision to resume academic study. The University of Leipzig at this time was ideally suited for his interest in serious scholarly inquiry and his desire to connect it closely to his socialist commitment. In this new setting, contrary to his academic experience in Belgium, he could choose freely from a wide variety of courses and work closely, in seminars, with professors who seemed congenial. For De Man three teachers proved to be most influential—the historian Karl Lamprecht, the philosopher and psychologist Wilhelm Wundt, and, most important, the national economist Karl Bucher. Under the direction of the latter De Man completed a doctoral dissertation in 1909 dealing with the Flemish textile industry during the Middle Ages. His study profoundly influenced his view of European history and particularly his understanding of the relationship between socialism and the bourgeois tradition.

During his years in Leipzig De Man was increasingly active in the wider European socialist movement. With two of his young German colleagues—Karl Liebknecht and Ludwig Frank—he formed an international organization for socialist youth and became its first secretary. He also served, by virtue of his command of French, German, and English, as a translator at international meetings of trade unionists and socialists. His growing awareness of national differences within the general movement—an important source of his later critique of Marxism—was heightened by a semester's study in Vienna and a longer stay in England during 1910.

De Man remained an orthodox Marxist, firmly opposed to those who wished to revise the theory, and committed to the task of nurturing a new mentality among the workers. This was his primary aim when, late in 1910, he returned to Belgium to head a newly formed "Center for Labor Education." The growth of the movement in Belgium had not been accompanied by a comparable increase in the skills required to administer the increasingly complex network of trade unions, cooperatives, mutual aid societies, and party branches. De Man was called on to coordinate and expand the study groups, libraries, and conferences that had developed more or less spontaneously. But he was also determined to bring to the movement, still marked by eclecticism in ideological matters, the "common doctrine" and inspiration provided by Marxism. He set out to build a strong Marxist wing of the party. It was, he recalled, a matter of communicating to the workers "truths about which they were still ignorant" and did not realize they needed.[26]

He also directed his apostolic zeal against the political opportunism that characterized the Belgium Labor Party, and specifically against those leaders who favored cooperation with the left wing of the Liberal Party. No wonder De Man's time as head of the party's educational work was stormy. Only the conciliatory role of Vandervelde saved him, on one occasion, from losing his post.

The outbreak of World War I shook De Man's faith to its foundations. Intimately involved in the desperate last-minute efforts by socialist leaders to avert war, he was dismayed by the rapid collapse of international working-class solidarity. What affected him most deeply, however, was the sudden dissolution of his own conscious principles. The pacifism that had been an essential part of his socialist faith was swept aside by the feelings aroused by the German invasion of Belgium. From his "sub conscious," he recalled, came elementary instincts that impelled him toward the field of battle.[27] He immediately volunteered for front line service as an infantryman.

Later, as an officer in a mortar battalion, De Man gained a deeper understanding of the kind of men who made up the rank and file of the socialist movement. His criticism of the Marxist view of human behavior would owe much to his observation of soldiers in combat. He came to appreciate attitudes and values that had little place in the Marxist view of the proletariat. The qualities of self-respect, the sense of honor, together with forms of emulation and discipline found at the front, would influence his psychological critique of Marxism. The economic determinism of orthodox Marxism was also undermined by two missions, to Russia and America, that De Man undertook on behalf of the Belgium government late in the war. It became clear to him that the profound differences in the development of the two countries could not be accounted for, as Marxists claimed, by economic factors. The war experience, as he put it, had "torn from my eyes the veil of doctrinairism" and freed him from "many things which were not part of my true self."[28]

But De Man's socialist faith, rooted in his bourgeois ethical sensibility, survived the collapse of Marxist orthodoxy. In his first autobiographical book, *The Remaking of a Mind*, published in English in 1919, he wrote of the need for a "new socialism."[29] Yet the meaning of the new socialism and that of his "true self" was still uncertain. Over the next few years De Man's course was erratic and frustrating.

In 1919 he returned to his educational post in the Belgium Labor Party. But he soon gave it up. His hopes for a peace based on Wilsonian principles faded rapidly amid the vengeful atmosphere within the victorious European powers. Even the working classes in Belgium and elsewhere, to whom he looked to lead the way toward a more enlightened Europe, offered no resistance to the resurgent nationalism.

His life now took a surprising direction. He decided to turn his back on Europe and move, with his wife and two children, to America. It was, he recalled, an attempt to find new "spiritual anchorage."[30] A chance meeting with a Canadian businessman during his travels in America had led to an invitation to take part in an expedition into the uncharted back country of New Foundland with the goal of developing its natural resources. De Man now joined an economic enterprise driven by those capitalistic motives and values against which he had rebelled twenty years earlier. It proved to be a rich experience, calling on the capacities for leadership and resourcefulness that De Man had displayed as an officer on the front lines. But the venture ended badly. His report on the expedition was distorted and misused by its financial backers and by corrupt politicians. "My brief Canadian adventure," he recalled, simply acquainted him with the grasping nature of "high finance on the young continent."[31]

De Man's attempt to make a fresh start was not over. But the next stage—following an offer from trade unions in the Pacific Northwest to start a school comparable to the one he had headed in Belgium—drew him back into the labor and socialist movement. Again the outcome was disappointing. The project for a school collapsed for lack of funds. And an appointment to teach a course on industrial relations at the University of Washington was canceled suddenly when De Man became a target of the political reaction that had begun to sweep across the United States in the postwar years. His love affair with America had ended; he abandoned his plans to become a citizen, convinced that the promise of democracy was being defeated by a new plutocracy.[32]

Returning to Belgium in the fall of 1920, De Man devoted himself once more to labor education, this time as head of a new School for Superior Workers. It was designed to train an elite body of functionaries for the movement. Selected for their leadership potential from local party organizations and trade unions, thirty students would be brought together for a year's study. Such subjects as political economy, history, sociology, and psychology were to be taught in close relationship to the practical work experiences of the students. The school also enabled De Man to develop the implications of his own movement away from Marxism. His new pedagogy stressed the capacity for critical thinking, encouraged the growth of moral and aesthetic values, and sought to "transform the whole life of the students."[33] De Man's model, as Karsten Oschmann observed, came directly out of his own way of life as an educated bourgeois man.[34]

De Man did not limit his activity to the school. Influenced by the "guild socialists" in Britain and by new notions of working-class participation in economic management in other countries, he now promoted a concept that would be central to his "new socialism"—industrial democracy.[35] Not only did he hope to develop the qualities needed by the workers when they conquered political power, but he saw their direct involvement in economic decisions at the local level as a counterweight to a parliamentary political system for which he had little respect.

Neither of De Man's new projects—the attempt to develop a nonbureaucratic elite and his efforts to advance working-class power at the factory level—made much headway against the entrenched ways of the trade unions and party. Moreover, his renewed attempt to promote conciliatory attitudes toward Germany and revitalize international socialism clashed with the views of party leaders and, indeed, with the feelings of the rank and file. Estranged from the Belgian movement, he decided to leave the country. His decision was influenced by the breakup of his marriage and a new union with a friend from the bourgeois circle of earlier years. In the fall of 1922 he took his two children and, joined by his new wife and her two children, moved to southern Germany. He had returned to the land he regarded as his "spiritual home."

Settling in Darnstadt, he obtained a teaching position at the Academy of Work in nearby Frankfurt and continued to lecture and write for the wider socialist movement.[36] But over the next three years he devoted himself mainly to a re-examination of the nature and meaning of socialism. What was the source of socialist ideas? What motives drew the workers into the movement? What were the means and prospects for a new socialism? *The Psychology of Socialism* was the outcome of his inquiry.

II

De Man described his *Psychology* as a "fragment of spiritual autobiography."[37] It was an attempt to resolve the "mental crisis" resulting from the collapse of his Marxist faith. He was convinced that his personal difficulties expressed a spiritual crisis in the socialist movement in general. Freed from the "Marxist way of thinking," he could address problems that faced "a whole generation" of socialists.[38] But his *Psychology* also expressed, as Madeleine Gravicz observed, "a need to demonstrate the truths of socialism and justify rationally his emotional need and ethical aspirations."[39]

The book dealt in large part with his recognition, based on his wartime experiences and his involvement in working-class education, that the mentality of the workers was not developing in the way Marx had forecast. He had discovered that the workers were being attracted, irresistibly, to the bourgeois way of life. It was, he confessed, "the most grievous disappointment of my life."[40] Out of his "black despair" came his effort to understand the psychological makeup of the working class. At the same time he was moved to re-examine the historical sources of socialism.

Early in his inquiry, De Man noted that the origins of socialism were not to be found in the "class interests of the proletariat but rather in the cultural wealth of instructed members of the bourgeoisie and the aristocracy."[41] Socialism was mainly a "bourgeois growth," the outcome of the "moral distress" of its intellectuals. Through a process that he likened to psychoanalysis, he traced socialist ideas, including the Marxist, to "cultural, ethical, and aesthetic sources." De Man was, in fact, recapitulating his own development. Socialism could be explained as an "antagonistic reaction of cultured bourgeoisie and aristocrats to their cultural environment." Later in his study De Man attributed that antagonism to the survival of precapitalistic values—notions of social justice, human dignity, and equality, that owed most to Christianity. Underlying Christianity and the other great religions, however, was an "absolute moral order," a "standard of values so general it can be regarded as inherent in human nature."[42] To account for the bourgeois values that had entered socialism, De Man thus fell back on metaphysical claims.

What then drew the workers to socialism? How did one understand what goes on "in the worker's mind?" What, more specifically, was the "emotive reaction of the worker to his social environment?"[43] To explore that reaction De Man turned to recent psychological theories—the physiological and experimentally based studies of Wilhelm Wundt, his teacher in Leipzig; the theory of instincts developed by the British social psychologist William MacDougal; and, most important, the psychoanalytical theories of Sigmund Freud and Alfred Adler. But he was also influenced by those European thinkers—Friedrich Nietzsche, Henri Bergson, the "life philosophers" in Germany, and his neighbor and friend, Hermann Keyserling—who had denied the primacy of reason in human beings in favor of an emphasis on the role of intuition, imagination, and the feelings. If the nineteenth century had been the century of science or logic, the new century would be the "century of psychology."[44]

At the center of De Man's social psychology was the concept of "disposition," a mixture of biological instincts and the modifications—the social and cultural meanings—added to these instincts through historical experience. The basic human instinct, he claimed, was "autovaluation," or self-respect.[45] All other instincts, such as the combative, the sexual, the playful, and what he identified as an instinct toward social solidarity, were secondary. The readiness of industrial workers to adopt socialist ideas could be traced to violations of the feeling of self-respect as this had been transformed into specific dispositions through a "long pre-capitalist past."

> The working class movement is not a product of capitalism. We must look at it as the product of a reaction which occurs when capitalism (a new social state) comes into contact with a human disposition which may be termed pre-capitalist. This disposition is characterized by a certain fixation of the sense of moral values, a fixation which can only be understood with reference to the social experience of the days of feudalism and the craft guilds, to Christian ethics and to the ethical principles of democracy.[46]

The clash between traditional values and the new economic system produced in the industrial workers a "social inferiority complex" that prepared them for socialist ideas.[47] For these ideas provided compensation for the loss of self-respect experienced by the workers with the coming of capitalism. Socialism reaffirmed many of the precapitalist values. But it also expressed what De Man called the "eschatological sentiment," the hope for a radically new way of life.[48] "The working class inferiority complex, intensified to a pitch of moral indignation against extant social conditions, gives birth to a new effect, that of a longing for a better future." Here, according to De Man, was the emotional tap root of the socialist movement. Expressed earlier in Jewish messianism and Christian chiliasm, socialism renewed the expectation of the "last days." Without the "eschatological sentiment," he claimed, "no socialist conviction can be explained." It constituted the "main motive force of the movement." It also indicated that the symbols and myths central to the "emotional life of the movement" could be traced in large part to Christianity.[49] But Christian values and hopes entered the movement only after being transformed into secular democratic aspirations. Christianity, democracy, and socialism were "three forms of one and the same idea."[50] Socialists who recognized this unity could tap "an inexhaustible source of spiritual energy."

To explain the origins and dynamic of the socialist movement in this way was also to illuminate its present crisis. For the eschatological sentiment had lost much of its force. The weakening of the movement's wellspring was reflected in the increasing preoccupation with the economic interests of the workers. And these interests were defined in terms of the values and tastes of the petty bourgeoisie.

De Man now accepted the inevitability of "embourgeoisement." The road to socialism, he wrote, "sets out from proletarian poverty, and passes by way of bourgeois mediocrity."[51] Only when the masses attained "a certain level of prosperity and well-being" could they be "directed towards ... loftier modes of life." In the meantime they were susceptible to the twin seductions of "reformism," their reintegration into the capitalistic system, and nationalistic feeling, or what De Man called "social patriotism."

The working class had ceased, in De Man's analysis of the movement, to play the role assigned to it by Marx. "The halo had vanished from the proletarian head."[52] The materialistic drives of the workers, expressed in the pragmatic policies of their political leaders and the strictly economic aims of the trade unions and cooperatives, had displaced the true goals of socialism.

De Man blamed Marxism in part for the loss of revolutionary elan. His *Psychology* was intended, in fact, to "liquidate Marxism" and, as the title of the French translation indicated, "go beyond Marxism." Running through the book was a critique of the "three pillars" of Marxist theory—rationalism, determinism, and economic hedonism.[53] Marx, he argued, had simply adopted the modes of thought, centered on the belief in mechanical causation, characteristic of the science of his day. By taking over the basic postulate of classical political economy, the claim that the rational pursuit of economic self-interest constitutes the fundamental human motivation, Marxism had unwittingly surrendered to the materialistic and acquisitive values of the bourgeois order it challenged. Marxism thus contributed to the reconquest of the movement by its capitalistic environment.

De Man claimed that his quarrel was "not with Marx but with Marxism," with the "forms of emotional valuations, social volitions, methods of action, principles and programs" that lived on in the movement.[54] He had, in fact, called into question the foundations of Marxist theory. At the same time he maintained that Marx had failed to recognize crucial elements underlying his own thinking: the eschatological and ethical impulses that enabled his ideas to function as a "new religion." Now, however, Marxism had ceased to inspire socialists; it simply provided "propaganda formulas" that rationalized the reformist policies of the Social Democratic leaders.[55]

How then could socialism be revitalized? De Man's solution demonstrated the continuing hold of his bourgeois past. The movement, he argued, could be saved only by those intellectuals, like himself, who embodied the ethical values and hopes that constituted the essence of socialism.

De Man defined the intellectual broadly. The term referred to all those individuals who, by virtue of their "brain work," assumed directing roles in economic and political affairs.[56] As such they constituted a distinct class, separated both from the capitalists and the proletariat. The failure to explain their crucial role in society, and within the socialist movement, had been a major deficiency in Marxist theory. For the intellectuals were the true "rulers of society." De Man even suggested that a "slight change" in the outlook or will of the intellectuals might "eliminate capitalism as an organizing principle of society."[57] But, of course, the great majority of the intellectuals had chosen to serve capitalism and submit to its "soullessness."

Still, the social nature of their work meant that intellectuals were naturally drawn to socialism. In terms inspired by the ideals of the bourgeois professions, De Man described the work of the intellectuals as intrinsically satisfying and directed toward service to the community.[58] Since capitalism thwarted those impulses and the self-respect derived from them, the intellectuals, like the workers, suffered from an inferiority complex. And like the manual workers they were attracted to a social system that promised to fulfill their deepest instincts.

De Man had discovered, through his analysis of the intellectual, the meaning of his "new socialism." Socialism ceased to be a distant goal; it could be realized in the "present happiness of ... living persons."[59] That discovery was "the last stage on the road which led me away from Marxism." His recognition that socialism found expression in service and joy in work also loosened his ties to the working class. Indeed, De Man claimed that the new socialism could be found initially only in "those unusual beings in whom moral passion dominates the whole of their intellectual activity."[60]

De Man had become convinced, through his educational efforts among the workers, that they were, with few exceptions, still incapable of embodying the socialist values and motives. "All we can hope from the adaptive and imitative instincts of the masses is that these ... will break a trail for the realization of vanguard minorities whose activities are the fruit of personal moral convictions."[61] In the meantime "all genuinely socialist ...

activity" was the "affair of a leading elite" that held up "before the masses samples of the kind of satisfactions for which the mass taste is not yet ripe."[62]

No doubt De Man saw himself as one of those rare individuals whose "spiritual metamorphosis" enabled them to inspire by example the new socialist way of life. What he described as a spiritual metamorphosis simply referred to his own protest against the social injustices, the selfishness, the hypocrisies, and the "degeneration of taste" of the bourgeois order, on behalf of its "loftier moral and intellectual values."[63] Confident that those values could be realized most readily among the intellectuals, De Man suggested at one point that the achievement of socialism would require "a change of proletarians into intellectuals."[64] He was engaged, in fact, in his own version of "embourgeoisement."

De Man's *Psychology* can be viewed as an attempt by a bourgeois intellectual to reclaim leadership in a movement, originating in the cultural and social tensions within the bourgeoisie itself, that had been diverted from its initial course by the materialistic drives of the workers. Although he still believed that the organized power of the workers would be necessary to overcome capitalism, and still assumed the correctness of much of the Marxist analysis of economic developments, he had adopted a highly idealistic interpretation of the socialist movement. In place of the Marxist emphasis on objective structures and forces, De Man had focused on subjective factors. Some critics charged that he had simply substituted a psychological determinism for the economic determinism of orthodox Marxism.[65] But he had reaffirmed the humanistic values of individual dignity and freedom derived from his own bourgeois inheritance. And he had anchored those values in metaphysical claims—in what he called the "divine power of the moral law."[66]

De Man's ethical idealism was expressed most clearly in his conception of the intellectual. Absent from his description of the "vanguard minority" was any suggestion that the intellectuals might have special interests or a distinctive will to power. His syncretistic psychology was extremely optimistic. It was virtually devoid of references to the baser tendencies in human nature, what in the Judeo-Christian tradition was understood as sin or evil, or what Freud identified as the human impulse toward aggression and self-destruction. Despite his attention to the nonrational forces in life, De Man was convinced that the passions, at least among the intellectuals, were subject to the control of conscience and reason.

De Man had not solved the problem of motivation. His claim that

Marxists had been unable to show how the material conditions of the workers, how the "is," gave rise to the "ought," could be applied to his own analysis.[67] To provide workers or intellectuals with an understanding of the historical sources or psychological conditions underlying socialism did not of itself generate a will to achieve socialism. Greater self-consciousness about the nature of the movement did little to counter the force of the immediate needs and desires that were pulling the workers down the path of embourgeoisement. Indeed, De Man's emphasis on the role of intellectuals tended to dilute that element in the socialist faith—the eschatological sentiment—which he had seen as the key to its dynamic. For the rationalistic bent of the intellectuals made it difficult, he noted, for them to sympathize fully with the "religious sentiments of the masses."[68] There were, he acknowledged, "two mentalities" in the movement.

Toward the end of his *Psychology* De Man seems to have recognized the limitations of his attempt to show the way to a deeper socialist motivation. In choosing "Credo" as the title of his final chapter, he suggested that his socialism was still, in large part, a personal faith. Nonetheless, he insisted that the future belonged to his form of socialism.

> For my part I firmly believe that there will soon be a swing of the pendulum and that the masses will return from the materialistic cynicism which now prevails to the religious feelings which animated socialism in its early days.[69]

Failing that, the fate of the working class would be a "demoralizing social parasitism and a generalized criminology."[70]

De Man conceded that "many days must pass before we can expect the masses, who are moved by instinct, to follow the gifted few."[71] And since the "psychical rebirth" of socialism could, at first, only be the experience of an elite, he addressed his book to the "small number of persons among whom are to be found the leaders of a coming generation." During the months following the publication of the *Psychology* he set out to find growth points for his ideas within the German movement. The "battle which rages around Marxist theory," he believed, was "going to be lost or won in Germany."[72]

III

A few weeks after the publication of the *Psychology,* De Man was invited to deliver the main address at the founding conference of the Union of Socialist Academics.[73] The occasion, he recalled, seemed perfectly suited for the practical application of his notion that intellectuals had a "special role to play in the realization of socialism."[74]

The "founder and soul" of the new organization was a young lawyer from Baden, Hugo Marx.[75] He had become convinced that the failure of the Social Democrats to carry out fundamental changes in German society when they held power just after the war could be attributed to their lack of experts. Without individuals trained in administration or law or capable of dealing with the complex social and economic problems facing the new regime, the socialist leaders had been unable to overcome the resistance of the established bureaucracy. Inspired in part by the Fabian Society in Britain, Marx hoped to develop a group of academically educated individuals who could advise the Social Democratic politicians on practical issues.

The choice of De Man to open the conference testified to the widespread interest in his ideas generated by the *Psychology*. But the book had also made him a controversial figure in the movement. His claim that Marxism had been superseded antagonized leading Social Democrats. They warned the conference organizers that De Man's appearance would be a "bad omen" for the future relationship between the party and the Union.[76] The threat moved Marx and his associates to ask De Man to withdraw. He refused. No doubt he saw the meeting as a unique opportunity to gain converts for his new socialism.

De Man's talk, "The Intellectuals and Socialism," repeated the main ideas of the *Psychology*—the critique of orthodox Marxism, his insistence that ethical values and motives constituted the true meaning of socialism, and his claim that the movement had degenerated into the narrow pursuit of material interests.[77] He focused, however, on what he described as the troubled relationship between the party and the intellectuals. The "academic question," he noted, went back to the Dresden party congress of 1903 when August Bebel, the party's leader, warned the delegates to be wary of the educated recruits lest they lead the proletariat astray.[78] Since that time the whole subject had been taboo, while the party's relationship to the intellectuals had deteriorated. Now the problem must be addressed. But the intellectuals could no longer be identified simply with those who had attended a university. "Today the question of the intellectual goes far beyond the question of the qualifications ... of a few academics to exercise ... offices in a working class party."[79] It was a question of the party's relationship to intellectuals in general.

Again, as in the *Psychology*, De Man defined the intellectual in a broad and vague manner. The term referred to those individuals who worked with their minds rather than with their hands. And he repeated his claim that socialist intellectuals embodied the goals of the movement. In contrast to the worker, with his "two souls"—one pulling him back into the capitalistic order, the other "struggling for a new culture"—the intellectuals transcended class interests.[80] They were moved mainly by ethical and cultural concerns.

De Man's talk at Weimar was received, he recalled, with "undivided applause."[81] Several of those present, however, defended a nondogmatic "living Marxism."[82] And the two Social Democratic leaders who attended urged the delegates to pursue the goal, advocated by Hugo Marx, of developing a body of experts and advisors for the party. But the readiness of the leaders of the new organization to bow to pressure from the Social Democratic executive and ask him to withdraw removed any illusions De Man had as to its capacity to challenge the outlook of the party. The "Marxist party church," with its dogma of the class struggle, was still too strong.[83]

De Man had helped, nonetheless, to turn the Union of Socialist Academics away from the course envisioned by Hugo Marx. The rift between the party and the new organization, evident at the opening conference, was never closed. Subsequent meetings of the Union demonstrated the preference of its members for the "ethico-religious" approach to socialism advocated by De Man. Even Hugo Marx, who continued to be the mainstay of the Union, gradually abandoned his hope of providing the party with expertise in favor of purely ideological concerns. Convinced that the German state could be conquered only "from below," the leaders of the Union increasingly viewed themselves as the "spiritual conscience" of the Social Democratic Party, charged with the task of reminding its leaders of their deeper cultural mission.[84] During 1930 the organization died. It had remained, according to Marx, peripheral to the party, incapable of supplying the "warning and more rational conscience" it needed.[85]

Even before the publication of the *Psychology*, De Man had identified another development in the German movement that promised support for his new socialism. In the preface to the first edition of the book he appealed directly to those within the new generation who viewed socialism as "an experience of the soul."[86] At a number of points in the book he noted the relative freedom of the younger socialists from the hold of "interests" that dominated the party leaders.

The emergence of a distinct outlook and spirit within the new generation of socialists was a striking feature of the movement in the years after the war. Forming more or less spontaneously in a number of German cities, associations of young socialists, many of whom had served in the army, were bringing new hopes and energies to the movement.[87] They were often impatient, even scornful, toward the political leaders who, they believed, had lost sight of the deeper meaning of socialism.

In the university student societies especially De Man recognized aspirations much like those he had expressed in his own revolt against the bourgeois world.[88] The leaders of these societies came "almost without exception" out of the educated sector of the bourgeoisie.[89] Like De Man they tended to be critical of the dry rationalism and determinism of orthodox Marxism and viewed socialism as a new feeling for life and the promise of a "new man." Here again was a socialism understood primarily in ethical and cultural terms; it meant human fellowship, joy in work, and made room for aesthetic values. Although these socialists continued to see the proletariat as the main vehicle for a new culture, socialism had ceased to be tied closely to a single class.

The new spirit found fullest expression at a meeting of young socialists in Hofgeismar during Easter week of 1923.[90] Held at a time when French and Belgian troops were occupying the Ruhr, the organizers shared in an upsurge of German patriotic feeling. In formulating their program they were determined to overcome the traditional hostility between the socialist movement and the nation. Indeed, they felt that the "Golgotha" suffered by the German people meant that they were uniquely situated among the European societies for the "spiritual rebirth" leading to socialism.

The hopes expressed at Hofgeismar soon faded. Within a year the new program was challenged by young socialists who reaffirmed an "unfalsified Marxism," the class struggle, and called for a "complete break with bourgeois ways" and the German state.[91]

Although the Hofgeismar group had failed to give a new direction to the younger generation of socialists, it was to one of its leaders, August Rathmann, that De Man turned in the spring of 1926 when he conceived the idea of starting a journal to express the new currents of socialist thought.[92] To be called the *Young Socialist*, the journal would compete directly with the official organ of the Social Democratic Party, *Die Gesellschaft*, which, he argued, had lost any "close ties with the times."[93] The economical and political issues that dominated the party press needed to be augmented by scientific and cultural discussions. Politics, after all, were "only part of their task." Unless the movement advanced beyond its "traditional interests" and expressed a "new world feeling," it could not realize socialism. There was, in short, a socialism that rested on "very differ-

ent grounds" than Marxism. It was time for "the two views to confront
each other on the intellectual and moral level." By means of the journal, De
Man also hoped to draw in a third current of new ideas within the German
socialist movement. In the group of "religious socialists" led by the theologian Paul Tillich, he saw an approach to the crisis of socialist thought that
had much in common with his own diagnosis. Tillich's religious socialism
merits closer examination here because it provides a critical perspective on
De Man's conception of socialism, and the bourgeois sensibilities that underlay it.

IV

The circle that formed around Tillich in Berlin during the early 1920s
was part of a wider development of religious socialism in Germany.[94] It had
begun before the war out of a growing concern among Protestant clergymen over the estrangement of the industrial workers from the churches.
For the interests and aspirations of the industrial workers had little place in
a Protestant tradition that tended, both in its Lutheran and Calvinist
forms, to be otherworldly and to emphasize individual piety. The collapse
of the old order in Germany at the end of the war seemed to a number of
the clergy to provide a new opportunity to reconcile the workers with organized religion. During the early Weimar years religious socialism embraced a range of activities, including charitable and settlement work, as
well as study groups. Its followers also attempted, within the representative bodies of the churches, to counter their traditional hostility toward the
Social Democrats.

The concerns of the Tillich circle were more limited, directed toward
questions of theology, history, and social theory.[95] It was a diverse group,
made up of clergymen and academics, and it included two men of Jewish
background, Eduard Heimann and Adolphe Lowe. Convinced that the
military defeat and humiliation of Germany opened the way for fundamental political and social change, they saw in socialism the promise of a renewal of the prophetic spirit within the Judeo-Christian tradition. Tillich
gave systematic expression to their attempts to connect that tradition with
the socialist movement.

Tillich's revision of his Lutheran faith had begun before the war and
then taken on new urgency through his experience as a chaplain at the
front.[96] He had come to question the traditional view of the "religious"
which, at least from the time of Schleiermacher, had been seen as a distinct

form of consciousness alongside the ethical, the aesthetic, and the cognitive. The religious, Tillich held, was a quality of human experience that made ultimate or "unconditional" demands on the individual. As such it erased the distinction between the sacred and the profane, or secular. It also gave meaning to life and was the source of human culture.

Viewed from this perspective Protestant Christianity ceased to be fixed within specific credal or institutional forms. What Tillich called the "Protestant Principle" expressed a dynamic relationship between the divine and the human.[97] It was also a critical principle, constantly calling into question the old religious forms and capable of discovering new manifestations of the spirit in strange and unsuspected places. Tillich saw in the socialist movement the promise of a redemptive spiritual force. It was the task of the religious socialists to make the movement aware of its own religious depths.

In his search for ways of thinking and experiencing that would overcome the seeming irrelevance of Protestant Christianity to modern society, Tillich was attempting to gain a fresh understanding of those characteristics of human existence that were prior to all social conventions, ideologies, and institutions. Influenced by Martin Heidegger—the two men were on the faculty of the University of Marburg in 1924—Tillich was engaged in an ontological quest.[98] Where Heidegger, however, interpreted the elemental condition of life, of "Being," in naturalistic and atheistic terms, Tillich remained a Christian. He viewed Jesus Christ as the unique source of meaning in life. But he argued that the moment when Christ entered history, the Kairos, might be renewed in secondary or derivative forms. Times like the present, when a profound crisis marked Western Civilization, were ripe for a new expression of the spirit, or a "secondary Kairos." Socialism held, according to Tillich, such a hope.

There were obvious affinities between Tillich's religious socialism and De Man's new socialism. Both men claimed that the socialist movement could realize its goal only by recovering its deeper inspiration. But there were, as Tillich's review of De Man's *Psychology* made clear, basic disagreements.[99] Although he praised De Man for certain features of his analysis—his realistic portrayal of the proletariat, his recognition that the socialist vision was losing its force, and his insight into the religious sources of the movement—Tillich maintained that De Man's psychology was superficial. He had failed to understand the "profound ontological level on which Marx had placed himself when he analyzed capitalism." De Man, and most contemporary Marxists as well, has lost sight of the dialectical understanding of reality by means of which Marx had grasped the concrete struggle of the workers and their developing sense of their destiny. The proletariat, by virtue of its embeddedness in the economic process, was the place where the fundamental conflict in modern history—the dialectical clash between the oppressive structures of capitalism and new social possibilities—was unfolding. According to Tillich, De Man's voluntaristic and rationalistic approach to socialism separated human will and knowledge from actual life. No wonder he had discovered the true meaning of socialism in the intellectuals rather than in the workers.

Tillich's ontology restored much of the Marxist emphasis on objective economic forces. But his account of human subjectivity differed profoundly from that of the Marxists. The Marxists, he argued, had failed to recognize the "religious forces ... hidden" in their dialectic and had surrendered to a materialism and determinism that denied the distinguishing features of human existence.[100] As a result Marxism had lost the "transcendental element ... the passionate eschatological tension ... the dynamic hopefulness present in its origins."[101] Tillich's ontology, in contrast, emphasized human freedom together with the uncertainties, the ambiguities, and, indeed, the demonic possibilities, that marked all human activity. Viewed from this perspective, socialism could only be seen as a venture of faith, subject to error and defeat, and ultimately dependent not on human will but on the grace of God.

By means of his synthesis of Marxism and Christianity, Tillich took aim at those features of De Man's socialism that owed most to his bourgeois inheritance—his reliance on the power of ethical motives and his confidence in the human capacity for self-mastery. De Man's ethical idealism was one expression of a development that, according to Tillich, underlay the crisis of modern civilization—the human claim to autonomy. He maintained that the drive toward complete self-sufficiency, which he identified with the bourgeoisie, would end in emptiness and sterility unless there was a recovery of religious inspiration, or what he called "theonomy." Tillich's summary statement of the cultural crisis could be read as a critique of De Man's conception of socialism.

> Autonomy is able to live as long as it can draw on the religious tradition of the past. ... But more and more it loses this spiritual foundation. ... At the end of this process autonomy turns back to the lost theonomy with impotent longing, or it looks forward to a new theonomy in the attitude of creative waiting until the kairos appears.[102]

Despite the differences between De Man and the Tillich circle, they hoped to find a common ground when, in the spring of 1928, they met at a conference in Heppenheim.

De Man had abandoned the plan for a new journal. But he and Rathmann, with the help of other socialist intellectuals, decided to organize a conference to discuss the state of the movement. They chose to limit the meeting to German speakers and to focus on the question of the foundations and the meaning of a socialist way of life, putting off until later the problems in the practical realm. De Man was asked to give the opening address. Concerned, however, that his controversial place in the movement might alienate those intellectuals who were still committed to Marxism, the organizers assigned a second opening address to a leading figure in the Tillich group—Heimann. The meeting became, in large part, a debate between De Man and the followers of Tillich.

The eighty men and women who gathered at Heppenheim came together out of a common belief that the socialist movement in Germany, and elsewhere in Europe, had lost its vitality. A "certain weariness," as the conference chairman, Hugo Sinzheimer, observed, had settled over the movement.[103] The earlier vision of radical social change had dissolved through the bureaucratization of the Social Democratic Party and its preoccupation with the immediate interests of the workers. Although socialists must, according to Sinzheimer, transform the economic system, the most urgent task at present was to clarify the "ethical spiritual" element in the movement. Only by connecting socialism once more with "the whole inner life of men" could the movement gain "a fresh impetus of will." Their task as intellectuals was to re-establish the ground of socialist belief.

De Man led off with an address on the "Foundations of Socialism."[104] His talk summarized the ideas he had been developing during the previous ten years. But he focused mainly on the ethical and religious sources of socialism. In Marxism, he argued, there was an "ethical passion" that "came only timidly to the surface ... in the use of words."[105] Underlying Marx's brilliant critique of bourgeois mores in the *Communist Manifesto* were "moral and legal ideas" that reached far back in Western history—to the thought of Plato, to late Judaism and early Christianity. Having appropriated these ideas unconsciously, Marx had then hidden his ethical values in his materialistic philosophy without, however, losing the "eschatological feeling." Here was the source of the enthusiasm found in the early movement.

A regrounding of socialism could only come, De Man argued, out of a fuller awareness of this background and an acknowledgement of "supra-historical eternal verities." De Man now described the ground of socialism as a "religious something," a feeling that could not be fully grasped by science or reason or critical analysis.[106] There were moments in life when "something more profound" than reason made claims on one. He cited his own decision, "proceeding from his whole being," to fight in Belgium in 1914 despite his conscious pacifist convictions.

Apart from his intuitions and metaphysical claims, De Man refused to say more about the nature of his faith. It was, he observed, one of the tenets of his religion that he could not "speak of it in public."[107] He maintained, moreover, in words drawn from George Bernard Shaw, that there was at the moment "no credible system of religious belief." This did not trouble him; the specific content of religious faith was, for socialists, irrelevant. Given the rational and ethical nature of the universe, all men of reason and good will, whatever their world views, would come to socialism. De Man even claimed that "anti-socialism is at bottom most profoundly an attempt to repress the torments of conscience"; the adversaries of the movement suffered from "troubled consciences."[108] Despite his insistence that socialism was grounded in religious feeling, De Man's socialism remained essentially ethical. This was the main target of his critics at Heppenheim.

Focusing on what he called De Man's "ethical voluntarism," Heimann argued that the meaning of socialism could not be found by bringing external standards to bear on the struggles of the workers; it could only be discovered within the "living movement."[109] Heimann attempted to reground socialism in a way that derived, as he acknowledged, from Tillich's theology. He accepted the Marxist analysis of capitalism and insisted that the development of socialism was inextricably bound up with the class struggle and the materialistic aspirations of the workers. Like Tillich, however, he rejected the determinism of "vulgar Marxism" in favor of a view of human subjectivity that emphasized both the "free moral resolve" of individuals as well as their proneness to error and discord. Socialism was a venture of faith which assumed that God worked in history. Indeed, Heimann viewed the historical conditions that were driving the workers toward socialism as a form of grace.

The discussion that followed focused mainly on De Man's conflation of the ethical and the religious, and his claim that all men of good will and reason would naturally gravitate to socialism. Not only was it a mistake, his critics argued, to reduce the religious to the ethical, but strong ethical convictions did not necessarily lead to a socialist belief. There were many in the antisocialist camp who were honestly and genuinely devoted to social justice.

Two figures at the conference attempted to mediate between the views of De Man and Tillich. Martin Buber suggested that neither the "religious way," as defined by Tillich, nor De Man's ethical way, provided a common ground for socialists.[110] Drawing on the ideas presented a few years earlier in his book *I and Thou*, he maintained that the "fictional differences" between socialists could best be overcome by examining the "actual way men lived together." What was needed was the building of local communities where individuals could meet in a spirit of love and reciprocity. Leonhard Ragaz, a Swiss clergyman who represented an older, prewar form of religious socialism, attempted to reconcile the religious and ethical approaches to socialism by calling attention to their historical roots in the thought of Luther and Calvin.[111] Socialism could best be seen as a synthesis of the ethical demands of Calvin, continuing through Kant and De Man, and the Lutheran emphasis on grace, as carried forward by Hegel and Tillich. In the "struggle of the proletariat" Ragaz saw a coming together of "unconscious ethical and religious goals."

De Man viewed the discussion at Heppenheim as a vindication of his position. In his concluding remarks he claimed that Tillich and his followers had simply confirmed his belief that individuals could "arrive at socialism from any honest religious conviction."[112] Their climb to the "lonely peaks" of metaphysical speculation had simply obscured the truth that socialism could be reached more easily "half way up the slopes"—at the ethical level.

The Heppenheim conference did not fulfill De Man's hope of giving new direction to socialist thought in Germany. The participants had failed to discover a common ground, and, moreover, the meeting did not generate the sense of fellowship necessary to continue the effort. Noting the "cold intellectualism" of the meeting, Ragaz commented: "I have never participated in a conference where there was less cordiality and humanity."[113] "No new, vital elan," he added, "could be born out of an atmosphere so cold," so lacking in tact, and the "socialist spirit." De Man concluded that the meeting "suffered, like so many academic enterprises, from an excess of intellect combined with a lack of will."[114] No wonder the plan to set up a committee to call further meetings and develop the practical implications of their discussion was abandoned.

The Heppeheim conference convinced De Man that there was little hope of gaining support for his ideas from other socialist intellectuals. He now decided to distance himself from the groups that had seemed to be his natural allies. Once more he turned away from a course of action that might have drawn him more deeply into the German movement. The essential loneliness of his intellectual journey was suggested at this time by the breakup of his second marriage, an event that convinced him that his was a life not suited for such a union.[115] His unwillingness, perhaps, inability, to engage in relationships of mutuality was noted by a young woman who observed him at a meeting in 1929. De Man, she wrote, was "rude and irreconcilable in discussion," at ease only with "intellectuals who were socially and intellectually inferior." He was "really an isolated man" who "avoided true human contact."[116]

The appraisal helps to explain some of the weaknesses of De Man's attempt to reconstruct the socialist ideology. The conception of society implicit in that attempt was extremely thin; he paid little attention to the texture of human relationships, ignoring, for example, the importance of the family and the role of secondary associations. He was largely indifferent to the function of institutions, the ways in which they made collective action possible or set limits to individual initiatives. His attitude toward the central institutions of the working-class movement, the trade unions, the cooperatives, and the Social Democratic Party, was mainly negative; he tended to dismiss the leaders as opportunistic, too ready to adopt bourgeois values and manners. One looks in vain through De Man's writings in these years for any sympathetic treatment of the dilemmas facing the socialist politicians in Germany as they struggled to protect the interests of the workers in a representative system that was increasingly paralyzed.

Although De Man continued to lecture widely in the German movement, he exercised, as one of his followers recalled, "only a modest influence."[117] The "directing cadres," locked into an orthodox Marxism, remained "irremediably hostile." But even the Marxist "revisionists" gathered around the *Sozialistische Monatshefte* failed to give him a hearing. He was dismissed as a "bourgeois individualist," even an anarchist. Indeed, despite De Man's study of social psychology and his insights into the ways in which historical experience had formed the common spiritual grooves for the socialists, his approach to social change remained individualistic.[118] What mattered most was the transformation of the values and motives of individuals. His own conversion to socialism remained paradigmatic.

De Man now abandoned his efforts to find intellectual allies within the German movement despite a promising new attempt to establish a rallying point for an ethically and religiously inspired socialism. The creation of the

Neue Blätter für den Sozialismus, which began publication in January 1930, was largely the work of Tillich and his followers.[119] But it would realize something of De Man's hope of bringing together the "Hofgeismarer" group, the religious socialists, and other socialist intellectuals to whom his ideas had appealed. Indeed, by attracting the "Mierendorff circle"—Julius Leber, Theodor Haubach, Kurt Schuhmacher, and Carlo Mierendorff— the journal began to bridge the gap between the practical problems facing the party and its intellectual critics.[120] It was, however, given the rapid deterioration of German economic, social, and political life in the early 1930s, a belated response.

De Man served on the editorial board of the *Neue Blätter* but he did not play an active role in its development, contributing only a few reviews and a single article, dealing with "embourgeoisement," during its three-and-a-half years of existence.[121] Meanwhile, he had accepted an offer to teach social psychology at the University of Frankfurt. There he resumed his solitary effort to rejuvenate the socialist movement.

V

De Man arrived in Frankfurt at a time, the late 1920s, when it had become one of Germany's most vital centers of intellectual and cultural life. The city's major newspaper, the *Frankfürter Zeitung*, as well as its new radio station, were open to new ideas in art and literature.[122] Frankfurt was also the site of a recently founded Psychoanalytical Institute and an important center for Jewish studies, with which Franz Rosenzweig and Martin Buber were closely associated. At the university, where Kurt Reizler had become rector, Tillich had just been appointed to the chair in philosophy, and Karl Mannheim was developing, in his "sociology of knowledge," an approach to the role of intellectuals that had much in common with that of De Man. The Institute for Social Research, founded there in 1923, had not yet begun its creative reworking of Marxist thought, but it was gathering a remarkable group of young intellectuals who were undertaking radical critiques of various aspects of contemporary social and cultural life.[123]

De Man did not find this setting especially stimulating.[124] Later he described Frankfurt as a place where a motley array of intellectual coteries had come together to worship the newest gods. Despite the brilliance of many of the figures there, it was a "tower of Babel," in which each group seemed to possess its own vocabulary.[125] He compared the thought of the Jewish intellectuals, in particular, to a "magnificent cerebral machine revolving in a vacuum." De Man did engage in long evening discussions with Tillich, but these simply confirmed the conclusion reached at Heppenheim—that there was, as Tillich told him, "an abyss between your mentality and that of ours."[126]

De Man continued to struggle with the questions that had occupied him throughout the decade—the psychological makeup of the industrial workers and the motives required for a socialist society. Both concerns had been central in his book *The Struggle for Joy in Work*, published a year after the *Psychology*.[127] Based on his involvement in working-class education, and, more directly, on questionnaires he had given to his students at the Academy of Work, the book proved to be a pioneering study of industrial psychology.[128] What he identified as "joy in work" was a "disposition," a transformation of a basic instinct—the instinct to find satisfaction in one's work—by historical experience.[129] In precapitalist Europe, he argued, that instinct had taken on a strong sense of social obligation. But this ethic of work had been eroded by capitalism. De Man expressed his surprise and pleasure at finding that something of this traditional disposition had survived in the modern world, that a majority of his working-class students, admittedly a highly selective group, reported that their own work was satisfying.

How then could socialists build on this surviving joy in work and find new ways to free the mass of industrial workers from unnecessary and unpleasant labor? De Man denied that the standard socialist solution, public ownership of the means of production, would be sufficient. What was needed was "socialization from beneath," changes in the immediate conditions in which men worked.[130] Here, as in his earlier writings, De Man advocated a form of industrial democracy, a sharing by the workers in the decisions at the factory level. The enhanced feelings of self-respect resulting from such participation would free the "old joy of work" from the purgatory of capitalism.

De Man reaffirmed, in his concept of work, a central element in his bourgeois inheritance. Indeed, the asceticism of the Protestant tradition found expression in his claim that the "painful sacrifice" entailed in work could be transformed into pleasure. Through the "performance of an action regarded as a sacred duty" sorrows "became joy."[131] De Man even claimed that the "miracle" of this transformation might give rise to an "eschatological transcendence" in which the individual experienced something of the socialist future.

At the University of Frankfurt De Man gathered a group of devoted students. They joined him in visits to factories where he continued his in-quiries into the nature of work in modern society. And by means of outings into the countryside and other informal settings, he developed a relation-ship with his students that was rare in German academic life. Later a mem-ber of the group attempted to capture, in fictional terms, De Man's person-ality at this time.

> Antoine de Barrenne [De Man] was tall, broad shouldered, and putting on weight a little. His curly hair was salted with grey and his face was so deeply tanned that his blue eyes shown out of his face. He gave a sense of physical struggle, but more than that, of inner vitality and at the same time of heroic tension, as if he was holding himself in leash.[132]

He remained, according to this portrayal, "profoundly revolutionary," still convinced that a "radical transformation of society" presupposed a "change in the mentality of the working class and the mentality of the human race."

The new mentality, however, was still essentially bourgeois. This was evident in a lecture, "Socialism and Culture," De Man delivered in Paris in March 1930, where he addressed the question of the "extent to which the working class movement contained the germs of a new culture."[133] Here he employed the distinction, fashionable in German thought, between "Cul-ture" and "Civilization"—the former representing creative forces in history and the latter the frozen and essentially sterile aftermath. Viewed from this perspective, socialists were charged with the task of renewing the creative forces, particularly the dignity of work, that the bourgeoisie had developed and then betrayed.

De Man still claimed that socialism would mean a "fundamental rever-sal of values," that it expressed a "creative process comparable to the leaven" Christianity had introduced into the world of antiquity.[134] But his radical claim was not supported by any argument that the socialist future would mean a dramatically new way of life. He simply stated that work in the future would be a right of all men and women and be "cooperative and collective." Apart from his insistence that socialism would realize a higher level of ethical conduct, he did not envision a world that differed signifi-cantly from that of an idealized bourgeoisie society.

In his attempt to guide socialists onto a new path De Man was caught in a growing contradiction. His recognition that the socialist movement drew its enthusiasm and energy from nonrational elements, particularly the "eschatological sentiment," was at odds with his own rationalistic bent, his determination to make the "unconscious motives" in the movement fully conscious.[135] This developing tension was evident in a lecture he delivered late in 1930.[136] There he cited Georges Sorel in claiming that "myths" were the "greatest force in history for creating values and fashioning reality." And he argued that the socialist movement must recover its mythical element if it was to "give new direction to the masses." But at the same time De Man denied that the socialist myth was irrational or unrealistic. The anticipatory or utopian feature in socialism was simply "an image projected onto an imaginary future in the light of present possibilities." To make the socialist myth, or utopia, rational, however, was to rob it of the spontaneous quality which, as Sorel had recognized, was the source of its power. A myth remains vital only as long as "its believers do not recognize it as a myth."[137]

The tension between De Man's rational outlook and his recognition that socialism drew its energy from nonrational beliefs appeared again in his lecture on "National Fascism," delivered in Berlin in December 1930.[138] The general election earlier in the year had demonstrated the extraordinary appeal of Hitler's movement. De Man was quick to see in its success lessons for the working-class movement. The rise of National Socialism could be explained in part, he claimed, by the failure of socialists to broaden their appeal to the impoverished sections of the middle class. But the dynamic of fascism came mainly from "impulses which the socialists had too much neglected during the previous ten years"—the need for a utopia, for a radical critique of capitalistic and bourgeois institutions, and for leaders who were "personalities." Why, De Man asked, had socialists "closed off access to such subjects?" Again he maintained that the ethical and spiritual elements in socialism had been set aside in favor of the pursuit of material interests and political power. The fascists, in contrast, had exploited the "anticapitalist motives" generated by the socialists as well as other motives ignored by socialists—aesthetic, heroic, and particularly, the "instinct for community" expressed in the fascist exaltation of the nation.

De Man employed the concepts he had developed in his *Psychology* to explain fascism. In its ideology, especially in its anti-Semitism and its anti-Marxism, certain sections of the middle class had found compensation for an inferiority complex. But while there were psychological parallels between the fascists and the socialists, the differences were fundamental. He contrasted the "false consciousness" of the fascists with the socialist attempt to achieve a "true consciousness."[139] While the fascists had regressed to primitive or prelogical modes of thought, the socialists sought a scientific understanding of society. "I join" the tradition from Socrates to Kant, De Man declared, in "viewing reason as the divine spark in man."[140]

During his stay in Frankfurt he attempted to connect what he had come to see as the "two mentalities" in the movement, the rational and the non-rational. The *festspiel*, or pageant, entitled, "Wir," which he wrote and produced in the spring of 1932, was designed to lift the participants and the spectators to his own level of socialist consciousness.[141] In this attempt to give his ethical socialism aesthetic or mythic expression he also sought to tap feelings comparable to those being mobilized by the fascists.

Performed on May Day, 1932, "Wir" drew on the rituals and symbols that had developed earlier within the German socialist movement.[142] Held in the largest hall in Frankfurt, the pageant has been described as a "psychodrama," portraying the passage of the working class from oppression to "liberation and redemption."[143] Over two thousand individuals participated, drawn from all ages, dressed in everyday apparel, and thus abolishing the "distinction between life and art." By means of films projected onto a large screen, alternating with the sounds of choruses and processions, the spectacle celebrated the life of the movement—the forces that drove it, the feelings that animated it.

"Wir" gave mythic form to the ideas that De Man had been developing for a decade or more. Hence the comment of one observer:

> All the doctrines of Henri De Man are condensed within it, under a form which became ... as in ancient Greece, a play, with the spectators participating. He has succeeded in presenting ... that which was perhaps the master idea in all of his doctrines ... the cultural ascension of the working class. Not as it is ... but as he dreamed it would be ... the bearer of new cultural values.[144]

To another observer it was "as if I were entering his mind piece by piece until the pattern became whole. I understood one thing—his idea that significant as economic factors are in motivating people to action, socialism will stand or fall by the idealism of its appeal."[145]

"Wir" expressed De Man's hopes for the movement. But it also proved to be the swan song of his decade-long effort to influence German socialism. Time for that effort was now running out. During 1932 the Weimar republic disintegrated and the socialists were increasingly divided and demoralized.[146] With the appointment of Hitler as chancellor in January 1933, the triumph of the Nazis was assured.

Before he left Germany De Man published the *Socialist Idea*, the culmination of his attempt to reinterpret socialism. The book was, in part, a response to the changing character of capitalism—its increasingly monopolistic structure—in part a response to the onset of the Great Depression. But the *Socialist Idea* also developed more fully De Man's claim that the central task of the socialists was to recover and revitalize bourgeois values.

There was a nostalgic, even reactionary tone in De Man's new portrayal of the precapitalistic bourgeoisie. Drawing on his doctoral dissertation, he argued that the cities of medieval Flanders, and their counterparts in northern Italy and France, had created institutions that expressed the belief, derived from Christianity, that work was the sole legitimizing source of economic reward. Never, according to De Man, had the original bourgeois values, expressed in the French Revolution's trinity of liberty, equality, and fraternity, "been so close to their realization as in the republican communes of the high middle ages."[147] With the development of capitalism, however, work and property were separated. The bourgeoisie "lifted off from the working class" and became a class of possessors and exploiters. Having discarded the values to which it owed its rise, the bourgeoisie ceased to be a progressive force in history. But the "spiritual currents" derived from the precapitalist bourgeoisie continued a subterranean existence and were constantly renewed by intellectuals capable of "penetrating into the realm of absolute values."[148] Marx was one of those intellectuals. The recent publication of his "Economic and Philosophical Manuscripts" confirmed De Man's earlier claim that ethical motives underlay Marx's socialism.[149]

De Man's vision of the socialist future was still recognizably bourgeois. In writing of the need to raise "the personal tastes of the masses," he advocated a "healthy asceticism," or a way of life in which hedonism and luxury would be rejected in favor of simple pleasures and comfort.[150] He continued to believe, too, that the immediate future of socialism was in the hands of the intellectuals. And he found fresh support for this view in Karl Mannheim's argument that intellectuals could rise above class and attain a "total vision of reality."[151]

Yet, De Man realized that he had reached an impasse in his attempt to revitalize socialism. Toward the end of the *Socialist Idea* he acknowledged that he had been mistaken in believing that a "renewal of the socialist impulse" could come from a "simple change of mentality."[152] He had also lost something of his confidence in the socialist intellectuals. In what was, perhaps, a confession of his own experience, he noted the tendency for intellectuals to become isolated from the "real movement of the masses."[153]

It was time, De Man declared, for a "new phase of socialist action."[154]

This was dictated in part by the "evolution of the capitalist social and economic order," the shift from a competitive to a monopolistic system dominated by financial interests. But the breakdown of the capitalistic system also challenged socialists to present practical alternatives. In the closing chapter of the *Socialist Idea* De Man outlined a plan for the legal overthrow of a capitalistic order that was "no longer susceptible of amelioration."[155]

De Man regarded his "Plan," therefore, as revolutionary; it called for two major structural changes in the economy—state control of the banks and other credit agencies, that he had come to see as the decisive forces in capitalism, and the nationalization of the monopolistic large industries.[156] But he departed from traditional socialist notions of public ownership by leaving much of the capitalist order intact. He believed that private property and the free market not only promoted efficiency in production but also protected individual liberty. His Plan thus carried over something of his respect for the union of work and property that he saw in the precapitalist bourgeoisie. He advocated, in short, a mixed economy, with the state playing a directing role through its control over fiscal policies and the major industries.

But while de Man now looked to institutional changes to advance the socialist cause, his Plan retained the essential features of his ideological reconstruction. He still counted mainly on the power of ideals to drive the movement. Although "interests" and the mass movement were necessary, they were subordinate to "the idea," which, as Dick Pels observed, "drew its revolutionary strength from its own private resources and thus realizes itself in history practically under its own steam."[157] Moreover, this voluntaristic or spiritual definition of socialism was still the possession of a disinterested intellectual elite guided by reason and conscience. In his renewed insistence on the role of intellectuals, De Man now called on that section of the middle class made up of "managers, engineers, and technicians" who were united in their pursuit of efficiency in production. De Man assumed, as Pels observed, a "natural union" of his earlier vanguard of socialist intellectuals and the intellectual elite of the capitalistic middle class. "The humanistic, normative rationality, which constitutes the basis for judgment of the former, finds a natural complement in the technical and productivistic rationality of the latter."[158] Both were viewed, in De Man's Manichean picture of society, as enemies of the "parasitic power of money."

De Man's Plan also required a new type of leader. It demanded men who were not "stuck in the old ways," who had not lost the capacity for creative initiatives.[159] Indeed, the very "lack of experience" would be an advantage to the new leader. What mattered most was audacity, "physical energy," and, above all, the possession of a plan that would avoid revolutionary extremism while going beyond mere reformism.

His description of the new socialist leader was a self-portrait. It also anticipated the next stage in his career. For several years Vandervelde had been urging De Man to return to Belgium and head the party's new Office for Social Research. In March 1933, De Man returned to his native country. A few weeks later the *Socialist Idea* was burned by the Nazis.

VI

He returned to a Belgium that was highly industrialized, dependent on exporting goods to a world market, and hence especially vulnerable to the recent collapse of international trade.[160] In the face of growing unemployment the Belgium government had adopted deflationary policies, cutting back on public expenditures, including those allocated to social welfare, in order to balance the budget and maintain the value of its currency. Confronted with mounting discontent among the workers, the Belgium Labor Party was helpless.[161] Neither its Marxist ideology nor its traditional reformist practices offered answers to the nation's economic and social difficulties. The situation called for bold initiatives. De Man seized the opportunity to propose a new political course for the party.

Politics was unfamiliar territory for De Man. Nothing in his experience up to this time had prepared him for its special challenges. He had never been a candidate for elected office, and his relationship to the political system, both in Germany and Belgium, had been essentially that of a critic. Not only had he become skeptical of parliamentary forms of democracy but he viewed most socialist politicians as opportunists, partly responsible for the enfeeblement of the socialist vision. He had shown little interest in, let alone understanding of, the efforts of Social Democratic politicians in Germany to protect working-class interests.

De Man's distaste for the intellectual give and take, and for the need to compromise, crucial to conventional politics, had not gone unnoticed. There were some individuals, one of his students in Frankfurt remarked, who "should never be in a political party."[162] De Man, she added, was a man of tremendous feeling, great ability, but he could not let any decision be made for him. "He must control every situation." His self-certainty, indeed, his arrogance, made it difficult for De Man to adapt to the mores of political life. But the traits that in normal times might have disqualified him for a political career served him well, at least initially, when he returned to Belgium. The leaders of the party were divided, the working class restive and receptive to calls for a general strike. The situation was ripe for De Man's approach to the crisis.

During the summer and fall of 1933, as head of the party's Office of Social Research, De Man developed his "Plan for Labor" in greater detail and attempted to sell it to the party leaders.[163] Vandervelde and most of the older socialists were critical of many of its features, most notably De Man's abandonment of the class struggle in favor of a wider socialist appeal, and his emphasis on the role of the state. But the trade union leaders, in desperate need of a policy to deal with rising unemployment, provided enthusiastic support. They were joined by the party's left wing, headed by a former assistant of De Man's at the Superior School for Workers, Henri Spaak. The latter's desire for action overrode his Marxist beliefs. With the strong backing of the trade unionists and the radicals, the Plan was adopted by an overwhelming majority when the party met for its annual conference at Christmas 1933.[164] At the same time De Man was elected to a newly created post of vice president and given powers comparable to those exercised by Vandervelde.

It was a remarkable ascent, a testimony both to the difficulties facing the party and to De Man's personal force and powers of persuasion. To many within the party he appeared as a savior, evoking feelings usually associated with a religious figure.[165]

During the first half of 1934 De Man formed a group of propagandists dedicated to his Plan and charged with the task of educating the party's rank and file. They would then undertake, according to his strategy, the larger mission of winning over those sections of the population—in the middle class, the peasantry, and the intellectuals—who had grievances against capitalism.[166] Neither of these goals was realized.

Having attempted in his campaign to bypass the established functionaries in the party and, indeed, to challenge their traditional prerogatives, De Man soon aroused strong opposition.[167] A number of his socialist colleagues were troubled, moreover, by several aspects of the Plan. His reliance on a strong state to counter the "bulwark of finance" seemed to some to be a "barely disguised form of fascism." Moreover, his introduction, in the summer of 1934, of corporatist ideas of economic representation also threatened the proletarian identity of the party.[168]

Nor did the Plan gain significant support outside the party. His efforts to form a "front of labor," in which Liberal and Catholic workers would join the socialists, failed. The old ideological loyalties that divided the working classes in Belgium were too strong. "From the beginning," as Oschmann observed, De Man's strategy was "more wishful thinking than a concrete analysis of possibilities."[169]

Nevertheless, De Man became a force in Belgium political life. When, in the spring of 1935, the government fell, its deflationary policies discredited, he was one of the socialists invited to join a new coalition ministry. For the Labor Party, which had made acceptance of the whole Plan a condition for entering the government, the offer presented a dilemma. But given the severity of the crisis and the possibility of providing some relief for the workers, the party leaders could hardly refuse the offer. For De Man, it was an opportunity to take the next step in what had become a long-term strategy to achieve socialism.[170] His conversations with the new prime minister, Paul Van Zeeland, a Catholic, had convinced him, moreover, that they agreed on the need for state control over the financial institutions and a program of public works to reduce unemployment. His new political role would last three years and include two terms as minister of finance. It ended suddenly in March 1938, when he was felled by illness.

De Man's political career has been judged harshly. Spaak, who was his closest ally in these years, maintained that De Man lacked, despite his presumed expertise in psychology, "political sense" and a "knowledge of men."[171] And Peter Dodge, noting his "extraordinary incapacity as a politician," attributed it to those qualities that set him apart from the practical politician—"dedication of his entire self to a cause, an overwhelming intensity of conviction which permitted no recognition of the legitimacy of other viewpoints, the horror of any attempt to strike a popular pose, as well as the principled indifference to material surroundings."[172] But De Man's performance in office deserves a more positive judgment. His policies as minister of public works helped to reduce unemployment, and despite his impatience with administrative routines and his distaste for parliamentary debate, he continued to be viewed as a valuable member of the government. Indeed, following the collapse of the second Van Zeeland ministry in the fall of 1937, De Man was asked to form a new government. His terms proved unacceptable. But once again he accepted the post of finance minister after being subjected to great pressure by his party.

Still, De Man's experiences in the cabinet left him profoundly disillusioned. The hopes with which he had joined the government dissolved amid the clash of interests, the ideological disagreements, and the cumbersomeness of parliamentary procedures. He placed much of the blame for the failure to enact bold measures on Van Zeeland.[173] What troubled him most, however, was the unwillingness of his own party, particularly its leader, Vandervelde, to support his Plan. Hence the bitterness of his assessment a few years after he left office.

> Forced to drain a swamp with the aid of a pitchfork and condemned to begin over and over again despite terrible fatigue ... seeing oneself demeaned by a leader who returns the confidence one has placed in him with lies, feeling oneself trampled on when one has been brought down by illness ... nothing of all that has been spared me.[174]

Later he would compare his life to that of Shakespeare's Coriolanus, who preferred to "serve in my own fashion rather than govern by means" of the common people.[175]

Although De Man felt betrayed by his fellow socialist and maligned by the Catholic and Liberal politicians, he concluded that the chief barrier to fundamental social change was the political system itself.[176] It had proven too weak to resist the pressures of the "money powers," the influence of a corrupt press, and the interference of the parties. What was needed was a much stronger executive, freed from constant dependence on parliamentary majorities, and allowed to develop a program over a period of several years. With the removal of the institutional obstacles, De Man still believed the future would belong to socialism.

Developments in Belgium during these years provided slight support for De Man's confidence. He had made little headway in mobilizing popular support for his Plan or, as a minister, in subjecting the country's financial institutions to political control. His efforts simply demonstrated where power lay in Belgian economic and political life. No wonder he felt at times that he was "not a socialist like the others" in the party and likened himself to a "savage animal" in a species that had been largely domesticated.[177]

Political responsibility often tames the radical. In the case of Spaak, for example, it brought out aptitudes and skills that would make him one of the most successful politicians of his generation.[178] Not so for De Man. His self-certainty, his conviction that he alone knew the path to socialism, remained largely intact. After leaving office he devoted himself, as head of the party following the death of Veldervelde late in 1938, to the task of liquidating the remains of its Marxist ideology and making it a vehicle for "a truly national socialism."[179] Disillusioned with the political system, he now held that such a goal could only be achieved by means of a much stronger executive, or what he called an "authoritarian democracy."

By the spring of 1938, however, the domestic political scene was overshadowed by the growing conflict between the fascist powers and the Western democracies. Faced with the threat of war, De Man and Spaak, now the foreign minister, championed a policy of strict neutrality for Belgium. Along with most of the country's political leaders, they believed that neutrality offered the best hope of staying clear of the struggles of the major European powers.[180] De Man, meanwhile, had returned to the pacifism of his earlier years, convinced that he had betrayed his principles in 1914. His neutralism, his pacifism, and his disenchantment with the parliamentary system prepared the way for the final and, as it turned out, disastrous stage in De Man's career as a socialist thinker and politician.

VII

When the war broke out in September 1939, De Man accepted a cabinet position in a new coalition government. But his activities as minister were limited to efforts, under the sponsorship of the Queen Mother, to strengthen the morale of the Belgian troops. He had grown close to the royal family during the late 1930s and now viewed the king, Leopold III, as a vital element in his conception of a new political order.[181] Not only did the king embody traditional values in Belgium, but, by occupying a position above the clash of political parties, he was, in De Man's eyes, an indispensable symbol of national unity.

In late May 1940, after the German armies had crushed the Belgian forces and occupied the country, De Man supported the king's decision to remain with his people and do what he could to mitigate their sufferings. Leopold's refusal to follow his cabinet into exile opened a breach in Belgian political life that was never healed and subsequently cost him his throne.[182] At the time, however, De Man saw an opportunity for the fundamental changes he had sought in vain through parliamentary politics. Hence his response when the king, shortly after the German conquest, asked him to outline a new form of government.

> The war has confirmed the debacle not only of a political regime, but of a social order characterized by the predominance of class egoism over the spirit of community, by the failure to recognize the duties of national and social soli-

darity, by a level of life too low for the dignity and culture of the mass of the population.[183]

De Man's hope that the German victory had opened the way for his new socialism was evident a few weeks later when, as head of the Labor Party, he issued a "Manifesto."[184] He took it upon himself, apparently without consultation, to define the policies the party should adopt in the face of the German occupation. "For the working class and for socialists, the collapse of a decrepit world is ... a deliverance." The political role of the Labor Party, he declared, was finished. For all the elements in Belgian society could now come together in a national renewal.

> In this world, a communal spirit will prevail over class egoism, and labor will be the only source of dignity and power. The socialist order will be ... realized, not at all as the thing of one class or of one party, but as the good of all, in the name of national solidarity that will soon be continental if not worldwide.

It was soon clear that German policy, dictated by Hitler, would provide little scope for De Man's hopes. The king, moreover, chose to view himself as a prisoner and refused to accept any political role under the Germans. But De Man's expectations and his illusions did not fade completely. During the fall of 1940 and the first half of 1941, he continued to collaborate, serving as a mediator between those individuals and groups in Belgium who sought his help and the German authorities.[185] While he recognized that any serious attempt to reconstruct Belgium's institutions would await the end of the war, he still envisioned a new Europe emerging from the German conquest, with supranational economic and political structures capable of ensuring peace and social justice. In the meantime he attempted to promote developments that would help Belgium participate in a new order. He played an important role, for example, in unifying the trade unions, long divided by socialist, Catholic, and Liberal affiliations, into a common organization.[186]

In the spring of 1941, De Man reaffirmed the hopes expressed in his "Manifesto" to the party. His "message to militant socialists" on May Day called on them to recognize the party's complicity in the collapse of the "decrepit and decadent" parliamentary system.[187] The war, he declared, was simply the "destructive phase" of a revolution; the death knell of capitalism had sounded. A socialist order that was no longer identified with a single class but with the whole nation was near.

De Man distinguished the "national socialism" he envisioned for Bel-

gium from the National Socialism of the Germans. While the latter expressed the hierarchical and militaristic features of the German past, socialism in Belgium would be based on its tradition of individual liberty.[188]
Yet he clearly admired certain aspects of the new Germany, its "superior
morale" and its greater unity and discipline.[189] He continued to hope that
the Nazi victory would open the way to a new Europe in which Belgium,
no longer viable in the old economic and political terms, would find a
place.

The hopes that De Man placed in Nazi Germany can only be seen, in
retrospect, as extraordinarily naïve. All the more so in view of his penetrating analysis of Hitler's movement ten years earlier. That he could close
his eyes to the terrorism, the persecutions, and the general oppression
within a country he knew so well, was, perhaps, a gauge to his disenchantment with parliamentary institutions.

By the late summer of 1941, however, De Man had earned the suspicion
of the occupying authorities. He was warned not to engage in further political activity. He did make one more attempt, in highly abstract terms, to
clarify his conception of socialism. In a series of articles he lamented the
process through which the socialist movement had been absorbed into the
liberal parliamentary tradition and argued once more that only an authoritarian or plebiscitarian form of democracy could break through the pluto-
cratic structures and achieve meaningful liberties.[190] But in November,
with the aid of friends, he left Belgium and settled in a cottage in the
French Alps. There he remained, apart from several furtive trips back to
Belgium, until the end of the war, reflecting and writing. Narrowly escap-
ing arrest as a fugitive from Belgian authorities in August 1944, he was
given sanctuary in Switzerland. There he also found, in a new marriage, the
companionship he had missed most of his life. During the years that followed, until his sudden death in an automobile accident in 1953, he devoted
much of his energy defending himself against the judgment, delivered by a
Belgian court in September 1946, condemning him as a traitor who had
"maliciously served ... the designs of the enemy."[191]

It was a miscarriage of justice. Not only did the court violate established judicial procedures, but the verdict was handed down at a time when
it was still virtually impossible to assess fairly the actions of those caught
up in the tragic ambiguities of wartime.[192] Moreover, De Man received no
help from the king in his efforts to justify his role during the occupation.[193]

In his last years De Man attempted to explain the failure of his lifelong
struggle to guide European socialism onto a new path. In his book *Mass*

Society and Cultural Decline, published in 1951, he situated that struggle within a new interpretation of European history.[194] His "diagnosis of our time" was, like the *Psychology* and the *Socialist Idea*, partly autobiographical, an interweaving of historical analysis with reflections on his experience within the socialist movement. The book was mainly concerned, however, with those forces which, he believed, had defeated his vision of an ethically grounded socialism.

VIII

Influenced by modern thinkers who had developed philosophies of history—Arthur Gobineau, Oswald Spengler, and Arnold Toynbee—De Man viewed Western civilization holistically, evolving from about A.D. 1000 and passing through distinct stages. Unlike Spengler and Toynbee, who had identified a plurality of civilizations, more or less self-contained, and realizing unique life cycles, De Man saw a confluence of civilizations and a unitary outcome in modern history. Western civilization had, by virtue of its global expansion, put an end to the plurality of cultural styles. The fate of the world was now inextricably bound up with Western civilization.

De Man's diagnosis centered on the concept of *Vermassung*, a condition in which the development of society was determined by "the behavior of the masses."[195] It was "the most striking phenomenon of our cultural epoch." Using terms that owed much to Ortega Y Gasset's *Revolt of the Masses*, De Man argued that the great majority of men and women had been reduced to objects, incapable of responding critically or creatively to the world around them. It meant a "general levelling from below," as the vulgar tastes of the masses, formed by mass consumption and advertising, overwhelmed the higher social and cultural values.[196] De Man, like Ortega, did not identify the "mass man" with a particular social class; it was a condition that affected all classes, rich and poor alike. As such, it called into question the assumptions underlying his earlier socialist faith—his belief in the capacity of all individuals to be guided by reason and conscience, his confidence that society was subject to man's control, and his conviction that history could be understood in terms of human goals.

The decline of the self-determining individual could be seen most clearly, he observed, in the development of the modern artist. For art, he claimed, was the "most direct ... and most naïve expression ... of the soul of an epoch."[197] With the "dissolution of style," a term De Man used to indicate a stable and enduring form of culture, the artist in the modern world was increasingly isolated and subject to a process of fragmentation that imperiled the very sense of self. Nietzsche, according to De Man, had been the "first cultural philosopher" to recognize the nihilistic tendencies of modern life and the way in which the "madness of the art world mirrored" the "madness of the epoch in general."[198]

In social life the outcome of Vermassung was atomization; community was replaced by aggregation. As the old social bonds disintegrated, individuals became disoriented and helpless, prone to primitive and infantile forms of behavior, and susceptible to anxieties that found expression in totalitarian politics and a constant readiness for war. The process also meant a loss of human control over society. De Man likened the condition of Western societies to that of a "steerless ship." With the loss of clear direction, however, there was also a feeling of being at the mercy of "nameless powers," gigantic technological and bureaucratic forces that followed hidden laws.[199]

The rise of mass society undermined the belief that history made sense. For "History," in any meaningful sense of the term, indicated the "capacity of men to know ... the forces that influenced them."[200] With the loss of this understanding, "History" was coming to an end. Western peoples were entering a "post history" era in which the old notions of human purpose and intelligible forces, indeed, the very idea of cause and effect, had collapsed. The threat of atomic warfare reinforced the feeling of living "in a time that no longer belongs to history."

De Man's diagnosis led him to the edge of what has been described as a "post modern sensibility," according to which previous notions of the self, society, and history have become problematical. But having called into question the assumptions underlying his socialist faith, he drew back from the radical implications of his diagnosis and reinstated the central features of his earlier interpretation of European history. What was fundamental to that history was again the development of the bourgeoisie and its central value—the "veneration of work."[201] This value, together with the closely associated affirmations of freedom, dignity, and equality of the individual, made Western culture unique. But the bourgeoisie had, in the form of capitalism, betrayed its values and left to the working class, inspired by socialist ideas, the task of renewing those values in the modern world. De Man conceded, however, that the hopes placed in the proletariat had been "illusory."[202]

De Man now maintained that Western civilization had "changed direction." It had turned away from "its original goal."[203] The shift was expressed in the internal reversal of the socialist movement itself, its capitulation to the capitalistic order it had challenged. It was, he suggested, in the nature of great creative and energizing ideas to be negated through their encounter with their surroundings and their subsequent institutionalization. A process that had taken Christianity a thousand years to complete had transformed the bourgeoisie in several centuries, and socialism in merely two or three generations.[204] In De Man's new dialectical reading of history it was the negative rather than the positive moment that had triumphed.

De Man's diagnosis of Western civilization at midcentury was bleak. He denied, however, that he was a pessimist. Since no one could predict the future with certainty, men and women were still free to choose their course of action. But given the "increasing velocity" of the changes encompassed by the concept of mass society, De Man offered little comfort.[205] He simply expressed the hope that the few individuals who could resist the "mass mind" and the process of depersonalization would "save our cultural heritage" and reaffirm what "conscience presents as duty."[206] Referring to the Old Testament story where Abraham asked God to spare the City of Sodom on behalf of a few righteous men, De Man asked: "How many are necessary" to save Western civilization?[207]

His portrayal of contemporary Europe was strangely one sided. By 1950, there were a number of developments—the movement toward European economic and political integration, the growth of welfare states, the creation of mixed economic systems, and the broadening appeal of the socialist parties—which corresponded closely to the changes advocated by De Man during the 1930s. Within a few years the German Social Democrats would acknowledge, at their conference in 1957, in Bad Godesberg, the importance of the ethical and religious sources of socialism that De Man had emphasized.[208] No wonder several of his commentators have viewed the development of the social democratic parties in Europe after the war as a vindication of De Man's ideas.[209] Some, in fact, have seen his influence, though unacknowledged, in these developments.[210]

That he could ignore those features of postwar Europe that he had favored earlier suggested the extent to which he remained fixed within his ethically centered vision of socialism. He still judged developments in Europe in the light of his earlier hope that the motives of ordinary men and women might be changed. He continued, moreover, to view European social and cultural life as a whole, shaped decisively by intellectual and spiritual forces that precluded significant variations among the individual countries. In 1950, he looked back with satisfaction on his refusal to choose between the fascist and the democratic powers in 1939.[211] The neutralist position he had adopted at that time was still a valid approach to the "cold war." There was little to choose between America, where the developments of mass society were most advanced, and Russia. Indeed, the domination of these two states after World War II simply confirmed De Man's pacifistic belief that armed conflict would settle nothing and bring results very different from the aims of the combatants.

Unwilling to acknowledge the continuing, indeed, increased strength of parliamentary forms of democracy in postwar Europe, as well as the renewed vitality of the underlying liberal and humane values, De Man retreated stoiclike to his old convictions. In the final version of his autobiography, published in the year he died, he took pride in the fact that he had remained faithful to the motives that had carried him into the socialist movement fifty years earlier. He had, to be sure, suffered many setbacks and frequently revised his view of the movement. But he claimed that he had been able, because of the "constancy of motives," to assimilate the new experiences and understandings without suffering demoralization or a loss of courage.[212] His life, he declared, could be viewed as "a curve which displayed ... many bends but no break." He was still, notwithstanding the changes in his views and the changes in the movement itself, a socialist.[213]

To be true to his deepest motives in the modern world meant, according to De Man, inevitable defeat. His attempts, as a politician, to translate his ideas into practical terms, had demonstrated that "truth" could not prevail in modern life.[214] In a different historical period, when cultures were creative and ascending, the innovative person might be effective and develop institutions that could serve his ideas. In societies dominated by the "mass soul," however, such an individual could only "swim against the stream." To maintain one's integrity in the contemporary world was to be, in the end, a victim.

De Man was, in fact, a victim of his own bourgeois sensibility. Fixed within its rationalistic and ethical outlook, he was unable to grasp the power and depth of the malevolent forces that overwhelmed Europe in the 1930s and 1940s. Supremely self-confident, he remained closed to the intellectual interchanges that might have led him to modify his views. And lacking any real sense of solidarity with the workers he refused to grant them the qualities of mind and spirit on which any advance toward a new kind of society ultimately depended. Increasingly isolated, he retreated into a psyche that, as one of his biographers suggested, bordered on the narcissistic.[215] In the end he could only place the blame for the failure of his socialist vision on those he had sought to lead.[216] Humanity itself, he concluded, had lost its way and entered a "post historical era." No wonder his *Vermassung* has been described as the "disenchanted postscript" of a disappointed intellectual who had lost his way.[217]

De Man responded to the "crisis of Marxism" in the years after World War I by reconstructing socialism on an ethical foundation. In doing so he reaffirmed central features in his bourgeois sensibility—its traditional ethos of work, its rationalism, and its ideal, exemplified by De Man himself, of the autonomous personality. Meanwhile, other Marxist intellectuals were taking up the challenge. How could the revolutionary project be revitalized? How could the working-class movement develop the consciousness and will required to achieve socialism? No figure during the interwar years searched so deeply into this problem as Max Horkheimer. His intellectual journey, however, would also take him beyond Marxism.

CHAPTER 3

Max Horkheimer

I

"There lives within each of us ... a deep indefinite yearning ... a voice that is noble and true and pure ... a voice which lifts us above other creatures. It is our God, the meaning of our existence; it speaks most powerfully in our youth."[1] The statement comes from a story that Max Horkheimer wrote in 1915 and included in a volume of youthful writings, *From Puberty*, published near the end of his life. He described the collection—novellas, imagined correspondence, and diary entries—as the "free fantasies of my youth," unconstrained by any "knowledge of complicated reality" or by psychological or sociological considerations.[2]

These writings, dating from Horkheimer's late teens and early twenties, expressed a "pre-ideological mentality." For they lay bare anxieties and aspirations, doubts and perplexities, that would be answered, at least for a time, by his faith in Marxism. Much of this mentality would persist as a "secret underground" in his thought as Horkheimer developed his Marxism into a "critical theory."[3] And after his Marxist faith in a socialist future collapsed during the devastating events of the late 1930s, his underlying attitudes and feelings would continue to influence his efforts to make sense of the world around him.

Horkheimer's pre-ideological mentality was shaped decisively by the bourgeois world in which he grew up.[4] Born into an affluent, conservative, Jewish household in 1895, he was raised with the expectation that he would succeed his father in the family's textile business. But his "inner voice," the conscience formed by his bourgeois upbringing, found expression in a growing spirit of rebellion. Like the young De Man, he came to judge the miseries and the injustices of the outer social world in terms of the ideals professed, and the happiness experienced, within his own home. An unbearable tension between his moral and religious values and the workings of social institutions pervaded the writings gathered in the volume *From Puberty*.

The tension between the two realms appeared most often in his accounts of the struggles of young men, or young women, to break free from a bourgeois way of life that they had come to see as hopelessly corrupt and hypocritical. They criticized their parents' generation for a variety of reasons—its preoccupation with material comfort, its indifference to intellectual and spiritual values, its complicity in the misery of the lower classes. For these rebellious sons and daughters the everyday life of the parents seemed little better than an animal-like existence. Most important, it stifled "what is honest and deep within us."[5] Thus several of the young women in these stories were repelled by the "slavery of marriage," and its self-effacing "duties and responsibilities."[6] Marriage denied their creative possibilities. The young men, on the other hand, recoiled from a life dedicated to "money and production."[7] For this would mean "the death of my yearning living soul."

The autobiographical element in Horkheimer's stories was obvious. It was most evident in the frequent presence of the businessman father who embodied the drive for worldly success, measured in terms of power or wealth. Thus in a story entitled "Adventure: A Posthumous Letter from a Millionaire to His Son," the father warns his son of the temptations that await him.[8] As a young man, he wrote, "my heart resembled yours and I suffered unbearably" from a recognition of the "immorality of riches" and "making other men your instruments." Initially he had dreamed of a life dedicated to the pursuit of truth and beauty. But in time he surrendered to base desires and fell into a life of "whoredom, carousing and degradation." Only for a brief period did he earn a "modest living as a writer," dreaming of a "great work of art" in which he would "sing a song of genuine living." In the end, however, he became a merchant "in spite of all" and gained great wealth. The father concluded his letter by advising his son to renounce the sinfulness of riches, give his inheritance to the poor, and "do only what is right for yourself." "Perhaps," the letter ended, "you are greater than I."

Horkheimer's stories express a radical individualism. His central figures are determined to live exclusively out of their own hearts or minds.

Thus one young woman resolves to "begin my life without any ... assumptions or prejudices," to simply express "what comes out of me as I am."[9] She is convinced that she is responding to "a secret force within," that she is engaged in a personal quest for perfection.[10] "Whether we sink or swim depends on ourselves alone."[11]

The other side of this strong commitment to autonomy—a central ideal in the nineteenth-century bourgeois outlook—was a contempt, or at least indifference, toward social institutions. The family, schools, religious organizations, the economic order, and the political system were all viewed as obstacles to the development of one's deepest self. In the typical bourgeois family, complacency and smugness prevailed; the older generation showed no tolerance for the aspirations of the young. Education offered no escape. "I hate the University and its pedantry," one figure declares.[12] The factories that dominated economic life were simply scenes of murderous work.[13] Nor did public life offer any hope for change. One young idealist expressed his hatred of "all political parties."[14]

Horkheimer seems to have been immune to the euphoria that swept across Europe when World War I broke out and seized so many in his generation. He had left school a few years earlier, at the age of fifteen, to enter his father's factory. And in 1912 he was sent abroad, first to Belgium and then England, to gain further training for a career in business. His experiences abroad made it difficult for him to feel any strong animosity toward the peoples who went to war against Germany in 1914. "One thing is clear," he wrote in that year, "I will not belong to any nation."[15] Slaughter on the battlefield was no more justified than murder by an individual. It was, after all, clearly contrary to the biblical command to "love your enemies."

Disengaged from institutions and conventions, Horkheimer's heroes and heroines were free to follow their deepest bent. But how then to fulfill their "yearnings," a constant feature of this sensibility? Art offered one alternative to the bourgeois way of life. For the artist understood the "inwardness of life and people."[16] He had "gained a deep insight" into the great game of the world without being bound to the necessities of practical experience. The poet, in particular, was "born to battle with his times."[17] Aware of the "criminality of the upper class," he was also capable of compassion for the unfortunate and disinherited. Horkheimer's artists were often torn, in fact, between the lonely pursuit of their own creativity and the sense of a social mission.

Nature provided another escape from the banalities of bourgeois existence. Horkheimer's characters are drawn to the fields, forests, mountains, and the sea as they flee from the strangulations of city life. Having left "all care and comfort in the valley below," they climb to a purer realm.[18] Or they might travel to the shores of the Mediterranean and the promise of cloudless skies and constant sunlight.[19]

For the young people in these stories, love and friendship provided other ways of overcoming the egoism and self-seeking of bourgeois life. The ties of love broke down the barriers of social class as well. For one young man, who renounced a "brilliant future" in his father's business, love was a "paradise" that erased the "borders between countries and classes."[20] The autobiographical element was again evident. For Horkheimer himself formed an attachment and later married a woman who did not meet the approval of his parents.

The three escapes from the everyday life of the bourgeoisie—love, nature, and beauty—converged in what has been seen as the most autobiographical of his stories, "The Island of Happiness."[21] It described the efforts of two young men and a young woman to live in such a way that "their own free convictions" were the source of all of their actions. United in their scorn for "practical life," they dream of an island to which they could flee from the "bonds of society." All they needed was a "small patch of earth" where they could "perfect themselves."

The setting for much of this story was England, and particularly Manchester, where Horkheimer and his childhood friend, Fredrick Pollock, had been sent to gain experience in commerce. But Manchester embodied the worst features of modern social and economic life.

> The people who live in this environment are self seeking and take joy only in things which increase their bodily well-being. ... "Business" is their god and for all else they are stupid and full of ancient prejudices. ... They are animals, who possess the gift of reason—a lowly transitional stage toward humankind. ... They lack just those precious things which make true men ... soul, yearning after truth, pure love, trust, compassion, joy in beauty, all that they don't have; they don't feel.[22]

The affirmations of love and friendship checked the fierce individualism that characterized much of this writing. Moreover, many of the stories showed a compassion for the poor and the weak together with a strong sense of social injustice. The yearnings of the young men and women might be satisfied through service for those in need. One young man, having reached an impasse in a life given over to sensuality and restless traveling, is urged by a friend to "forget yourself" by helping others.[23] He discovers that compassion is the "highest, holiest feeling" and "thinks no more of himself."

In several of the stories the model for this way of life is Jesus, the man "who hung on the cross."[24] Indeed, in these stories the hero assumes, through a close identification with the "crucified one," a messianic role himself. Thus a prisoner on the eve of his execution dreams that the cell doors open and he goes out into the countryside to preach a gospel of love and peace.[25] The dream enables him, on awakening, to accept his death confident that he has finally understood the true meaning of life. Another young man is lifted into a "purer realm" during a concert and imagines himself engaged in a similar mission.[26] Like the one "who died for others," he teaches his followers the meaning of redemption—the turning away from self-seeking and possessions. The people recognized him as an apostle and "kissed his hands." The messianic was a distinctive feature of Horkheimer's sensibility in these years.

But while these early writings centered on young idealists with a sense of mission, they were constantly prey to doubts and treacherous "demons" within.[27] The artist might turn out to be a "dry egoist";[28] nature might become a new refuge for a narrow egoism;[29] love affairs often ended in betrayal. Those young men and women who repudiated the bourgeois way of life frequently surrendered in the end to its claims or blandishments. The dream of an "Island of Happiness" collapsed when the parents called on the authorities to deal with their wayward offspring.

Horkheimer's characters were, in fact, deeply divided, torn between their spiritual aspirations on the one hand and their earthly appetites, even baser impulses, on the other. "We want to be released from the earth and yet we love it with our whole heart."[30] There was, moreover, a strong strain of eroticism in many of the stories. The young men often found solace in the arms of prostitutes.

No wonder many of the central figures suffer from feelings of guilt and sin. The sense of guilt arose in part out of an awareness that the lives of the affluent bourgeoisie rested on the exploitation and suffering of the masses.[31] But a number of the stories express a traditional religious understanding of human limitation and the capacity for evil. "We are sinners," one character declares, "and must suffer as long as we breathe."[32] Hence the "unspeakable torment of life." The "boldest of utopias," therefore, could not touch the "kernel of life" which was "torment and death."[33]

The pessimistic side of this sensibility owed less to the Christian or

Jewish belief in the fallen state of human beings than to the influence of Schopenhauer. Horkheimer had been introduced to the philosopher by his friend, Pollock, in 1914 and found there views of the human condition that ran counter to his strong idealistic and romantic outlook.[34] Schopenhauer's claim that men and women were slaves to the will, together with his special sense of human compassion and solidarity, proved congenial to Horkheimer in his attempt to deal with the contradictions in human nature. One of his characters endorses Schopenhauer's "religion of nothingness" as "more consoling, joyful and lighter than the whole dumb heavy earth."[35] Running through the pages of *From Puberty* was a dual outlook, an optimistic, at times messianic hope for a radically new way of life, on the one hand, and a pessimistic view of the human condition on the other.

Yet his characters were, for the most part, insulated from the exigencies of everyday life. They tended to float in a kind of spiritual or aesthetic space where they were free to occupy themselves with questions about the meaning of life, love and beauty, suffering and death, while lamenting the spiritual desert they see around them. "What I love about the skylark," one figure declares, "is its weightlessness, its freedom from the pull of the earth."[36] Even the stories that expressed compassion for the lower classes and demands for social justice lacked any genuine understanding of the lives of the poor and the oppressed. His working-class characters were stick figures, projections of a romantic or idealistic imagination. This remoteness from the real world was reflected too in an implacable scorn for those who exercise the social, economic, and political functions in the societies where these stories took place. Political activity, in particular, was unworthy of any serious effort to improve the human condition.

By the summer of 1916, however, Horkheimer began to connect his characters more closely to the war and political developments in Germany. Political revolutionaries now appeared, men who were determined to overthrow the existing social order and bring justice to the suffering masses. But the main goal of any popular uprising was to give the masses "access to true culture" and create a society in which "love will awaken in mankind," and all would be united in their appreciation of nature and beauty.[37] As for conventional political activity, it was dismissed as the mere pursuit of power and money. Even the socialists, who set themselves up as "spokesmen for the people,"[38] were distrusted. Like their opponents they were concerned only with the satisfaction of animal needs. Revolution, one character declares, is necessary, but its place "must be in one's own soul."[39]

Sympathy in these stories was given mainly to young men who renounced violence and were, therefore, at the mercy of the brutal forces, military and political, that raged around them. As soldiers they faced three possibilities—death in combat or, if they refused to fire on the enemy, life in prison, or suicide. Martyrdom became, in fact, a central theme in several of the stories after 1917.[40] Closely related to this theme was the appearance of the Jew, virtually absent from the earlier stories. By virtue of his isolation, his spirituality, and special sensitivity, the young Jew was particularly vulnerable in a society caught up in the turmoil of war and revolution.[41] Horkheimer's awareness of the dangerous potential of anti-Semitism in Germany was suggested in two stories where enraged mobs wreaked their vengeance on rich Jews.[42] Their houses went up in flames, and the streets outside were littered with the bodies of the victims.

These stories suggested Horkheimer's own sense of vulnerability as a Jew and may have reflected personal experiences. He had been drafted into the army in 1917, and his experience of life in a military barracks was described in several of his stories as an animal-like existence. He was declared unfit for military service, however, and spent the remaining months of the war in a sanitarium. Discharged in Munich, he witnessed at close hand the revolutionary uprising there in November 1918.

A military sanitarium provided the setting for the developing tensions in Horkheimer's thought, and, at the same time, his fears for postwar Germany. In a play, *Peace*, a political agitator, Zech, calls on a convalescent soldier, "Claude," who is also an artist and a Jew, devoted to the gospel of love, to join him in revolutionary action.

> Were the times milder, the use of force not a burning necessity, compassion might be appropriate. But the courage of the battlefield must not ebb, passion must flow unweakened into the stream of popular rebellion. Given the harsh reality, aesthetics must take part or go under. The time for individuality is over.[43]

In order to build a future society, Zech declares, blood must flow.

The dialogue between Zech and Claude is interrupted by the appearance of Norbert, a Prussian officer who had won the affection of Claude's former girlfriend, Germaine. Norbert claims the German future on behalf of a set of values that will put an end to the dreams and the self-indulgence of both Claude and Zech. What would come out of the war and the sacrifices of thousands, according to Norbert, was a new kind of discipline. The German people would find a new sense of duty and responsibility; they would recognize that "their body, their spirit, do not belong to themselves," that they owed all to the state.[44] An officer in another story put it this way:

> Each among you must understand that he belongs to the state with skin and hair and soul. ... No other thought can be accepted. ... The individual is impotent, the state invincible. ... What remains to the individual if he loses the state?[45]

The contrast between such a vision of Germany's future and Horkheimer's commitment to individual autonomy, as well as his affirmations of love and compassion, could hardly have been greater.

The oscillation between pessimistic and optimistic viewpoints continued throughout *From Puberty*. Toward the end of the volume several of the characters lament once more the pervasiveness of cruelty in the world. "I know that we are cursed, condemned to dreadful things, that mankind is wicked and that evil always triumphs."[46] To a poet who declares that man is good, one figure responds, "Man is cruel, tyrannical, deceitful, a murderer, greedy for power, insatiable, evil, scornful, capable of all vices."[47] Yet Horkheimer's other voice continues to be heard. In a world where one no longer believed in the old gods and all the old meanings had been lost, love alone might make life worthwhile.[48] Love was still a force capable of dispelling the darkness and gloom that surrounded human beings.

The more positive voice, presumably that of Horkheimer himself, appeared in the final diary entries, dated during the closing months of the war.

> I will again believe in my future, in the values for which I struggle. ... If there is a future everything will again have meaning [and] I must have a task to fulfill . ... Nothing is necessary, nothing must remain the same, all can be changed. I will take up the fight against the enemies of freedom and the spirit, against all the fixities of the old order.[49]

At one point the diarist likens his condition to that of a "ship on a blue Swiss lake," setting out on a voyage "without a clear destination."[50] Mankind, he declares, "remains a potentiality." Hence "our task"—that of finding the path to true happiness.[51] Only then will the world cease to be a madhouse and our yearnings be stilled.

These passages point ahead toward Horkheimer's lifelong struggle to discover such a path. But at the end of the war he remained, as the final sections of *From Puberty* suggested, a discordant mix of attitudes and feelings. It was a mentality that had much in common with the romantic anticapitalism found in much of German intellectual and cultural life in the early years of the century.[52] Here too was the passionate ethical and aesthetic protest against a society increasingly dominated by the values of materialistic acquisition and competition. Like other romantic anticapitalists, Horkheimer challenged the bourgeois order in terms of social and spiritual values drawn from its own religious and humanistic traditions. What distinguished him, however, was the deep antinomy in his thinking, his inability to resolve the contradictions between his messianic aspirations and his Schopenhauern pessimism. He was ripe, therefore, for an ideology that would point the way out of the impasse and give direction to his intellectual and emotional energies.

The Horkheimer who is present in *From Puberty* was incapable of returning to his father's factory. He was determined rather to continue his education. In 1919, after a semester at the University of Munich, he and Pollock enrolled in the University of Frankfurt. Horkheimer had no intention at that point of pursuing an academic career. He was simply eager, as he recalled, "to learn what is known about mankind at present."[53] To this end he turned initially to the study of psychology, which, at Frankfurt, was dominated by the new school of "gestalt psychology" and the claim that particular phenomena could be understood only in terms of a presupposed whole. This approach to knowledge would deeply influence Horkheimer's way of thinking and be reinforced by his attempt as a Marxist to view social life holistically.[54]

Horkheimer soon settled onto a path, guided by the neo-Kantian philosopher at Frankfurt, Hans Cornelius, leading to an academic career in philosophy. But he was not attracted to conventional notions of philosophical inquiry. In a letter to his fiancé, "Maidon," in the fall of 1921, he expressed his distaste for prevailing forms of philosophical analysis in favor of a way of thinking that was more closely related to everyday life.[55] He was influenced by Heidegger, having spent some time in Freiburg with the philosopher, who viewed philosophy as springing forth "anew each day out of one's own experience." Horkheimer confessed his sense of "feeling myself in a cage," barred from my intentions and playing a "shameless role ... out of piety" and hence "outside myself." "I must live daily," he added, "in the service to an idea."

Horkheimer completed the work—two dissertations dealing with aspects of the Kantian system—necessary for an academic career.[56] But his philosophical development, on the one hand, and his existential and ethical concerns, on the other, remained separate for some time. It was only after

1924 that he began to find, by means of Marxism, a way of connecting his " inner voice" and the external world.

II

Horkheimer never gave a detailed account of his conversion to Marxism. Nothing in his writings suggested any intellectual or emotional upheaval comparable to that experienced by De Man. In an interview in 1970 he recalled, in general terms, the appeal of Marxism in the years right after World War I.[57] It provided, he observed, the "best critical" perspective on German society at that time and drew the "true consequences" from the war. It offered, moreover, a counterforce to what he saw as the growing threat from the political right in the early Weimar republic.

A concern for social justice had found expression in *From Puberty*. And the later sections had indicated his growing sympathy for the revolutionary left. Karl Liebnecht appeared in one of the late stories as a martyr.[58] But Horkheimer's adoption of Marxism was "slow and deliberate."[59] He did not, like several of his close friends, take part in the group of Frankfurt intellectuals who set out in these years to revitalize the Marxist doctrines and then created the Institute for Social Research. Horkheimer's caution, a continuing characteristic of his relationship to Marxism, has been attributed to his concern for his academic career. But it also reflected his struggle to reconcile Marxist theory with the attitudes and feelings expressed in *From Puberty*. That struggle can be followed in his "Notes" and diary entries during the 1920s. They were, as one of his editors commented, "a continuation of his earlier literary efforts on a new theoretical level."[60]

By 1925 there was, however, "a new orientation in his thought."[61] Its implicit presuppositions and organized center now came from Marxist theory. Yet his fuller appropriation of the theory in the years just ahead was marked by numerous doubts and hesitations.[62] For his moral protest against bourgeois society did not blend easily with the Marxist doctrines. The tension was evident in the published version of his "Notes," the *Dämmerung*, which appeared in 1934, and even more intimately in the reflections and diary entries that remained unpublished until near the end of his life.[63] They record his efforts to connect his "inner voice" with the Marxist analysis of capitalism.

Horkheimer was still engaged during the late 1920s in the soul searching apparent in his earlier writings. Life, he observed, was a "fearful dark journey," subject to many hazards and temptations.[64] He worried lest he be seduced by the "pseudo security" offered by the bourgeoisie and betray his quest for truth. He noted, in particular, the dangers presented by academic life with its "self-deceptions" and "official functions" that might "take him prisoner." In these years he traced the roots of his inner conflicts to his family. At one point he lashed out against his parents, denouncing the "grim malicious egoism of my mother and the petty cowardly egoism of my father."[65] "Between my parents and myself," he wrote, there existed an "unbridgeable yawning spiritual gulf" that could never be filled.

What continued to move him most deeply were his "moral intuitions."[66] He conceded, however, that the "language of the heart" lacked any metaphysical grounding. And he rejected the efforts of contemporary philosophers "to press to the center of Being" in hopes of finding, as in earlier times, "a deep and united … world view" capable of giving meaning and direction to life. The "materialist," with whom he now identified himself, realized that the quest for this kind of "spiritual support" was no longer possible. Horkheimer was content, therefore, to accept the love of mankind, together with feelings of compassion and human solidarity, as a "natural fact."

Horkheimer's moral sensitivity made it especially difficult for him to embrace what, for Marxists, was the crucial force in history—the proletariat. How can one love or "even come close," he asked, to a class that is lacking any spiritual life and is mired down in the "brutality, stupidity, and meanness" of present conditions?[67] But the very fact of these conditions, he answered, made bourgeois society, which "cannot exist" without them, unbearable. It was one's "moral duty" to identify oneself with the "little people … besmirched" by bourgeois institutions. "Higher individuals today," he insisted, "necessarily stood on the side of the political left."

Yet the gulf between bourgeois intellectuals like himself and the workers continued to trouble him. In one of the early "Notes" he contrasted the "idealistic and religious character" of the former with the "primitive needs" underlying the struggles of the proletariat.[68] While the "philosophical socialists" dreamed of the transfiguration of humanity, the workers turned to socialism only when they recognized that "they had nothing to expect" from capitalism except continuing misery. Horkheimer suggested that the "utopian exaggerations" of the intellectuals would have to be set aside for the moment in order to concentrate on the betterment rather than the alteration of mankind. After all, a new socialist man could only come through a change in social conditions.

Horkheimer was not content, however, to give up the messianic long-ings that underlay his thought and to view the socialist movement simply as the pursuit of the material interests of the workers. He could adopt the basic Marxist doctrines only with qualifications. Thus he accepted the Marxist claim that economic activity was the decisive force in social life, affecting "everything down to the delicate tendrils of the individual soul," while rejecting any extreme version of economic determinism.[69] He denied that there was a logic "immanent in history" leading to socialism.[70] The fu-ture was still open. At the present, he wrote, Europe faced the possibility that it might descend into a new barbarism. What mattered was the indi-vidual will. He worried lest the preoccupation of Marxists with class lead them to forget the "reality of individuals."[71]

"How little," Horkheimer wrote at one point, "economic factors have to do with the inner life."[72] He scolded Marxist intellectuals for failing to acknowledge the "secret mainsprings of their own thoughts and acts"—compassion for the sufferings of others.[73] Socialism, after all, was simply the "form that morality has taken in our time." He denied, moreover, that Socialism could be viewed merely as the "redistribution of goods."[74] Such an interpretation was vulgar, a "thinking laden with resentment." Marxism was "more noble, more profound and inward" than the mere satisfaction of "material needs." The higher values could be viewed, in fact, as part of man's material needs. No wonder one commentator has observed that Horkheimer, as a Marxist critic of bourgeois society, remained "to some extent outside the critique."[75] Horkheimer even suggested that one might have to be disloyal to Marxism as currently understood in order to do jus-tice to its insights.[76]

Despite the continuing force of his inner voice, the romantic anticapi-talism of Horkheimer's earlier years was giving way to a much more ration-alistic view of social transformation. "Without insight" into the nature of social relationships, he observed, "moral ideas play the role of fetishes," in-capable of offering guidance for action.[77] Marxism had given new meaning to the moral indignation aroused by his hatred of bourgeois society. It ex-plained the stunted lives within the capitalistic order. Most individuals had become "mere functionaries of property relations," incapable of acting as "real autonomous human beings" except when they were at play or en-gaged in activities that did not matter.[78] Marxism offered a vision of a "classless and planned economy" in which the "free subject ... consciously creates social life."[79]

Socialism could only be realized, therefore, by "men trained in theory."[80] But theory should not be viewed as an absolute; it was simply a tool for understanding society and subject, therefore, to historical changes. He criticized orthodox Marxists for failing to recognize the provisional nature of their doctrines. Indeed, he grouped them with various religious and political sects—Christian Scientists, Psychoanalysts, National Socialists, and others—who were "gripped by theory."[81]

Still, there was the problem of the proletariat. Was it possible, he asked, in one of his diary entries, to find "men among the poor who can escape the intellectual order of capitalism?"[82] He thus acknowledged the dilemma that occupied all serious Marxist thinkers in these years—the widening gap between their theory and the actual development of the working class. It had become clear that the workers had not become, as Marx predicted, a unified and self-conscious revolutionary subject. In the face of this development Georg Lukács, the most creative and influential Marxist theorist of the period, had accepted the Communist Party as an agent capable of embodying a genuine socialist consciousness.[83] Although strongly influenced by Lukács, Horkheimer set out, in contrast, to clarify the relationship between the working-class movement and the theorists who were charged with the task of guiding it onto the right path.

Once more he noted the profound divide between the intellectuals and what he called the "proletarian elite."[84] The latter usually lacked "clear-sightedness about the realities" around it and tended, therefore, to act blindly. The "revolutionary career" was often a "passage toward the unknown, with misery, disgrace ... and prison as its way stations." Indeed, the moral character of the working-class leaders might not be the best. Those who came out of the "bourgeois circles," in contrast, tended, because of their acute moral sensibility, to stay "away from the political fight." Do the men on this higher plane, he asked, have a basis for condemning those who are actually engaged in the struggle?

The question was ironic in view of Horkheimer's own relationship to Weimar political life. For he could find no point of contact with the practical struggles of the German workers save one that was critical and hostile. He complained, in fact, that the "wretched intellectual and moral state" to which the ruling class had reduced the workers made them "ready to tear to pieces" those who "undertake to free them from their tutelage."[85] Horkheimer's own distance from the political struggle was apparent in a short essay in which he attempted to explain "The Impotence of the German Working Class."[86]

The advance of technology, he argued, had divided the German workers into the employed and the unemployed and thus destroyed their "community of common interest."[87] While one section, represented by the Social Democratic Party, was increasingly integrated into the capitalistic system, the other section, the unemployed, represented by the Communist Party, had "nothing to lose but their chains." This development had meant a split between "the interest in socialism and the human qualities necessary for its implementation." Although the Social Democratic workers still possessed the capacity for education and organization, and hence the possibility of a "clear theoretical consciousness," they had ceased to recognize that the "human condition cannot be effectively improved under capitalism."[88] Their leaders had come to hate "any precise theoretical point of view." The communists, on the other hand, still held onto the socialist goal but they had lost the intellectual and practical capacities to implement it. Their leaders threatened to turn the Marxist doctrines into "a mindless and contentless cult of literalism and personality." In short, "the two elements of the dialectical method" in Marxism—practical experience and "clarity concerning fundamentals"—had ceased to be integrated.[89]

Having distanced himself from the political struggles of the German workers, Horkheimer focused mainly on what orthodox Marxists called the "superstructure," the forms of consciousness or, to use his own terms, "those ideas which play a role in the psychic economy of the individual" and thus facilitate "the domination of the ruling class."[90] Employing the Marxist conception of ideology, or "false consciousness," he criticized traditional religious and metaphysical notions for what he saw as their debilitating effects on human understanding. By proclaiming "the existence of a power which was independent of history yet governs it," the old ways of thinking discouraged social insight and creativity.[91] Contemporary efforts by the "life philosophers" and others to reflect anew on the fundamental characteristics of human existence were no better.[92] But while the Marxist critique of ideology had come to play a central role in Horkheimer's thought, he drew back from any crude form of reductionism. Even as he denounced the older theological and metaphysical notions, as well as their contemporary surrogates, he acknowledged the debt that Europeans owed to their religious past. Without the "idea of justice" bequeathed by Christianity, he observed, "mankind would be deprived" of the energies required through the ages to challenge social injustices.[93]

Horkheimer had turned away from the formalistic preoccupations of conventional academic philosophy in order to consider the ways in which ideas "flow out of the material traffic of actual men" and were "interwoven with their real behavior."[94] But he continued to be deeply influenced by the German idealists, particularly Kant and Hegel. He adopted the Kantian notion that the mind is an active force in the shaping of reality as well as his commitment to reason. He embraced, too, Kant's vision of a rational society in which the free, autonomous individual would find a place. But Horkheimer held, following Hegel, that the meanings and values enunciated by Kant could be understood only within a concrete historical and social setting. He also accepted Hegel's claim that society can only be understood as a whole while rejecting Hegel's metaphysics—his belief that history expresses a transcendental spirit.[95] From both Kant and Hegel came the conviction, reinforced by Marx, that the truth and significance of events lies beneath the surface, beneath "mere facts." To uncover the deeper, hidden meanings was the task of rational inquiry.

In developing his own conception of materialistic philosophy, Horkheimer, therefore, carried over much of the German philosophical tradition.[96] But he also retained, from his earlier reading of Schopenhauer, something of the latter's skepticism toward the grand systems of Kant and Hegel, as well as his profound pessimism.[97] Schopenhauer's continuing influence was suggested by Horkheimer's observation that Marxists were too quick to disregard the existence of evil because they had a "theory which accounts for it."[98]

Horkheimer had become convinced, as a materialist, that metaphysical speculations—judgments about the absolute or essential nature of things—were fruitless. But this did not prevent him from making metaphysical statements of his own. It was obvious, he declared, that the universe is "senseless … unfeeling and remorseless," that man is simply the "plaything of blind nature."[99] Indeed, the aloneness of man in the universe means that he is the only source of reason in the world.

Horkheimer's two voices—the promptings of his moral feelings and the new rational or theoretical voice provided by Marxism—could be heard in a series of lectures, "The Beginnings of the Bourgeois Philosophy of History," presented at the university in 1928 and published two years later.[100] They were, he stated at the outset, an exercise in "self-clarification." Although Marx was not mentioned in the lectures, they were firmly grounded in Marxist theory. Horkheimer was concerned mainly, however, not with economic and social developments but with what he referred to as the "effective use of ideational instruments of power."[101] Applying the Marxist conception of ideology, he attempted to demonstrate, through analyses of major "bourgeois" thinkers—Machiavelli, Hobbes, and Spinoza—the ways in which "intellectual notions" rationalized and justified the social process, particularly the changing modes of production.[102] He recapitulated the Marxist narrative, according to which the bourgeoisie freed itself from its subservience to the aristocracy, became the dominant class in European history, and subjected the lower classes to its will.

Horkheimer's narrative also made room for the protests of the early European utopians—Thomas More and Tommaso Campanella—against the developing property arrangements of the bourgeoisie and the miseries it inflicted on the lower classes. Although the utopians lacked an understanding of history and, hence, lived in a fantasy world, they recognized that "true misery" could not be eradicated within the bourgeois order since its causes "lay in the economic realm."[103] They recognized, too, that only a "revolutionary upheaval of foundations could create unity in the place of a fragmented human existence and justice in the place of injustice." But the revolution, Horkheimer added, must come from below.

> However, those who understand the roots of the evil that utopians reveal, as well as the goal to which their emancipation is connected, are not the legislators but precisely those groups of individuals who suffer privation as a consequence of their position in the social life process.

Horkheimer's account ended with a discussion of the seventeenth-century Italian philosopher Giambattista Vico. What appealed to him in Vico was his search for "history's inner laws ... and its hidden tendencies."[104] Although Vico attributed these laws and tendencies to God, he had anticipated Marx in fixing on a "historical process in which humans act," as well as in his attempt to find "purposive laws and relationships." He had anticipated Marx, too, in recognizing that "human creations," meanings and institutions, originated in "material conditions."[105] Vico had arrived, therefore, at the "most modern views." But for Vico, and Horkheimer as well, in contrast to orthodox Marxists, the future was uncertain.

> We must follow him in his conviction that the possibility of a return to barbarism is always open. External catastrophes can play a role in its return but so can the events that humans themselves bring about. ... Beneath the deceptive veneer of the present age, tensions are at work ... that very likely could bring about horrendous setbacks. ... There is precisely as much meaning and reason in the world as human beings realize within it.[106]

The refusal to hypostatize history in favor of an emphasis on subjective and volitional qualities of individuals would continue to characterize Horkheimer's Marxism.

By the end of the 1920s Horkheimer had found in Marxism a compelling explanation of the moral failings and social deficiencies that he had described in *From Puberty*. Something of the hold of his Marxist faith can be gauged from the way he defended it against the attempt of Karl Mannheim to subject Marxist theory to the kind of critique that Marx had leveled against the bourgeois ideologies.[107] In pointing out that Marxism, like its rival systems of thought, was rooted in the experiences and interests of one section of society, Mannheim sought to show the limitations of the proletarian perspective as well as the possibility that "free floating intellectuals" might rise to a more comprehensive and objective point of view. In defending the uniqueness and validity of Marxist theory, Horkheimer ignored Mannheim's claim that it could, by virtue of its historical rootedness, offer only limited insight into social conditions. Instead he pointed to the aspects of Mannheim's thought that carried over elements of "classical idealist philosophy" and its metaphysics. Marxism, according to Horkheimer, had overcome the idealist preoccupation with the analysis of concepts and had investigated the "actual conditions that determine the relations between the real struggles of human beings and their ideas." The "question of the correctness or falsity of equally situationally determined ideologies can only be put in terms of a judgment of their appropriateness for their time."[108] Convinced of the unassailable nature of the Marxist doctrines, Horkheimer refused to grant any merit to Mannheim's argument.[109]

Horkheimer's academic career and his Marxist faith—the exoteric and the esoteric parts of his life—were joined in the fall of 1930 when he was chosen as the new director of the Institute for Social Research. He had played no role in the development of the Institute but he now shared the goal of its creators—"the study and extension of scientific Marxism."[110] He also possessed the academic credentials necessary to occupy a professional chair and thus fulfill the required connection between the University of Frankfurt and the Institute. With the help of Paul Tillich a chair in social philosophy had been established for Horkheimer in July 1930. Early the following year he set out to define the future work of the Institute.

III

Before his appointment as head of the Institute, Horkheimer had planned to write a book entitled *The Crisis of Marxism*.[111] Although the book was never completed, the remarkable series of essays he wrote during the 1930s was a sustained effort to overcome what he saw as the deficiencies in the dominant form of Marxism and thus to contribute to a renewal of its revolutionary drive. He identified the deficiencies of Marxism and defined the work of the Institute as well, early in 1931, when he presented his inaugural lecture as its new director.

Horkheimer approached this work as a philosopher, determined to "carry out anew the exalted role" that Hegel had assigned to philosophy.[112] Its task was, in short, to provide "a new interpretation of life," to explain the "vicissitudes of human fate ... not as mere individuals, however, but as members of a community."[113] From this standpoint Horkheimer re-examined orthodox Marxism and what he saw as its failure to do justice to the subjective aspects of human behavior. Marxist theory, he observed, had been unable to explain "the connection between the economic life of society, the psychical development of individuals, and the changes in the realm of culture."[114] Horkheimer was, at the same time, addressing the central problem facing Marxist theorists in these years—the failure of the working class to develop the consciousness necessary for it to fulfill its historic mission. His essays during the 1930s would be concerned mainly with the exploration of consciousness, with the ideas that mediated between the economic determinants emphasized by Marx and human action. Here, in what Horkheimer referred to as the "psychical linkages," one can follow the interplay between his moral sensibility and the Marxist ideology.

To correct "a badly understood Marx," in which "the psyche of human beings" was viewed as "mere reflections of the economy," Horkheimer called on the members of the Institute to combine "philosophical theory and specialized scientific praxis."[115] They must take up again the task initiated by Hegel—that of understanding the "individual interests, drives, and passions of human beings" within the context of a collective whole.[116] For the collapse of the Hegelian synthesis during the second half of the nineteenth century had meant a split between a narrow positivistic fixation on mere facts, on the one hand, and a series of new metaphysical speculations on the other. It was time to bring back together genuine philosophical inquiry and empirical investigation. Horkheimer urged the members of the Institute "to pursue their larger philosophical questions on the basis of the most precise scientific methods, to revise and refine their questions in the course of their substantive work, and to develop new methods without losing sight of the larger context."[117]

Given the Marxist concern over the state of proletarian consciousness, it was not surprising that Horkheimer proposed that members of the Institute undertake research into the "psychic structure" of the significant social groups.[118] Their initial task, he suggested, was a study of "the skilled and white collar workers in Germany." He was, in fact, endorsing a project that was already underway. During 1929, Erich Fromm, with the support of the Institute, had distributed an elaborate questionnaire to thirty-three hundred individuals in order to gain insight into the relationship between "the objective situation, the psychic structures, and the political conviction of the workers."[119] Bringing his psychoanalytical training to bear, Fromm and his assistants hoped to gauge the readiness of the German workers for revolutionary action. Their findings were disappointing, for they indicated the weakness of genuinely radical motives, even among those workers with a left-wing political outlook. Horkheimer opposed publication of the study, fearful, according to Fromm, that its Marxist color might damage the public image of the Institute.[120] If so, the episode illustrated a paradox that would characterize Horkheimer's leadership of the Institute—his attempt to maintain the appearance of objective scholarly inquiry even as he employed Marxist theory to explain and provide a critique of the existing social order.[121]

In his own effort to gain a fuller understanding of the present content of human consciousness, Horkheimer also turned initially, in an essay published in 1932, to psychology as an "indispensable auxiliary science."[122] By means of Freudian psychology, in particular, he hoped to answer the crucial question facing Marxists—how to explain the "psychic mechanisms" that "keep latent" the class conflicts generated by "the economic situation."[123] Psychology, he argued, could penetrate to the deeper layers of consciousness and "uncover ... the irrational powers" that prevented individuals or groups from envisioning "a higher and more rational form of society." The Freudian concept of the unconscious promised insight into the formation of a "false consciousness." For those individuals, on the other hand, whose actions were "motivated by insight," there was less need to "revert to psychological explanations." Confidant that Marx had provided such insight, Horkheimer denied the general applicability of the Freudian view of the unconscious.

Psychology, Horkheimer argued, could also counter the damage resulting from an excessive emphasis on the "economistic principle."[124] Although he accepted the Marxist claim that "the economic situation affects the most intimate aspects of human life," he resisted any extreme form of reductionism or determinism. Human beings could not be "dissolved into mere functions of economic relationships."[125] Psychology was needed to correct such views by providing "insight into the forms and conditions" of human initiative.

> It must differentiate within each epoch the total spiritual powers available within individuals—the strivings at the root of their physical and intellectual efforts—from those relatively static psychic characteristics ... that are determined by the overall social structure.

In his reference to "spiritual powers" Horkheimer was taking aim at those Marxists, and liberals as well, who explained the behavior of individuals "exclusively on the basis of their material advantage."[126] "Economic egoism," he insisted, was "historically conditioned and subject to radical change." It should be possible, therefore, for psychology to demonstrate a different psychical reality "no less intense than that of material gratifications."[127] Human beings might, he argued, "experience a sort of happiness in the solidarity with like minded souls that makes it possible for them to assume the risk of suffering and death."[128]

Horkheimer continued to be moved, as these remarks suggest, by strong moral feelings. At one point he noted the special sensitivity of "refined individuals," like himself, who were not involved in "the crude tasks necessary for the reproduction of society."[129] "Their mental apparatus" was such that "an insignificant moral conflict in their own lives" might result in "the greatest upsets." Here, too, he observed, was an object for "psychological work."

At the end of the essay Horkheimer expressed the hope that the psyche might "gain greater weight" in the future.[130] "At critical moments in history" it could become "a more decisive factor than is usually the case." Horkheimer was attempting, as a Marxist theorist, to reassert the role of conscious factors, the understanding and the will, in the development toward socialism. His emphasis on individual autonomy and volition—indications of his continuing debt to German idealism—expressed the "implicit normative" concerns in his thought.[131]

In his attempt to advance those values Horkheimer relied less on psychology, which simply described the content of consciousness, than on his own reflections as a philosopher. Rejecting Marx's claim that philosophy had come to an end, he reaffirmed the role of the philosopher in his effort to recover the revolutionary subject.[132] In the essays that followed he set out to reconstruct Marx's materialistic philosophy in a way that made room for his moral commitments and, at the same time, restored the human will.

The two essays published in 1933, "Materialism and Metaphysics" and "Materialism and Morality," developed the conception of materialism he had advance a few years earlier in his "Notes."[133]

The year 1933 was critical for Horkheimer and other members of the Institute.[134] In January of that year Hitler became chancellor and during the following months the Nazis tightened their grip over German society. Anticipating a time of troubles, the leaders of the Institute had moved its assets out of the country, and when, in March, it was shut down by the authorities, Horkheimer continued to administer its program, first from Geneva, and, after 1934, from New York. Despite the altered settings and the dispersal, for a time, of its members, the work of the Institute went on with Horkheimer still assuming the main responsibility for developing its theoretical framework.

In "Materialism and Metaphysics" Horkheimer distinguished his form of materialism from that of earlier materialists who, like their idealistic opponents, were chiefly concerned with metaphysical questions. In wrestling with the "enigma of being" or the "totality of the world," the older metaphysical ways of thinking had attempted to establish the ultimate grounds for human values and behavior.[135] But the modern materialist, according to Horkheimer, required no such justification. Aware of the "fundamental role of economic relations," he simply sought "insight into the earthly order of things."[136] He replaced the old justifications of human action with "an explanation of it through an historical understanding of the agent."[137]

Horkheimer's conception of materialism has been described as a way of thinking that enabled him to take up matters ignored by the earlier mechanistic and deterministic forms of materialism.[138] He accommodated what he referred to as the "spiritual powers" of human beings. He cited with approval thinkers who had criticized the earlier forms of materialism for their failure to explain "the fact that the psychic processes we experience are something totally different from anything material."[139] But while the modern materialist acknowledged the existence of spiritual and moral phenomena, he viewed them simply as aspects of "man's striving for happiness," as natural facts "requiring no justification."[140] "Feelings of indignation, compassion, love, solidarity and so on" could be accepted without reliance on religious or metaphysical claims.[141] Horkheimer's form of materialism thus brought together the two main strands in his intellectual development—his moral protest against the bourgeois order, and his Marxist understanding of capitalistic society. The way in which his earlier sensibility had entered into the Marxist ideology was evident in his formulation of the dialectic.

The dialectical materialist, he argued, in contrast to the detached observer postulated by the idealists, and the older materialists as well, immersed himself in the effort to "improve the human situation."[142] Since his views "are essentially determined by the tasks to be mastered at the moment," the traditional distinctions between subject and object, fact and value, as well as theory and practice, disappeared.[143] By virtue of his direct engagement in the social struggle, the dialectical materialist was also in a position to recognize new possibilities arising in history. The philosopher, or theorist, became the agent through which society achieved self-consciousness, and served as a force for revolutionary change.

Horkheimer attempted to recover the revolutionary subject by emphasizing the role of the theorist. By virtue of his unique capacity to understand the turnings of the dialectic, he could guide the workers toward a rational and just society.[144] This conception of the dialectic also carried forward the "totalizing impulse" derived from Hegel and reinstated by Lukács.[145] Horkheimer rejected any claim to an absolute understanding of society; total understanding could only be provisional. But he was confident that Marxism enabled one to grasp, however fleetingly, the essential structure and direction of society as a whole.

Horkheimer's conception of the revolutionary subject was, however, one sided.[146] It was confined to the realm of consciousness, and lacked any clear connection with the actual struggles of the workers, which, according to Marx, served as a corrective to theory.[147] As several commentators have pointed out, theory for Horkheimer functioned as a substitute for political praxis.[148]

By 1933, to be sure, political developments in Germany precluded any direct engagement between the members of the Institute and the proletariat. But what one critic described as Horkheimer's "aristocratic aloofness" from the working-class movement, his failure to identify any fruitful point of contact with the working-class parties, had characterized his Marxism from the beginning in the Weimar years.[149] Hence the conclusion of Michael Löwry. Horkheimer's Marxism, lacking any "concrete, material support ... was condemned to become more and more suspended in the air, socially rootless, and abstract."[150]

In his second essay on materialist philosophy Horkheimer focused directly on the moral concerns that had led him to Marxism.[151] How, he asked, had the "highly developed European individual," capable of judging the world in personal moral terms, arisen?[152] It was an inquiry into his own outlook. He was attempting to explain his own rebellion against bourgeois society—his sense of the discrepancies between its moral values or ideals and its social practices.

He had found the answer in the Marxist analysis of capitalistic society. Marx had disclosed a fundamental conflict between the "possessive in-stincts of individuals under capitalism" and the "needs of the community as a whole."[153] The resulting tension in the "inner lives" of men and women had been overcome in part by the creation of moral codes that checked in-dividual self-seeking. But this had meant, as in the ethical thought of Kant, a conflict between duty, the "categorical imperative," and the self-interest or desires of the individual. It reflected the profound rift in bourgeois soci-ety. And since the gulf between its professed values and its social practices was an inescapable feature of capitalism, it could only be overcome by a radical transformation of society and the "systematic incorporation of each member into a consciously directed labor process."[154]

Such a transformation, Horkheimer believed, was already underway. The bourgeois epoch was "about to end." He described its dialectical over-coming, however, not in terms of the concrete struggles of the workers but as a consequence of the moral goals produced by the bourgeoisie itself. "Bourgeois morality," he wrote, "presses toward the superseding of the or-der that first made it possible and necessary."[155] With the passing of that or-der the moral code of the bourgeoisie was destined to disappear or, "at the very least, step into the background."[156]

Although Horkheimer had found, in Marxism, a rational explanation of his moral protest against bourgeois society, the "inner voice" of his early years had lost little of its force. It could still be heard in the rhetoric with which he denounced the existing social order.

> The struggle of great economic power groups … is conducted amid the atro-phy of kind human inclinations, the proclamation of overt and covert lies, and the development of immeasurable hatred. … The need to veil this state of af-fairs … gives rise to a sphere of hypocrisy which … penetrates into even the most private of relations. … At no time has the poverty of humanity stood in such crying contradiction to its potential wealth. … It appears as if the world is being driven into a catastrophe … which can only be compared … to the fall of antiquity.[157]

But while he contemplated the dark turn in European life, he still held, as a Marxist, an optimistic view of the future. Virtually absent now was the

ontological pessimism, influenced by Schopenhauer, that marked his earlier writing. Not only could Horkheimer attribute the destructive impulses
in human beings to social causes but he had identified, in the human capacity to reason, the crucial mediating forces, neglected or at least devalued
by the orthodox Marxists.

The concept of reason or rationalism was the subject of the two essays
that followed his discussion of dialectical materialism.[158] It provided another way of exposing the self-serving ideologies of the bourgeoisie and the
psychic imprisonment of the working classes. But his new inquiry into the
"psychic links" also moved further away from the immediate struggle of
the workers to that of the intellectual or theorist.

Bourgeois rationalism, which Horkheimer traced back to Descartes,
had been built on the false premise that the human being was "capable of
producing valid knowledge out of itself."[159] The bourgeois confidence in
the isolated ego, itself a reflection of the individualistic and competitive
ethos of capitalism, was also found in the British variant of rationalism—
the empiricist tradition reaching back to Locke. Both versions of rationalism expressed the "attitude of enlightened bourgeois strata which hoped to
put all questions of life under their own control."[160] In emphasizing the
"pure processes of consciousness," however, bourgeois thinkers had ignored vital human experience and avoided "all great human questions." No
wonder the "life philosophers"—Nietzsche, Henri Bergson, and Max
Scheler—had protested against the "deadening effect" of bourgeois philosophy.[161]

Dialectical materialists remedied the defects both of the traditional rationalists and their "irrationalist" critics. Through an awareness of their
own embeddedness in the social process and their recognition of the tasks
it presented, they could develop theory as "a critical, corrective, forward
driving and strengthening element" in the struggle for a better social order.[162] Indeed, "without the correct theory of society as a whole, social action" was reduced to "mere accident."[163] The "refinement of theory" continued, therefore, to be Horkheimer's answer to the question he had posed
in his inaugural lecture. It was the indispensable "psychic link" between the
objective social situation and progressive action. At the same time he had
elevated the intellectual, or theorist, to the commanding position in the
movement toward socialism.

Horkheimer continued to hold the fundamental Marxist doctrines.
The "whole of social life" depended ultimately "upon economic factors."[164]
History was driven by the struggle between social groups. The decisive fact

of the present was the divorce between the "human productive process" and the "human will." "Chance and death rule over life" for society "confronts individuals as an alien power of fate, as nature."

Horkheimer's confidence in the capacity of the proletariat to develop a higher consciousness, always rather limited, had diminished further in the face of the Nazi success in gaining the support of Germans in all classes. He had become convinced, in fact, that European workers in general had developed, by virtue of their place in the productive process, a "psychic constitution" that diverted them "from insight into the most important questions of life, and thus also from their own true interests."[165] It was up to the intellectual, therefore, to function as a liberating force. Truth had power. The "process of cognition" itself "included real historical will."[166] It was the responsibility of the intellectual, or theorist, "to stand by it [truth] unbendingly, apply it ... act according to it, and bring it to power against the resistance of reactionary, narrow, one-sided points of view."

Horkheimer now conceded that "the strivings of progressive social groups toward the realization of a more rational society" had been "brought to a standstill" and probably "for some time to come."[167] But he still claimed that "when the right word is sounded" some, at least, of the "psychic fetters under which human beings suffer today" might be broken.[168] The liberating message came not simply from Marx's "fundamental insights into the essence of society," but from materialistic philosophy. "By unmasking the metaphysical idols which have long constituted a center piece" of traditional thought, modern materialism would direct "the human capacity for love away from the products of fantasy ... toward real living beings."[169]

Horkheimer still believed in 1934 that the Marxist analysis of capitalism was being confirmed by contemporary history. The "agglomeration of great amounts of capital, as against the declining share of the average individual," the increase of unemployment, and the "diversion of productivity from constructive to destructive purposes" had all been forecast by Marx.[170] Those "involved in this struggle," therefore, could see in these developments corroboration of their "unswerving faith."

Despite Horkheimer's attempt, by means of his materialistic philosophy, to establish the importance of theoretical understanding as the crucial mediating factor in the struggle for socialism, the problem of the "psychic links" remained. His preoccupation with the subjective or conscious factors had meant a comparative indifference toward those social and economic developments that had been central to Marx's analysis of capitalism.

He showed little interest, as a number of critics have pointed out, in "the critique of political economy."[171] He ignored the "already mounting corpus of political thought and economic analysis" developed by other Marxist thinkers in the 1920s and 1930s.[172] What Axel Honneth referred to as the "sociological deficit" in his thought led, paradoxically, to Horkheimer's failure to examine closely what should have mattered most to him—the moral elements in social life that could not be explained in terms of a "blind compliance with functional imperatives."[173]

Hence the irony of his criticisms of those socialist intellectuals who distanced themselves from the "questions of a strife-ridden humanity."[174] When he noted the resulting "mistrust toward intellectuals" he might have been referring to himself. For he and his colleagues increasingly resembled, in the words he applied to others, a "free floating intelligentsia" that had lost any "conscious connection" to the actual struggles of the workers.[175]

IV

During 1935 and 1936 Horkheimer continued his exploration of the intellectual and spiritual failings of the bourgeois way of life, and its baleful effect on the psyche of the working class, in two essays dealing with "Philosophical Anthropology."[176] This school of thought in Germany provided another foil against which Horkheimer developed his conception of dialectical materialism. Although the philosophical anthropologists— Scheler and others—agreed with the dialectical materialists in recognizing "one's own historicity," they had attempted to find enduring elements in human nature that could provide norms for individual and social behavior. They failed to see, according to Horkheimer, how "conceptions of the human" varied with "changing historical conditions."[177] Not only was the "fate of human beings ... infinitely varied," Horkheimer insisted, but "we cannot predict what potentials mankind has yet to fulfill."[178]

The concept of a fixed human nature also opened another avenue for Horkheimer's ongoing exploration of the psychic subjection of the masses. Pessimistic views of human nature, he argued, had helped to internalize the beliefs and values that, along with physical coercion, had held bourgeois society together. For example, insistence on the depravity of human nature by the Protestant theologians Luther and Calvin had provided a rationale for keeping the "dangerous wickedness of human nature" in check.[179] The Protestant ethic was not, as Max Weber had claimed, an independent factor in historical development, but essentially ideological; through the "spiritualization" of the masses they were more easily integrated into the capitalistic mode of production.[180] Although the bourgeoisie professed "religious and ideal values," they were, in fact, "atheistic … vulgar materialists."[181] At few points in his writing was Horkheimer so extreme in his demonization of the bourgeois class. Its "unrestrained egoism" resulted in a way of life marked by cruelty, coldness, and indifference; it was increasingly insensitive to spiritual existence.[182] It lacked any qualities that could prevent the "repression and annihilation of one's fellow human beings."

In order to gain a deeper understanding of the moral degeneration of the bourgeoisie, Horkheimer turned to Nietzsche. For the latter grasped more clearly than any modern thinker the process through which European societies had fallen into "hypocrisy and indulgence toward … error and injustice."[183] Horkheimer now dismissed Freud's contention that the aggressive and destructive tendency in human beings was "a basic fact of psychic life" and "determined by biology." This view could be seen as a surrender to "social and religious conventions."[184] Nietzsche, in contrast, had provided, in his account of Christianity and the "genealogy of morals," a "magnificent analysis."[185] He offered unmatched insights into the "psychic connections" between social developments and the harsh practices of bourgeois society. But given Nietzsche's lack of "historical understanding" or "clear theoretical knowledge," he could not explain the social causes of the "spiritual decay."

The major problem remained—how to liberate "huge masses of people" who were still caught up "intellectually, within the old forms" created by the bourgeoisie.[186] It had become clear to Horkheimer that the workers could not free themselves by their own efforts. Hence the need for theorists to uncover the "social contradictions" and find the "means of overcoming them."[187] Once again Horkheimer called on those intellectuals "in whom theory and historical practice" formed a unity.[188] "With their help" humanity might enter "a higher form of existence" and "acquire the freer psychic constitution." No doubt he included himself among those for whom "the dark ethos of a dying epoch … no longer has any power."

In a long essay, "Authority and the Family," published in 1936, Horkheimer examined the "psychic makeup" of the masses from still another perspective.[189] The essay was the introductory and theoretical section of the major interdisciplinary project undertaken by members of the Institute in the mid-1930s, designed to gain a deeper understanding of fascism.[190] By focusing on three mediating factors—culture, authority, and family—

Horkheimer attempted to illuminate the ways in which the inner lives of individuals were being shaped by social and economic forces.

Although Horkheimer defined culture as coextensive with civilization itself, he was chiefly interested in the "so-called spiritual expressions of the life of peoples."[191] How did moral ideas, religion, art, and philosophy serve to internalize and rationalize the power relations of bourgeois society and thus "supplement physical coercion?"[192] Only in this way could one explain why the "subject classes" had "borne the yoke of an oppressive social order for such a long time."

Culture, for Horkheimer, however, held ambivalent possibilities. It contained values that might move the individual to oppose "existing conditions."[193] But again it was the intellectual, in whom "an established psychic makeup does not play the decisive role," rather than the proletariat, who pushed the cultural dialectic forward.[194] Horkheimer did not explain the independence of the intellectual. He simply noted the "immense psychic energy" and the "strength and courage" required to "leave the old way of life."

"Authority" too was ambivalent and dialectical; it might mean submission or liberation. But it was, according to Horkheimer, a "central category" for understanding the psychic formations that condemned "the greater part of mankind to senseless wretchedness."[195] Nietzsche had shown how bourgeois forms of authority had led to "an idolatry of the actual."[196] And yet, a new authority, which challenged those forms, could arise out of theoretical understanding. Once more it was the possession of those intellectuals who, by virtue of "great psychic energy," had escaped "the prevailing outlook" and envisioned a "higher form of society."[197]

The family occupied a special place in Horkheimer's attempt to understand the "psychic character of the vast majority of men."[198] It was the "germ cell of bourgeois culture," the main mediating force between bourgeois society and the "authoritarian oriented conduct" that helped to sustain it.[199] The bourgeois family, dominated by the father, inculcated those qualities of obedience, duty, and work—the type of character required by a capitalistic economy. The child in such a family was taught, moreover, to trace all failings back to personal rather than social causes.[200] The "great mass of proletarian families," according to Horkheimer, had adopted the bourgeois model.[201]

The autobiographical strand, apparent in much of Horkheimer's writing, was especially evident in his treatment of the family. His reference to the clash between bourgeois notions of marriage and the "erotic desires of the young" recalled his own conflict with his parents.[202] But his discussion of the family also indicated a nostalgic and conservative turn in his thought that would become increasingly visible in the years ahead. For now he claimed that the bourgeois family held values that challenged its own predominant paternalistic and competitive ethos. In the figure of the mother he saw an alternative set of values—love and caring—that might serve as a refuge from the ruthless competition of the market economy.[203] The mother might even "sow in the children the seeds of a lasting spirit of rebellion" and nurture the hope for a different form of society. Such a hope found support in Horkheimer's belief that the "original orientation to the family," centered on the father, was coming to an end as capitalism left its liberal and entrepreneurial phase behind.[204] With the growth of monopolies and the decline of the entrepreneur, the father was losing his traditional role. But while Horkheimer suggested that "this last stage of the family" might make way for a new form of community, his analysis lacked any clear relationship to the Marxist account of social developments.

The next essay, "Traditional and Critical Theory," published in 1937, has often been viewed as the definitive statement of Horkheimer's form of Marxism.[205] But it also marked a further retreat from the optimism expressed in the earlier essays. He now used the term "critical" rather than the term "dialectical materialism" to indicate the essential character of his thought. In a time "like the present," he wrote, "true theory is more critical than affirmative."[206] Virtually gone now was the promise contained in his dialectical reading of history. The main task of critical theory was to explain the inhuman social practices of the present, which form the "individual's life down to its least details."[207]

The essay recapitulated much of the material in the previous writings, emphasizing once more the ways in which bourgeois modes of thought had influenced the psychic conditioning of the masses and prevented any genuine social understanding. Horkheimer still claimed, as a Marxist, that "the despair of the masses" would act as "the decisive factor" at the "major turning points" in history.[208] But such a point was far off at best. For the wretched condition of its life, "imposed on the proletariat from above," prevented it from becoming a "social force."[209]

Much of the essay dealt with the "tension between the theoretician" and "the class which his thinking is to serve."[210] Theorists, he claimed, still sought a "dynamic unity with the oppressed class." But they tended to oscillate between an "exaggerated optimism" toward the proletariat, on the one hand, and a deep pessimism, resulting from "periods of crushing defeat," on the other. Indeed, more and more, the intellectual who really grasped the "social whole" was engaged in an "aggressive critique ... against the distracting, conformist, or utopian tendencies within his own [socialist] household."

Horkheimer had not abandoned his attempt, as a Marxist philosopher, to give "voice to the mystery" contained within the dialectic of history—the promise of a "rational and just society."[211] But he now conceded that the "course of events seems to be leading far away from such a future."[212] To believe in the socialist future in the present situation resembled fantasy. Given his "obstinacy" toward the world around him, the theorist was likely to be treated as "an enemy and criminal" or perhaps as a "solitary utopian."

No wonder Horkheimer felt increasingly isolated. "Truth" in the face of the "conditions of late capitalism and the impotence of the workers" could only find "refuge among small groups of admirable men."[213] In that thought he found some hope and, indeed, something of his earlier messianic bent. "History teaches us that such groups, hardly noticed even by those opposed to the status quo, outlawed but imperturbable, may at the decisive moment become the leaders because of their deeper insight."[214]

Horkheimer had reached an impasse in his attempt to rejuvenate the revolutionary subject. His hope, always tenuous, that the working class might become the historical agent forecast by Marx, had shifted decisively to the intellectuals. But having redefined his Marxism as critical theory, he had also become more aware of the personal grounding of his Marxist faith. Critical theory was, "in its totality," he now acknowledged, "the unfolding of a single existential judgment."[215] He still insisted that this judgment, which endorsed Marx's analysis of capitalism, was "generated by the [social] order itself." But he had lost confidence in the development of objective social forces. In a postscript to his essay he simply fell back on his faith that "the thrust toward a rational society" was "really innate in every man."[216] Given the growing strength of fascism, however, it was becoming very difficult to maintain that faith.

After moving to New York, Horkheimer had established the Institute as the center of a remarkable group of emigré scholars. His success owed something to the generosity of Nicholas Murray Butler, president of Columbia University, who provided facilities for the Institute and whose faculty offered other forms of encouragement.[217] But Horkheimer and his closest colleagues kept their distance from American academic life, committed to working out the German philosophical tradition as they had interpreted it.[218] The Institute's journal, *Zeitschrift für Sozialforschung*, continued to publish articles mainly in German. And Pollock periodically reminded Horkheimer, in a series of "Memoranda," of their special mission: the members of the Institute constituted a unique community. "Only conscious pride in the truth and value of our community over against a hostile world," Pollock wrote, would enable them to press forward with joy and courage.[219]

During the mid-1930s, however, Horkheimer found a particularly congenial thinker in a friend from his student days in Frankfurt, Theodor Adorno. Their correspondence in these years, while Adorno studied at Oxford, provide an illuminating account of their intellectual developments.[220] In the years ahead the three figures, Horkheimer, Pollock, who carried much of the administrative burden of the Institute, and Adorno, would determine the direction of its work, while the remaining members—Erich Fromm, Walter Benjamin, Herbert Marcuse, Karl Wittfogel, Franz Neumann, Leo Lowenthal, and others—fell away or played secondary roles.[221]

In 1938 Horkheimer shifted the main focus of his thought from the ways in which the bourgeoisie had inhibited and thwarted the revolutionary potential of the workers to what he now saw as its natural political outcome—fascism. In two essays written in that year—"Montaigne and the Function of Skepticism" and "The Jews and Europe"—he employed the orthodox Marxist doctrines to explain the growing strength of authoritarian political systems.[222] As industrial societies moved from competitive to monopolistic forms of the economy, he wrote, dictatorship became the "appropriate form" of government.[223] Fascism was "simply the agent of big business," a late stage in the process through which an economic elite, having subjected much of the middle class, as well as the workers, to its power, had created a powerful state capable of protecting its interests.[224] Fascism, Horkheimer declared, was "the truth of modern society." It was the inevitable outcome of the power relations and exploitive features which, under the liberal and free market phase of capitalism, had been disguised and inhibited to some extent. Now the "cultural lies that poisoned" the earlier times had "either become transparent or have been abolished."[225] The "false securities of the past"—property, family, religion—had been replaced by the "terror in which the ruling class now takes refuge." Even in those parts of Europe where fascists had not gained power there were strong tendencies making for an authoritarian state.

The continuing hold of the Marxist doctrines was evident in Horkheimer's treatment of anti-Semitism. The persecution of the Jews in Germany and elsewhere could be explained in terms of their declining economic importance. With the ending of the free market they were being stripped of their "power as agents of circulation" and became the targets of various resentments.[226]

Yet Horkheimer parted from those Marxists who saw in the rise of fascism the final crisis of capitalism and its imminent demise. He was influenced by the studies of Pollock, who now argued that the new authoritarianism, in the form of state capitalism, might provide a long-term solution to the conflicts generated by the free market.[227] By means of a planned economy it might satisfy the needs of the people and thus demonstrate that an evil system could function effectively.

Horkheimer developed his view of fascism more fully in an essay, "The Authoritarian State," published in 1940.[228] In this new discussion of the capacity of capitalism "to outlive the market economy," he emphasized the process through which the working-class organizations had allowed themselves, during the Weimar years, to be integrated into the capitalistic order and thus had given up their revolutionary vision. Even if capitalism came unexpectedly to an end, he wrote, and a "resurrected mass party" took over, little would change since the working-class leaders had themselves adopted authoritarian principles.[229]

Despite Horkheimer's new awareness of the possible durability of capitalism, he had not abandoned his faith in the capacity of intellectuals, even in the context of the authoritarian state, to "build the cells of a new world."[230] In each of the three essays dealing with fascism he reaffirmed the capacity of critical theory, as an "active humanism," to confront society with the rational "possibility which is always concretely visible within it."[231] Such a possibility could only be envisioned, however, as a "qualitative leap" out of "existing material conditions." Horkheimer still anticipated a day when the "narrow minded and cunning creatures that call themselves men" in the present, would be seen as "caricatures, evil masks behind which" lay higher human possibilities.[232]

Still, the "lesson to be learned from fascism, and even more from Bolshevism," was the fact that "what seems like madness" from the standpoint of a "detached analysis" can become reality.[233] Toward the end of the essay on the authoritarian state Horkheimer suggested that the only option for the working class was an alliance with the state capitalists. After all, their planned economy was "closer to socialism than liberalism."[234] Given the failure of the proletariat to make its own revolution, there remained no choice for it and its theoreticians but to follow the *weltgeist* on "the path it has chosen." That the words were to be taken ironically was suggested by his final sentence. "As long as world history follows its logical course it fails to fulfill its human destiny." By 1940, however, Horkheimer was losing his Marxist faith in the future.

It is against the background of his assessment of fascism that Horkheimer returned to the problem that had occupied him throughout the 1930s—the deficiencies of individual and collective psyche under late capitalism. In an essay, "The End of Reason," written late in 1940, he focused on what had emerged in the earlier essays as a crucial mediating force between social conditions and revolutionary action—the "gift of reason."[235] But reason had ceased to be a reliable force for positive social change.

By the phrase "end of reason," Horkheimer referred to a process through which traditional notions of reason had been stripped of older meanings and values and been reduced to purely instrumental functions. This development, he argued, had been implicit in the use of reason from the beginning. For it had entailed a skeptical attitude that inevitably called into question the notions of freedom, justice, and truth, which earlier thinkers had identified with reason.[236] In time this self-critical bent had purged it of "so much of its content" that reason had virtually destroyed itself. As a consequence, Horkheimer argued, "the fundamental concepts of civilization are now in a process of rapid decay." What was left was simply the "pragmatic significance" of reason, its capacity to promote "the optimum adaptation of means to ends" regardless of their origins or character.[237] It came to be "regarded as a matter of subjective preference whether one decides for liberty or obedience, democracy or fascism."[238]

To explain the process through which reason had turned "against itself" and taken on the "form of skepticism," Horkheimer still relied on the Marxist analysis of capitalism. The causes of the new "bond between reason and efficiency" lay "within the basic structure of society itself."[239] By splitting society into "groups with competing interests," economic developments had prevented any universal application of reason and turned it into an ideological tool for a privileged class.

In this new discussion of the development of consciousness under capitalism, the problem with which Horkheimer had been most concerned in the earlier essays—the "psychic links" between economic determinants and human actions—ceased to be relevant. He now argued that the inner conditions for human freedom and initiative, still present to some extent under the liberal phase of capitalism, had been eliminated. The rise of fascism had meant a "leap from indirect to direct forms of domination."[240] Under the "new and naked form of command and obedience," the "rule of economy" had been extended "over all personal relations."[241] With this development most individuals had lost the capacity for self-awareness and personal development. "Neither conscience nor egoism is left."[242] All that remained for the individual was the ability to adapt. Since "the individual no longer has any future to care for, he had only to be ready to … follow orders, to pull levers."[243]

What mattered most to Horkheimer in this process was the loss of the capacity for reflective thought and theory. Absent now was his earlier confidence that one could, through a dialectical understanding of reality, perceive and work for a more rational and just social order. At a time when "the exploration of meanings" or the "speculative sense" had been displaced, at least for most individuals, by an "acquaintance with functions," all that remained was technique.[244] Only philosophy, Horkheimer wrote in another essay at this time, might still serve a critical function, preventing "mankind from losing itself" in those ideas and activities that the existing organization of society instills into its members.[245]

The virtual disappearance of any mediating factors, and hence the reduced capacity of human beings to resist the ever greater encroachment of external forces, was evident, according to Horkheimer, in the fate of the bourgeois family. Again he visited the starting point of his own moral protest against bourgeois society—the clash between father and son. But that kind of rebellion, generated by the contradiction between the professed values of the father and his social practices, "can no longer crop up."[246] For the process through which fascism broke down individuality was now taking place "tacitly and mechanically" everywhere by means of mass culture so that by the time "children come to consciousness everything is settled." The relationship between the father and son had been reversed; it was now the "child, not the father," who "stands for reality."

With the end of the conflicts within the family, other values were lost as well. The vestiges of matriarchy, the values of caring and nurturing, which Horkheimer had seen earlier as countering the harsher features of patriarchy, were being liquidated by the National Socialists. Indeed, love itself, an "irreconcilable foe of the prevailing rationality," had become an object of scorn.[247] The fascist "emancipation of sex," which instrumentalized the most intimate of human relationships for the purpose of population growth, had no tolerance for the unique heroism of true lovers, their "loyalty without prospect and reason."

The mutilation of the human personality resulting from the "pragmatic rationality" of industrial capitalism had found its completion in fascism. The pain and torture employed in the concentration camps was simply the final stage in a long historical development. That development had now gone so far that "reason does not dare to doubt it."[248] Injustice had come to be "blindly accepted as a visitation of supernatural fate." In a world where reason had been "purged of all morality … no one may remain outside and look on." Hence the need to bring the "resistant and the wayward, the phantast and utopian" into the fascist form of reason, by pain if necessary. The existence of "one solitary 'unreasonable' man" was an indictment of the whole society. This explained, according to Horkheimer, the "hatred of Jews." It derived, ironically, from their stubborn and "unintelligible faith in a God who has everywhere deserted them."

Did Horkheimer see any hope in the face of the darkness that was "gathering over the whole sphere of private life?"[249] Despite his diminished faith in reason, and dialectical materialism, he held that "even in fascism" morality had "left its traces" in those individuals who were "conscious that the reality to which they yield is not the right one." Toward the end of the essay he maintained that there was still more to reason than "the alienated life that preserves itself in the destruction of others and of itself."[250] And he suggested that "in the inferno to which triumphant reason has reduced the world" men might be able to see through its illusions and recognize it "for what it is." The extent to which the self had been dissolved might also mean a liquidation of the prudence and stupidity of the form of historical reason that had made economic domination possible. If so the self-destructive process of reason would come to an end leaving a clear choice between "barbarism and freedom."

V

The essay "The End of Reason" represented a radical reversal in the course of Horkheimer's thought. Not only had he lost his confidence in the capacity of a dialectical understanding of the social process to point the way ahead, but he had reverted to a form of Marxist determinism, to the claim that the modern consciousness was little more than a reflection of economic developments.

There were objective as well as subjective reasons for the striking turn in Horkheimer's thought. Developments in Europe at the end of the 1930s—the triumph of fascism, the tyranny of Stalin in Russia, the capacity of capitalism to integrate the working class, and the descent into war—made it difficult for him to sustain his earlier optimism.[251] To explain the shift in Horkheimer's outlook some commentators have noted the influence of his colleagues. Pollock's studies of capitalism, which had called into question the causal primacy of economic factors, had clearly shaped Horkheimer's view of fascism.[252] At least one student of his thought has seen in his changing conception of history echoes of Benjamin's pessimistic reading of the past.[253] Others have emphasized his increasingly close relationship to Adorno, who had never shared his confidence in the power of reason.[254]

Horkheimer's openness to such influences was itself, however, a sign that he had reached an impasse in his attempt to renew the revolutionary drive in Marxism. In the essay "Traditional and Critical Theory," which was the climax of that attempt, he conceded that the socialist intellectual had become an isolated voice, relying only on his existential judgment, and appealing in vain to the working class. Indeed, with the "uncoupling of Marxist social theory from proletarian class consciousness," Horkheimer's relationship to the workers had simply been reduced to a "moral decision."[255]

It is hardly surprising that Horkheimer found it necessary to re-examine the foundations of his thought. He continued that re-examination and developed the implications of his new view of reason and history in two books published during the 1940s—*Dialectic of Enlightenment*—a volume of "philosophical fragments," coauthored with Adorno, and *The Eclipse of Reason*.

In their introduction to the *Dialectic of Enlightenment* the authors conceded that they had "trusted too much in the modern consciousness" and failed to recognize the extent to which the growth of modern science had diminished "theoretical awareness."[256] For Horkheimer it was an acknowledgement that he had been unable to show how intellectuals and the proletariat might come together for revolutionary action. He now joined Adorno in an effort to discover "why mankind instead of entering a truly human condition, is sinking into a new kind of barbarism."

Horkheimer's struggle with the question can be followed in the two essays that probably owed most to his thinking—the opening, theoretical chapter, "The Concept of the Enlightenment," and the third chapter,

"Juliette, or Enlightenment and Morality."[257] He continued to rely on the Marxist analysis of capitalism, noting at a number of points the way in which changes in consciousness reflected the "corresponding conditions of social reality."[258] And he maintained again that the triumph of instrumental reason, now identified with the Enlightenment, had meant the virtual disappearance of the possibilities for free and creative action. "On the road to modern science," he wrote, mankind had renounced "any claim to meaning"; modern science "managed without such categories" as "substance and quality, activity and suffering, being and existence."[259] Indifferent to the "hidden qualities" in reality, what Horkheimer now referred to variously as the "other" or the "alien," human experience was reduced to "computation and utility." But a life that was incapable of transcending "the confines of experience" was impoverished. What was left, according to Horkheimer, was simply an "arid wisdom that holds there is nothing new under the sun, because all the pieces of the meaningless game have already been played out in thought."[260]

To explain mankind's imprisonment in the disenchanted world of instrumental reason, Horkheimer and Adorno emphasized the fallacies of the Enlightenment "way of thinking no less than ... the social institutions with which it is interwoven."[261] Indeed, they now interpreted human development as a kind of fall, inseparable from social progress. "The curse of irresistible progress," as Horkheimer put it, had meant "irresistible regression."[262] The closing down of the human capacity for self-reflection, and hence initiative, had made possible the "political error and madness," the "charlatanism and superstition," expressed in fascism.[263] The proletarian masses, having become pliable objects of the "smoother automatic control mechanisms" established within consciousness, could no longer "hear the unheard of with their own ears."[264] Socialism too fell victim to this process. Having been caught up in the "legacy of bourgeois philosophy," socialism had been reduced to the "merely quantitative and mechanical."[265]

Was anything left then to support the hope, expressed by the authors in their introduction, that their "philosophical fragments" might contribute to a "more positive notion of enlightenment?"[266] Certainly Horkheimer found little in the cultural landscape that promised any renewal of the spiritual qualities—the "aura" or "mana"—that had once nourished human beings. Religion, the traditional guardian of such qualities, was sterile. It had, according to Horkheimer, degenerated "into a swindle," into little more than an instrument of the new administrators.[267] Art, on the other hand, "still had something in common with enchantment," for it maintained "its own self-enclosed area," not subject to the laws of "profane existence." But for Horkheimer the main hope still lay in the human capacity, however diminished, for reflection. In the face of the "wholesale deception of the masses" he again claimed that the theoretical enterprise constituted the only "true revolutionary practice."[268]

But "revolutionary practice" for Horkheimer had been reduced to a critique of the Western tradition of rationalism. That critique had displaced the dialectical understanding of history he had drawn from Marx. And with the collapse of his Marxist faith in the future he turned back to the moral concerns in which his thought had been grounded from the beginning. In his essay "Juliette, or the Enlightenment and Morality," his "inner voice," suppressed in large part during his passage through Marxism, could be heard again.

The essay initially addressed a problem that had continued to occupy Horkheimer—the failure of modern philosophers to provide meanings and values capable of filling the spiritual vacuum resulting from the decline of "objective reason" and its religious or mythological sources. Thus he noted the "hopeless attempt" of enlightened bourgeois thinkers in the nineteenth century "to replace enfeebled religion" with "moral teachings."[269] It had been futile, he argued, because a form of reason that had become no more than a means of self-preservation lacked any criteria for distinguishing between good and bad, right and wrong, justice and injustice. Such a concept of reason, expressed in modern science, could only be neutral toward values; moral claims, therefore, became arbitrary.

But the skeptical spirit of the Enlightenment had not stopped at "the minimum of belief, without which the bourgeois world cannot exist."[270] Together with the workings of the competitive and acquisitive economic order, the new rationalism had destroyed all "bonds and obligations." Enlightenment thought undermined the bourgeois order it had helped to create. With the reduction of society to mere power relations the way was open for the kind of domination exercised in fascism and totalitarianism.

To explore what interested him most—the moral consequence of this process and the ways it anticipated the barbarities of fascism—Horkheimer turned to the "black writers" of the bourgeoisie, the Marquis de Sade and Nietzsche. They had recognized most clearly the implications of the loss of the religious sanctions for traditional moral values. De Sade, in particular, had initiated, through his spokesperson, Juliette, a "transvaluation of values."[271] She undertook a radical reversal of those bourgeois values to which Horkheimer remained committed.

In place of the ideals of "freedom, equality and justice," which Hork-heimer had hoped to redeem from their betrayal by the bourgeoisie, Juli-ette proposed the opposites. Freedom, she declared, was not the natural condition of most men, but rather slavery or at least domination by oth-ers.[272] Rejecting the claim that everyone "should be treated exactly" the same, she defended those individuals who were naturally contemptuous of society and "were endowed by nature with an eminent capacity for crime."[273] As for justice, she dismissed it as simply a "defensive reaction," a refuge for the weak; for the strong it represented fetters.[274]

The private virtues—compassion, love, sympathy for the sufferings of others—which had been part of Horkheimer's moral sensibility, were also called into question by Juliette. Whoever surrenders to compassion, she declared, "perverts the general law," for this upheld cruelty, violence, and oppression as natural.[275] Cruelty for its own sake, the pleasure of inflicting pain on others, was simply a fact of life. Love, within the new table of val-ues proposed by Juliette, was reduced to mere sexuality, indeed, simply to "genital and perverted sex."[276] No place remained for romantic love, ex-tolled by Horkheimer for its "unnatural, immaterial" qualities as well as its "utopian exuberance." With the devaluation of love went the extinction of the family as a place where the gentler values of caring and nurture, associ-ated with the mother, might flourish.

Juliette practiced her countermorality, however, not as natural behavior but as "tabooed activities."[277] She took "intellectual pleasures in … attack-ing civilization with its own weapons." She was devoted to science and, in fact, to the bringing of "one's emotions and inclinations" under the control of reason. In undertaking her "work of sacrilege" she had disclosed not only the "subterranean existence" of the "primeval behaviors which civili-zation had made taboo" but also their transformation into the "destructive tendencies" within bourgeois development. Later, Nietzsche would cele-brate the "courage to do what is forbidden" and describe the "profound pleasure … in all the debauchery of conquest and cruelty."[278] In revealing the actualities of bourgeois life as against its ideology, De Sade and Nietzsche anticipated the "cult of strength" that the German fascists had raised to new heights.[279]

But unlike Juliette, or De Sade, whose critique of traditional values tended toward nihilism or anarchism, Nietzsche had attempted to "save European civilization."[280] His notion of the superman, or a "higher self," could be seen as an effort to "rescue God" and reconstitute spiritual bonds.

Nietzsche had, in his own words, drawn from "the torch lit by ... Christian belief," and reverted to mythology.

In the writings of De Sade and Nietzsche, Horkheimer had found a "predictable chronicle of the public virtues of the totalitarian era."[281] The "black writers of the bourgeoisie" had "declared the shocking truth"—the indissoluble relationship between instrumental reason and the forms of domination culminating in fascism. The honesty of the two thinkers was, therefore, to be preferred to the attempts of the "moralistic lackeys" of the bourgeoisie to hide or cover up the essential features of their society.

Notwithstanding the deep pessimism of their diagnosis, Horkheimer and Adorno were still attempting to advance theoretical understanding and, indeed, draw out of the Enlightenment itself a more positive concept of reason. But their critique of instrumental reason required, as a number of commentators have pointed out, a principle in terms of which their critique could be justified.[282] The attempt to identify such a principle was one of the problems Horkheimer struggled with in his volume of essays *The Eclipse of Reason*.

Initially presented as a series of lectures at Columbia University in March 1944, the essays developed at greater length his critique, not only of fascism, but of modern Western societies in general.[283] His opening chapter recapitulated the argument, introduced in the "End of Reason" and developed further in the *Dialectic of Enlightenment*, that industrial society was increasingly dominated by a narrow conception of rationality that was incapable of making value judgments and hence simply served the goal of individual self-preservation. He now used the term "subjective reason" to describe this form of rationality and contrasted it with the traditional form it had eclipsed—"objective reason." The latter, expressed in classical philosophy and Christian theology, had recognized "a spiritual power living in each man" that reflected "the true nature of things ... to which we should devote our lives."[284] Again he told the story of how reason had "liquidated itself as an agency of moral and religious insight."[285] For the attempt of modern philosophers "to replace traditional religion" with a "secularized Christian ethic" had failed.[286] The triumph of subjective reason had meant the "atrophy and shrinkage," indeed, the extinction of the "inner life."[287] Having lost the spontaneous capacity to "discover and assert new kinds of content," modern man had entered into a profound cultural crisis.

There were, Horkheimer observed, two contemporary attempts to deal with the crisis—positivist philosophy and Neo-Thomism.[288] But the positivists, he argued, had abandoned any effort to "disclose the underlying reality" and simply "glorified existing reality."[289] The Neo-Thomists, in contrast, were engaged in a futile attempt to reconstruct a form of objective reason on the basis of an outmoded religious tradition. The "transition from objective to subjective reason" was, according to Horkheimer, "a necessary historical process." There could be "no going back."[290]

Horkheimer found a new "reference point" for his critique of subjective reason in what he called the "revolt of nature."[291] In the "Juliette" chapter of the *Dialectic of Enlightenment* he had noted an overpowering longing "to return to nature" in those individuals who had been "forced to become part of the social order."[292] Now he maintained that there were, even among the great majority who bowed to "irresistible reality," "natural impulses … antagonistic to the various demands of civilization," which still led "a devious underground life."[293] To these impulses he looked for qualities to replace those lost through the "eclipse of reason." Nature became, as Georg Lohmann has argued, a stand-in for objective reason.[294]

The drive to master the physical world, fundamental to the Marxist vision of human emancipation, and the central function of instrumental or subjective reason, had meant, according to Horkheimer, a disempowerment of nature parallel to that which had impoverished objective reason. A subjugated nature was being stripped of all "intrinsic values and meanings."[295] For nature, "if rightly read," held lessons for mankind. Through its "tale of infinite suffering," in particular, it might raise human beings above a mere concern for self-preservation.[296] For Horkheimer, as for his early teacher in moral questions, Schopenhauer, nature possessed the capacity, by making one aware of suffering, to generate compassion.[297] Nature thus became a possible new source of the moral values formerly associated with objective reason. Man's changed relationship with nature promised a way of recovering the lost human qualities.

What troubled Horkheimer most about the attempt to master the physical world was its impact on the human personality. For the disciplines and forms of adaptation required to subdue nature also entailed the repression of the spontaneous impulses and personal aptitudes that constituted genuine individuality. "Domination of nature," he wrote, means "domination of men," not only of others but of one's self.[298] "Emptied of content," the individual was reduced to the functions imposed by the dominant minority.[299] "Economic and social forces" took on the "character of blind natural powers."[300]

Horkheimer's central concern—the loss of personal autonomy—was developed in a chapter entitled "The Rise and Decline of the Individual." Through a survey of notions of individuality, beginning with Socrates, followed by its Christian forms, down to modern concepts of the entrepreneur and engineer, he again told a story of human impoverishment. The "depth and complexity" of the individual, expressed most fully in Christianity, had gradually dwindled to a merely functional view of man.[301] The "loopholes for individuality," still present to some extent during the liberal phase of capitalism, had now virtually been closed.[302] With the integration of human beings into modern forms of social organization, the bourgeois ideal of autonomy lost whatever content it had, and "minds were closed to dreams of a basically different world."[303]

Horkheimer refused to allow the individual to "entirely disappear in the new impersonal institutions."[304] Man was "still better than the world he lives in." There were still "forces of resistance," if not in groups, at least in individuals.[305] And he suggested that a "new era" of individuality might come from those who had experienced most directly, from fascist persecutions, the "terroristic annihilation" that most individuals were undergoing "unconsciously through the social process."[306] The "anonymous martyrs of the concentration camps," in particular, having experienced "the infernos of suffering and degradation" because of their resistances, were the "symbols of the humanity that is striving to be born." The victims of fascism thus came to occupy a position resembling that assigned earlier to the proletariat.

In the final essay in the *Eclipse of Reason* Horkheimer turned again to the intellectuals—to those individuals who were capable of understanding the "antagonism between self and nature."[307] A "philosophical awareness of the process," he maintained, might "help to reverse it." But the underlying problem remained: where was the "comprehensive concept of reason" by means of which one could judge "all that mutilates man?"[308] Lacking such a concept, Horkheimer simply fell back on the claim that philosophy was "mankind's memory and conscience."[309] As such its task was to "defend culture against the barbarians at the gate."[310] But culture, which included the "great ideals of civilization—justice, equality, freedom"—could be preserved only, in Lohmann's words, by means of a "relapse into metaphysics."[311]

Horkheimer's major writings during the 1940s indicated his steady movement away from the orthodox Marxist doctrines.[312] His faith in the proletariat as a redemptive force, never very strong, had collapsed by the end of the 1930s and with it his confidence in the dialectical unity of theory and practice. Not only had economic factors ceased to occupy the decisive role they played in Marxist theory but capitalism was no longer the main object of inquiry. It had been replaced by a philosophy of history centered on the regressive results of mankind's effort to dominate nature.

Horkheimer's break with Marxism was furthered by the major research project that occupied the Institute during the 1940s—an ambitious inquiry into the nature of anti-Semitism.[313] It was the "Institute's most extensive and sustained concentration on empirical research."[314] Supported financially by the American Jewish Committee, the project initially promised to give new purpose and vitality to the Institute, which, by 1940, had lost much of its coherence and direction. In fact, the project turned into the Institute's "central business and pushed everything else into the background."[315]

Horkheimer, who had moved to Los Angeles in 1941 for reasons of health, assumed directorship of the project. He still hoped, however, to develop further the philosophical reflections presented in *Dialectic of Enlightenment* and the *Eclipse of Reason*. His letters in these years expressed his continuing frustrations over the distractions of administration. Pollock reminded him from time to time of the special mission to which they had been called.[316]

The anti-Semitism project was not only a distraction but it "slipped more and more out of their hands" into those of the American social scientists who had been recruited for the study.[317] For they relied on methods— psychological and survey techniques—toward which Horkheimer had been skeptical. The theoretical concerns that he had always placed uppermost, together with the essential impulse of the Institute—its critical spirit—faded into the background.

But Horkheimer's own understanding of anti-Semitism shifted, within the context of the project, away from the orthodox Marxist approach he had adopted in his essay, "Jews and Europe." The economic interpretation presented in that essay gave way to an analysis, developed mainly by Adorno, that employed the psychoanalytic concepts of projection and paranoia to explain the Nazi treatment of the Jews.[318] Anti-Semitism was also integrated into the negative philosophy of history—centered on the theme of domination—developed in the *Dialectic of Enlightenment*. The special vulnerability of the Jews, according to Adorno, could also be explained in terms of the peculiarities of their history and the "prohibition of mimesis" that was fundamental to their religious tradition. By 1944, in fact, Horkheimer had come to see the Jews as both the "martyrs of civilization" and the symbol of "everything mankind stands for."[319] They had re-placed the proletariat as "the focal point of world history"; their fate was "inseparable from the survival of culture itself."

The extent to which Horkheimer, and Adorno, had parted from the Marxist doctrines can be measured by their changing relationship to the individual who remained the most orthodox among the members of the Institute—Marcuse. He had, not surprisingly, been baffled by the *Dialectic of Enlightenment* when he received a copy late in 1944.[320] And when, two years later, he pushed for a renewal of the Institute's journal and the need to focus once more on the "absent revolution," he found Horkheimer cool and evasive.[321] Indeed, Marcuse's draft for a fresh theoretical orientation, in which the goal of communism, a soviet-style republic, would be achieved through a revolutionary upheaval, simply demonstrated how little unity was left among the critical theorists. Horkheimer and Adorno had long since lost the hope of identifying a revolutionary agent and, as the view of history presented in *Dialectic of Enlightenment* indicated, simply looked for individuals who could resist the advance of instrumental reason.

Horkheimer's reaction to Marcuse's proposals was not simply a reflec-tion of his "long march away from orthodox Marxism."[322] For he and Adorno retained enough of the Marxist analysis of modern social and eco-nomic developments to share much of Marcuse's view of global politics, according to which fascist and totalitarian outcomes were seen as inherent in the liberal bourgeois order.[323] Horkheimer and Adorno were careful, however, lest any open expression of such views offend the academic and political groups on whom they depended for support. The self-censorship that had always characterized Horkheimer's employment of Marxist con-cepts was again evident in the late 1940s, when he was negotiating with the leaders of the University of Frankfurt regarding the possible return of the Institute to its original home.[324]

The question of whether to leave America was the cause of much heart searching during 1948 and 1949 as Horkheimer and Pollock considered the pros and cons of the move.[325] Would the move serve what remained, after all, their main desire for the future—the "prospects for the undisturbed" continuation of philosophical reflection?[326] As Horkheimer observed, however, their close ties to the German tradition had never really been bro-ken by their stay in America.[327] And during 1949 he concluded that Ger-many offered the best hope for carrying forward the work of the Institute.

VI

In 1950 Horkheimer settled once more in Frankfurt and with the support of the American and German authorities re-established the Institute for Social Research.[328] He reoccupied his chair in philosophy, served for a time as rector of the university, and resumed the directorship of the Institute. Along with his closest colleagues, Pollock and Adorno, he welcomed the opportunity to contribute to the reconstruction of Germany and its reintegration into the development of the Western democracies. At the same time he hoped to renew the program envisioned for the Institute in the early 1930s—combining empirical social research, enriched now by the methods of the American social sciences, with philosophical development. Thus in his address at the official reopening of the Institute in 1951 Horkheimer spoke again of the need to link specialized studies with the broader viewpoint and critical attitude appropriate to the work of the social theorist.[329]

The Institute did not realize that goal. Although it undertook a series of research projects, dealing with such problems as political awareness among the Germans and industrial relations in the reconstructed capitalistic economy, it did not advance the "critical-theoretical thought" of the earlier years.[330] Between the practical work of the Institute and the critical mission, which had always been its primary reason for existing, there was a widening gap.

This can be explained in part by the altered circumstances in which the leaders of the Institute found themselves. At first dependent on the German educational establishment and the American officials for financial support, and later on research contracts, Horkheimer and his colleagues were reluctant to present a radical critique of German society. Horkheimer, however, could no longer offer a systematic challenge to capitalism, for the critical theory of his earlier years "was in ruins."[331] Indeed, he now regarded the essays of the 1930s with a certain embarrassment, convinced that they had lost much of their relevance to developments in Europe after the war. In the years ahead he would strenuously resist the efforts of younger intellectuals—most notably, Jurgen Habermas—to reinstate "the utopian perspective of a radical critique of dominant conditions" that had been "the essential impetus behind Critical Theory."[332]

Yet there was a marked difference between Horkheimer's public role in Germany during the 1950s and 1960s—that of the recipient of many honors and a respected though rather conservative commentator on political, social, and cultural questions—and his "inner voice," which could be heard again in his private reflections.[333] Although he was no longer engaged, as in the 1930s, in systematic theoretical and philosophical inquiry, he continued to struggle with the questions that had occupied him earlier.[334] That struggle can be followed most clearly, not in his public lectures and writings but in his "Notes" and, particularly, in the private conversations, the "shavings," recorded by his friend Pollock.[335] It was here, as Alfred Schmidt observed, that one finds the deepest layers of Horkheimer's thought.[336] They also reveal a process of self-excavation, a search into the sources of the values and aspirations, which, for a time, had found expression in Marxism.

Despite the dramatic change in his situation and that of the homeland to which he had returned, Horkheimer held firmly to the diagnosis of Western civilization presented in the writings of the 1940s. In that diagnosis he argued that Western societies were caught, through their commitment to instrumental reason and the domination of nature, in a downward spiral of social atomization, spiritual impoverishment, and political authoritarianism. The end of the war and the defeat of fascism had not altered his gloomy view of the future. When Adorno declared, in 1945, that Hitler had simply anticipated a development that the victorious bourgeois societies would follow in the years ahead, he spoke for Horkheimer as well.[337] As noted earlier, they did not go so far as Marcuse, who described liberal capitalism as "pre-fascist," lest such pronouncements hinder their efforts to renew the work of the Institute.[338] But Horkheimer continued to be occupied, as his "Notes" and the "shavings" indicated, with the implications of the diagnosis presented in the *Dialectic of Enlightenment* and *The Eclipse of Reason*. Convinced that Western societies were moving inexorably toward a completely administered order, Horkheimer doubted that the liberalization of German political institutions, which he strongly supported in public, could reverse the process of spiritual decay.

Democracy, he declared at the end of the 1950s, had no historical future.[339] Given the manipulation of the masses by the media, democracy could only contribute to the movement toward a new tyranny. Nor was he impressed by the "economic miracle" experienced by Germany during the 1950s.[340] The increased material comfort was small compensation for the "rancor and rejection of every kind of decency" that was spreading through society.

Horkheimer's notes and private conversations are sprinkled with apocalyptic statements. "European history," he declared at one point, "is finished."[341] A "totally dark world" threatened, for the death of the "European spirit" was imminent.[342] Although Horkheimer had, in the essays of the 1930s, rejected any form of historical determinism, he now saw the "bourgeois mentality" disintegrating through the operation of "immanent laws."[343] Hitler had represented the beginnings of the "last phase of bourgeois society," while the "Russian caricature of socialism" could be viewed as a model for its ending.[344]

Only the American military presence and German rearmament, he observed in 1961, had prevented a Russian invasion.[345] But given the immanent logic of modern history, there was little to choose between the two superpowers; Russia and America were becoming "more and more alike."[346] The Europeans, having lost any unifying purpose, could only receive a "new will ... from outside." It would come, Horkheimer contended, from "barbarism and spread in a barbarous fashion," and more likely out of the East, from the despotic systems developing in Russia and China.[347] "Russia," he declared at one point, "under the pressure of the Chinese masses, will overrun Europe."[348]

What still troubled Horkheimer was the loss of individual autonomy. This concern runs like a litany through the late writings. [349] He believed that the triumph of instrumental reason and the growth of the administrative society meant an emptying out of the inner self. Hence the readiness of most men and women in modern society to respond like marionettes or robots to external signs, or any ideas presented to them.[350] Language itself had become sterile, for individuals no longer had anything significant to say to each other. They were being reduced to "functions of the social machine," mere cogs on an "assembly line."[351] A "despiritualized society" meant, in short, the end of individualism.[352]

The shadow of the failed socialist revolution darkened Horkheimer's late reflections. Despite his insistence that developments within modern civilization had been inevitable, he claimed that a great historical opportunity had been missed.[353] After the bourgeoisie had been unable to "develop beyond itself," the socialists had failed to fulfill its spiritual legacy.[354] Not only had the socialist leaders been captured by nationalistic loyalties and thus betrayed their international mission, they had surrendered to the "cult of the state."[355] The socialists had, in short, been absorbed into capitalism.

Marxism bore some, at least, of the responsibility for the failures of the socialists. Horkheimer continued to believe that the Marxist critique of political economy was "a perfectly rational basis for an understanding of social development," at least until a "better [theory] replaces it."[356] But he also maintained that Marxist theory was simply a passing phase of historical understanding that might function as a "false consciousness."[357] He now recognized, moreover, that the Marxist prediction that administrative relations would replace the old forms of domination had turned out to be "dismayingly true."[358] For Marxists, as for their capitalistic opponents, the hope they had placed in the mastery of nature had proved to be misguided.

"We are no Marxists," Horkheimer declared at one point, for Marx "was interested in quite different things than we are."[359] Unlike those individuals for whom "Marxism is the whole truth, for us it is only a tool for knowledge of men in society." He was, moreover, increasingly aware of the messianic impulses underlying Marxism, or what he referred to as its theological "a priori."[360] But its "secularized messianism" now seemed to him pathetic, "infinitely inferior to the authentic one."[361] Marxism had become, in short, a "false religion."[362]

The fundamental error of Marxism, he concluded, was metaphysical; it lay in the claim that all human problems "can be solved" if only the "social problem is solved."[363] Horkheimer had now rejected the optimistic anthropology implicit in Marxism in favor of a belief in "radical evil in human nature."[364] Mankind, he observed, was "a rapacious race, more brutal than any previous beast of prey." Not surprisingly, Horkheimer turned back in these years to Schopenhauer as the most reliable of philosophical guides.[365] For Schopenhauer had exposed the rationalistic and moralistic illusions of the philosophical idealists. He was, Horkheimer claimed, "the teacher for modern times," one whose thinking was shared instinctively by the younger generation. Schopenhauer appealed, moreover, because he had drawn from his grim assessment of the human condition a deep compassion for those who suffered.

As his return to Schopenhauer suggested, Horkheimer was peeling away much of the ideological cover by means of which he had attempted to resolve the antinomies of his early years. The "inner voice," largely silenced or expressed indirectly during his passage through Marxism, could be heard once more. He now likened it to what Hegel had described as the "mystical element in truth."[366] Horkheimer cited the Christian notion of grace and the mystic's sense of an "inner light" as comparable examples. Without this "mysterious, spontaneous, active" dimension of consciousness, he insisted, there could be "no truth" or, indeed, no genuine human existence. To rely on the inner voice was, to be sure, dangerous, for truth was never fixed. One must avoid the tendency of those, like believing communists, who were caught in the dogmas proclaimed by the party. The pursuit of truth required constant human activity and what he called "creative fantasy."[367] He even suggested that in "periods of decline such as the present, the higher truth lies in madness."

Horkheimer's reaffirmation of the inner voice amidst the general gloom of his diagnosis indicated that he had not given up his hope that a critical theory might counter the dehumanizing tendencies in modern civilization. But the old problem remained. What grounded or justified a faith in a form of reason that transcended the value neutrality, indeed, the nihilistic bent, of instrumental reason? The question of the "foundation of Critical Theory," as Wiggershaus observed, had "become urgent" once more.[368]

Horkheimer continued to view philosophy as one way of combating the destructive forces of the time. He was critical of most forms of modern philosophy, condemning in particular the later versions of positivism for their implicit acceptance of conventional views of reality.[369] And he noted again the failure of philosophers to accomplish the task, forfeited by religion, of providing meaning in life and pointing the way to a "new heaven."[370] But he could still hope for a vanguard of intellectuals who, having withdrawn "from the bourgeois crowd," might "run ahead" and serve as "beacons in the prevailing darkness."[371] Although they had "long since lost those entrusted to their care"—an obvious reference to the proletariat—philosophers were still charged with the task of developing a "kind of knowledge no longer merely instrumental." An "Association of the Clear-sighted," as he described it, might play a role comparable to the early Christians who had gone "into the catacombs."[372] Horkheimer had not abandoned his critical enterprise. Criticism, after all, was "the soul of all experience of history."[373] But the nature of his criticism had changed. It no longer functioned, as in the dialectical materialism of the 1930s, to identify and advance the rational possibilities discerned in the social process. It now served mainly in a negative fashion—to question the existing order of things. The "saddest thing" about the present, he maintained, was the loss of the "capacity to imagine that there was 'another.'"[374]

To challenge the "unreflectively positive" outlook Horkheimer turned in his last years, before his death in 1973, to religious questions. In a series of interviews in the early 1970s many of the private reflections of the 1950s and 1960s found public expression.[375] The interviews indicated his continuing struggle with the problem that occupied him following the collapse of his Marxist faith in the future—the status of the moral values and spiritual qualities that seemed to him essential for any genuinely human existence. Convinced now that one who viewed the world from a strictly scientific or positivistic standpoint lacked any criteria for choosing between "cruelty and love of neighbor," he attempted to find, through his reflections on religion, new support for his inner voice.[376]

Religion had played a continuing, though ambivalent, role in Horkheimer's thought.[377] In its Christian form it had been an integral part of the oppressive institutional and ideological structures that accompanied the growth of capitalism.[378] And he continued in the postwar years to see the Christian churches as negative forces; they were a "gigantic ossified piece of machinery" that helped to maintain the social order and contributed to the administrative tendency of modern life.[379]

But Horkheimer's protest against bourgeois society had, as his early writings indicated, been inspired in large part by religious values and attitudes. And even as he developed, by means of Marxism, a naturalistic explanation of morality, he acknowledged the debt owed to the Jewish and Christian traditions. In a short essay, "Thoughts on Religion," published in 1935, he had observed that although "mankind loses religion as it moves through history," the loss "leaves its mark behind."[380] And he claimed that the "drives and desires which religious belief preserved" could be detached from the old forms and "become productive forces in social practices." The failure of philosophers to fill the vacuum of meaning resulting from the decline of religion constituted a major theme in his writings. This was, as he declared in his inaugural lecture in 1931, one of the main challenges facing the members of the Institute.

With the fading of his Marxist optimism, the problem of meaning—the ideas and values capable of motivating and giving direction to human action—became more acute. Horkheimer doubted that one could return to the old religious beliefs. Religion, he declared in 1962, "is finished."[381] But he was troubled by a sense of what had been lost. With the ending of traditional forms of religious life the basis for distinguishing between "good and bad, love and hatred," had disappeared.[382] The very concept of truth, and "thought itself," lacked a foundation. But something even more important had been lost—the capacity of human beings to look beyond the world of phenomena or mere appearances. For the "great religions" had been the source of an essential human disposition—that of rebelling against "things as they are."[383] And despite the compromises and betrayals of its adherents, Christianity still meant an "internal independence from the world"; it was "utterly opposed to conformity" to secular authorities.[384] Horkheimer even suggested at one point that those who were fighting a rear-guard action against oppressive institutions might "make common cause with the churches."[385]

Horkheimer's late reflections brought out what several students of the Frankfurt school have seen as its "occult theological element."[386] Yet theology functioned for Horkheimer, not to refer to any positive religious belief, but to move outside the world of phenomena. In what he described as the "yearning for the wholly other" he could preserve those moral commitments that had been the driving force of his life and, indeed, preserve something of the eschatological hope he had once placed in Marxism.[387] He thus made room for "other standards than those given by nature or society" and his hope that "the injustices which characterized the world" were not "the last word."[388]

Horkheimer justified his refusal to give content to the "wholly other" by appealing to the ancient Jewish prohibition against any attempt to name or describe God.[389] But he had concluded that human beings needed some form of transcendence, that the "consciousness of our loneliness and abandonment" was "only possible through the idea of God."[390] Still, Horkheimer allowed, at most, only for the "shadow of God."[391] Given the growth of science and technology, he did not believe that it would be possible to "revive religion."[392]

This was a strange end to Horkheimer's intellectual journey. For he continued to believe that Western peoples were moving inexorably toward a totally administered society—a world without meaning, love, spirit, or individuality.[393] Against that coming world of "ice and steel" he could oppose only his innermost yearnings for transcendence while rejecting the religious terms in which they had traditionally found expression. He was, in Habermas's terms, seeking "to salvage an unconditional meaning without God."[394]

After leaving Marxism Horkheimer had returned to the moral and metaphysical questions with which he had been occupied in his early writings. He could say at the end of his life that the deep concerns of his earliest years had not changed, even though his judgments as to what was possible had altered.[395]

Despite the self-searchings of his late years Horkheimer had never moved outside his bourgeois moral and cultural sensibility. He, and his colleagues, had never entered sympathetically into the lives of the working classes they sought to liberate. No wonder one critic has charged them with the "worst form of European intellectual snobbery."[396] Others have described them as epigoni, suffering from nostalgia for a Central European social and cultural world now irretrievably lost.[397] Indeed, despite the ways in which their Jewishness set them apart, Horkheimer and his colleagues remained committed to the values, summed up in the concept of Bildung, held by the Mandarin section of the German bourgeoisie.[398] Faithful to those values, however, the members of Frankfurt school represented "an exceptional center of resistance" to the totalitarian tendencies, both left and right, of their time.[399]

The problem that defeated De Man and Horkheimer—how to renew the movement of revolutionary socialism—was taken up a generation later by a young Marxist intellectual in Poland, Leszek Kolakowski. He faced the crisis of Marxism in a different form than that experienced by his predecessors. But his attempt to revitalize the ideology also led to its dissolution. And after leaving Marxism Kolakowski continued the inquiry, begun by De Man and deepened by Horkheimer, into the nature of Marxism and the historical implications of its breakdown.

CHAPTER 4

Leszek Kolakowski

I

During an interview with Horkheimer in 1971 focused on the "future of critical theory," Claus Grossner suggested that the Institute's earlier mission—that of combining theory with empirical social research—might be revitalized by calling the young Polish philosopher Leszek Kolakowski to Frankfurt.[1] A year earlier, in fact, Habermas had proposed that Kolakowski be invited to fill the chair in philosophy occupied earlier by Adorno. His proposal had evoked vigorous opposition from left-wing students at the university who maintained that Kolakowski had ceased to be a genuine Marxist.[2]

The students judged Kolakowski correctly. By 1970 he had moved far from the Marxist convictions of his earlier years. His doubts were initiated by his recognition of the contradictions between the communist order established by Lenin and Stalin, and the Marxist promise. He went on to question not only the legitimacy of the Marxist system in Poland but also to re-examine Marxist theory.

Born into a bourgeois intellectual family in the industrial city of Radon in 1927, Kolakowski grew up in an atmosphere of free thought and political radicalism.[3] Still a schoolboy when the war broke out, he soon lost his father, murdered by the Nazis. Cared for by relatives, he spent much of the time of the German occupation in a country house with a large library "which he used voraciously."[4] At the end of the war, when he began to study philosophy at the University of Lodz, he adopted Marxism and joined the communist youth organization.

This was not an obvious decision for a young philosopher. Up to this time Marxism had been a minor current in Polish thought, dominated as it was by Catholicism and by a rationalist tradition, influenced later by the neo-positivism of the Vienna Circle.[5] Kolakowski's commitment to Marxism presupposed values and aspirations that made him receptive to a comprehensive ideology. Thus one student of his development has distinguished "two layers in his thought"—an "original grounding and guiding impulse" made up of the values of freedom, equality, and social justice, on the one hand, and the Marxist world view on the other.[6] Between the two layers, the ethical and the ideological, a tension would soon appear; it provides a key to Kolakowski's development.

The young Kolakowski was recognized early as one of the most promising in a new generation of Polish philosophers, both by representatives of the positivist school and by the leading Marxist theoretician in Poland, Adam Schaff. Following Kolakowski's completion of the degrees required for an academic career, he was appointed to the faculty of Warsaw University and joined the editorial board of a leading philosophical journal. In the early 1950s he identified himself fully with "the truths familiar to every Marxist," understood in the materialistic and deterministic form developed by Engels and Lenin.[7] The proletariat, Kolakowski declared in an early essay, was "the only class which is interested in absolutely objective knowledge of the world." "Because of its origin," it was free of the "mystifications and distortions" that marked Western bourgeois philosophies. Equipped with "an unreflective dogmatic Marxism" and a Promethean attitude toward the world, Kolakowski saw his main role in these years as that of a polemicist, doing battle with the rivals to his faith.[8]

It was a battle on two fronts. Positivism, which had outstanding representatives in Poland, was one target. Although Kolakowski had served as a teaching assistant to one of its leading figures, Tadeusz Kotarbinski, and had developed skills in logic and linguistic analysis that would serve him well in his future philosophical work, he attacked the positivists both for their claims about the nature of genuine knowledge and for their intellectual caution. In the form of positivism called "conventionalism," which left open those areas of experience not amenable to logical analysis, or the principle of verification drawn from the sciences, Kolakowski saw a tolerance for religious and metaphysical ideas that challenged the Marxist claim to provide an exclusive and exhaustive interpretation of reality.[9]

But his main target was Catholicism.[10] For Catholicism, with its total interpretation of life, presented the only serious rival to his Marxist world view. Like most Marxists, Kolakowski deplored the traditional domination of the Polish people by the Catholic Church, seeing it as a force for obscurantism and conservatism, standing in the way of a socialist society. Its doctrines—particularly that of original sin—discouraged human efforts at self-improvement, denigrated reason, and sanctioned unjust social arrangements. It offended the Promethean outlook that was central to Marxism.

Kolakowski immersed himself in the Catholic theological tradition, studying in particular medieval philosophy. Two-thirds of the score of essays he wrote during the late 1940s and early 1950s dealt with aspects of Catholic thought. He displayed, according to one observer, an almost obsessive interest in religion.[11] In 1954 he even traveled to Rome to attend a congress of Thomistic philosophers. Kolakowski's interest in religious questions would become, after the collapse of his Marxist faith, central to his thought.

During the early 1950s Kolakowski followed the political line laid down in Moscow; he was, in his own words, a Stalinist of the "purest water."[12] Later, however, he recalled stirrings of doubt, citing a trip to Russia in 1951 when he was sent, with a group of Polish intellectuals, for indoctrination in Marxism. He was dismayed by the low level of intellectual and cultural life evident among his hosts.[13] And when, after the death of Stalin, the communist order in eastern Europe experienced a "thaw," a loosening of Russian domination, Kolakowski began to re-examine his Marxist faith.

The first clear sign of his departure from orthodox Marxism came at a philosophical conference in East Berlin in March 1956 dealing with "The Problem of Freedom in the Light of Scientific Socialism." In a gathering that included a number of leading communist intellectuals, Kolakowski caused consternation by questioning the optimism of the Marxist view of the future.[14] He denied that there would be any easy reconciliation between the interests of the individual and those of society under communism. The individual, he argued, could not be understood simply in terms of the class struggle. Nor would the satisfaction of material needs dispose of life's existential anxieties—the realities of suffering and death and questions of ultimate meaning. In the future society, Kolakowski predicted, human beings would still be vulnerable to moral failings.

Kolakowski's talk in Berlin indicated the first cracks in his monolithic Marxist world view. It also marked the beginning of his intensive philosophical re-examination of the ideology, centered on the problem of individual freedom and responsibility. He was, at the same time, increasingly critical of the communist system.

By the early weeks of 1956 several Polish intellectuals were speaking out against the order imposed by Russia.[15] Their criticisms were given a sharper edge by Khruschev's disclosure, at the Twentieth Congress of the Communist Party of the Soviet Union in March, of the crimes of Stalin. During the spring the fires of discontent in Poland widened, fed by a general resentment toward Russian control, the frustrations of the intellectuals and artists over censorship, peasant hostility to the collectivization of farming, and growing economic difficulties culminating in a bloody uprising by workers in Poznan in June.[16]

This was the setting for a bold act by Kolakowski, one that made him overnight a leader in the rising wave of dissent. Emulating the action of Martin Luther in the sixteenth century, he posted a number of theses, under the title "What Is Socialism?" on the bulletin board of Warsaw University.[17] His theses described socialism in terms of what it was not, in ways that pointed to the oppressive political system that had been constructed in Russia and Poland. Kolakowski's array of negations included those policies of the communist state that denied legal protection for individuals; curtailed freedom of speech, association, and travel; and imposed a stifling conformity on its subjects. He described an order in which the leaders had become a privileged elite with high salaries, jealous of their power. He charged that they had turned Marxism into a mere ideology, a tool of their own interests, and had lost all respect among those they ruled. Communism had become, in short, a regime guilty of many of the historic wrongs and injustices it had promised to overcome—a caste system, even slavery, racism, and anti-Semitism; aggressive nationalism and imperialism; enforced ignorance and conformity. Through its total control over the means of production, distribution, and exchange, it had become a new system for exploiting the working class. Socialism, in contrast, Kolakowski concluded, was simply "a good thing."

Kolakowski's critique was, as rhetoric, effective. He had exposed the glaring contradictions between the realities of the communist order and the values professed in its Marxist ideology. Although the authorities did not permit the publication of "What Is Socialism?" it circulated in manuscript form among students and intellectuals in Warsaw. Kolakowski thus became a major voice in a rising chorus of criticism, made up of artists and intellectuals, representatives of the working class, and even members of the communist party leadership.

The intellectual protest, together with growing social and economic discontent, provides the background for the "October Revolution" in 1956 that brought the reformist communist Wladysaw Gomulka to power.[18] Gomulka convinced the Soviet leaders that the calls for greater independence and democratization in Poland could be contained without serious damage to the communist order. For progressive groups inside of Poland, however, the way seemed to be open for far-reaching changes.

Shortly before the October Revolution Kolakowski attempted to state the significance of this time for Marxists. His essay "Intellectuals and the Communist Movement," published in September, addressed those individuals who were "professionally engaged in theoretical work" and concerned with the whole "life of society."[19] He declared that intellectuals had an indispensable role to play in the movement toward a truly communist society. He cited Lenin's claim that it was necessary to bring Marxist theory to the workers from outside, since they lacked the opportunity for prolonged study.

But Marxist theory, Kolakowski argued, had reached an impasse. The task of intellectuals, therefore, was to reconstruct "a Marxism adequate to the needs of this era"—to deal with such issues as the actual condition of modern capitalism, and the proper role of the Communist Party in the state.[20] He called for the "rebirth of sociology as an independent science," capable of providing guidance in the realm of politics. The function of the intellectuals, however, was not limited to theoretical work. They were also the "creators of socialist culture," shapers of a new "socialist consciousness." At the moment, Kolakowski observed, the "spiritual life of the new society" was threatened by the "tastes and habits" of the peasants and the lower middle class. The intellectuals were charged to "rebuild completely all areas of human life."

By emphasizing the responsibility of intellectuals for the movement toward a genuine communism, Kolakowski was distancing himself from orthodox Marxism. For he now focused mainly on the realm of culture, viewed to a large extent as autonomous. It was, he claimed, "the most sensitivized tissues of the social organism" and expressed "most keenly" the destructive and degenerative forces at work in society.[21] As he went on to present a harsh criticism of the communist order in Poland, he concentrated on its cultural life.

The communist leaders, he maintained, had transformed Marxism into a "mythology, an object of worship, surrounded by a ritualistic cult and immune to criticism." Marxist theory had become "hermetically sealed"; it had been reduced to "a whole stock of permissible fetishistic concepts inaccessible to analysis."[22] Not only had theoretical progress become impossible, but Marxism had been turned into an "instrument of apology" for those in power. As a result the "individual and collective abilities that might have been used in economic, political, and intellectual life" had been paralyzed.

Kolakowski urged his fellow communist intellectuals to "combat pseudo-Marxist mythology and bigotry, as well as religio-magic practices," and "rebuild respect for completely unrestricted secular reason."[23] He offered several principles for correcting the misconceived relationship between science and politics, each of which affirmed the freedom of rational inquiry. There were no "untouchable truths," no "assertions that are 'a priori,' exempt from criticism, discussion, or revision."[24] One of the crucial tasks facing Marxist intellectuals, therefore, was to recover "the general principles of rational thought" and apply them "to all theoretical work."

Still, there was the problem of propagating Marxism "on a mass scale."[25] Kolakowski denied that the working class was merely a "passive object of cultural creation." He believed that a new "social culture" was being "formed spontaneously in the process of the class struggle." But since most individuals were not able to grasp Marxist theory on "scientific grounds," they were dependent on the "scientific truths" discovered by specialists. The faith they needed was quite different, according to Kolakowski, from that provided by leaders who simply propagated "politically correct truths."

Convinced that only the "socialist consciousness of the intelligentsia" could "banish mythology" from communist cultural life, Kolakowski had now freed himself as a philosopher from the political claims that had dominated his thought earlier.[26] At the same time the two layers of his thought, his moral concerns and Marxist theory, had ceased to be integrated. Both were subjected, in a second essay written in the fall of 1956, to closer philosophical scrutiny.

His essay "From What Lives Philosophy?" expressed his new intellectual independence as well as the return of moral questions to the central place in his thinking.[27] At the outset he rejected Marx's claim that philosophy, having served historically as an ideological tool in the class struggle, was destined to die out in a classless society. What, he asked, had been the actual function of philosophy in social development? His answer constituted a defense of the relative autonomy of philosophy and its indispensable role in history.

Philosophy, he argued, had emancipated human beings from the religious mythologies with which they had attempted to compensate for the shortcomings of everyday life. Philosophers had also laid the foundations for the natural sciences. The various scientific disciplines had usually risen out of the "badly founded generalizations" of philosophers, generalizations that then took on a more rigorous life of their own.[28]

The main contribution of philosophy, however, had been "the building up of moral attitudes."[29] Kolakowski traced this role back to the efforts of Greek philosophers to teach virtue. But moral foundations were required for other aspects of life as well. Even scientific activity presupposed moral norms that had been formulated earlier by philosophers.

Although he was breaking away from orthodox Marxism, Kolakowski continued to view human beings from a strictly naturalistic standpoint. "Man knows that all that surrounds him, including himself, arises out of the mud."[30] It was still necessary, therefore, to free the "social consciousness from the nightmare of religious delusion" and to recognize that man was "the most valuable product of materiality," engaged in a struggle to fulfill and perfect himself. The goal of a radical transformation of human existence remained central to Kolakowski's outlook. "We do not want to simply revolutionize the political, economic, and technological spheres," he wrote, but man's will itself.[31] He continued to view that goal from a Marxist perspective. But having recognized the perverse uses to which the Stalinists had put Marxism, he was reconsidering its central doctrines. His essays during 1957 and 1958 were attempts to reformulate Marxism in a way that made room for his moral commitments. He was, moreover, increasingly open to currents of philosophical thought in the West.

Kolakowski's essay "Permanent vs. Transitory Aspects of Marxism," published early in 1957, was a "revisionist" manifesto.[32] In a discussion bristling with sarcasm, he described again the ways in which the Communist Party leaders, or what he called the "Office," had distorted the Marxist doctrines. He sharply distinguished "institutional Marxism" from "intellectual Marxism."[33] While the former, defined by those in power, had assumed the form of religious dogma, the latter carried forward the Marxist attempt to "analyze every social phenomenon that might ever occur."

Insofar as Marxism had been transformed into an institutional concept, it had ceased, according to Kolakowski, to offer a "specific world view."[34] What meaning then, if any, he asked, was left in Marxism? Kolakowski went on to argue that Marxism was simply a "methodology of the social sciences."[35] It provided a new form of social analysis through its notions of determinism and historical materialism, and its explanation of political institutions and cultural life as outcomes of "the social divisions arising from the system of ownership."

Having lost his belief in Marxism as a world view and reduced it to a methodology, Kolakowski concluded that the "borderline between Marxism and non-Marxism" was "extremely fluid."[36] Indeed, "to speak of a compact and uniform Marxist camp," set off from the rest of the world, no longer made sense. He even suggested that "the concept of Marxism as a separate school of thought will in time become blurred and ultimately disappear altogether."

Kolakowski now introduced the concept of "the left," in contrast to "the right," as "the most significant division" in social and political life.

> By the intellectual left ... we mean intellectual activity distinguished by: radical rationalism in thinking; steadfast resistance to any invasion of myth in science; an entirely secular view of the world; criticism pushed to its ultimate limits; distrust of all closed doctrines and systems ... a readiness to revise accepted theses, theories and methods.[37]

Although Kolakowski no longer viewed Marxism as "a doctrine that must be accepted or rejected as a whole," he was still committed to the task of displacing the pseudo Marxists, who had become dominant, with those who truly understood Marxism.[38] For Marxism continued to serve as "a vital philosophical inspiration, affecting our whole outlook on the world" and providing "a constant stimulus to the social intelligence and social memory of mankind." It enabled human beings to "unmask myths of consciousness as resulting from ever recurring alienations in social existence and to trace them back to their real sources."

Through his revision of Marxism Kolakowski was surrendering much of the world view that had given meaning to his life. He had lost as well the confidence that he had found a way of realizing his moral aims. In the major essays ahead he addressed both the larger problem of meaning in life and the status of the moral values to which he was dedicated.

II

By 1957 Kolakowski had become the leading figure in the new current of Marxist revisionism in Poland.[39] The revisionists were, however, increasingly at odds with Gomulka. Their hopes for the further relaxation of censorship in cultural life and for democratic forms had been based, in fact, on fundamental misunderstandings.

Gomulka was in a difficult position. He had convinced the Russians that he offered the best hope of maintaining order in a volatile political situation, while assuring them that he could be relied on to maintain close ties between the two countries. He recognized that the Poles depended on Russia to resist German claims to the territories that had been ceded to Poland at the end of the war. The Russian invasion of Hungary in November 1956 was a harsh reminder of the danger the Poles faced if their increased sovereignty and greater internal democracy posed any threat to Russian security.

But Gomulka was not simply a political realist. He remained, for all his ideological flexibility and his humanism, an orthodox Marxist, firmly committed to a one-party state as the means of achieving socialism.[40] In a speech shortly after he assumed power he made it clear that there were strict limits to the process of reform. No opposition parties would be permitted, and the state would continue to exercise control over cultural life. In the course of 1957 the communist government in Poland retreated from a number of the promises made in the previous October.

The revisionists presented a danger to Gomulka's government. At a meeting of the party's Central Committee in May he attacked those who threatened the ideological solidarity of the regime.[41] He signaled out Kolakowski, in particular, as a "talented young philosopher" who was distorting Marxism and ignoring the crucial distinctions between "bourgeois democracy" and "socialist democracy." During the spring and summer of 1957, as the government tightened its control over cultural life, there was a deterioration in the area of political liberties that had been won earlier.

Nevertheless, the October Revolution had enlarged the scope for criticism and dissent in Poland. Despite the reimposition of cultural controls, Kolakowski became even bolder on his revisionist course. In the face of official attacks, and even private conversations with Gomulka himself, he sharpened his critique of orthodox Marxism.[42] He also continued to reflect on the moral concerns that, having been loosened from Marxist theory, still drove his thinking. His development can be followed in two major essays published during 1957, "World View and Daily Life," and "Responsibility and History."[43] These essays provided, according to one observer, the "center around which a great ideological debate" was now underway among Polish Marxists.[44]

In the first of the essays Kolakowski acknowledged his own loss of the world view provided earlier by Marxism. And he posed the question—"Can one find the feeling of a meaningful life again?"[45] Once the question arises, he added, "one cannot draw back from it."[46] The "yearning must be satisfied." It constituted, in fact, "the secret life nerve of philosophy."[47] This was not simply a personal matter. The problem of meaning, Kolakowski argued, had important social and political implications. In a reference to conditions in Poland he suggested that the loss of meaningfulness in life was directly related to feelings of powerlessness and to a "dying of initiative and a general slackness" in contemporary society.[48]

How then did people recover meaning in a time when "the active experience of the world and its moral affirmation" had been torn apart?[49] Kolakowski dismissed religious or other transcendental solutions. Religion, he declared, was an "insatiable sponge of the spirit."[50] Nor could one find meaning in the natural world. For there was a "radical dissonance between nature and human strivings."[51] He rejected as well the turn to history for answers. In a clear indication of his abandonment of orthodox Marxism, he denied that "history as a whole ... has meaning."[52]

What remained was simply "man himself" as a source of meaning.[53] Kolakowski went on to affirm "freedom as the highest good for man" and free rational activity as the "basis for the meaning of existence."[54] He conceded that there were many areas of life—matters of love and friendship, the choice of vocation, artistic impulses—that could not be "grounded rationally."[55] He also suggested that "the consciousness of a meaningful life" could not develop without passion or love. Such a life demanded, moreover, a willingness to take risks and a suspicion of a "completely hierarchically ordered" existence.[56]

Kolakowski's thought had taken an existential turn, indicative of his growing interest in Western European thinkers—Martin Heidegger, Karl Jaspers, Jean Paul Sartre, and others—as he attempted to fill the vacuum left by the dissolution of orthodox Marxism. But he was also addressing aspects of human experience that had been ignored in Marxist theory. Hence his reference to the more intimate features of human relationships and his recognition of the anxieties with which individuals contemplated the inevitability of death.[57]

Kolakowski still viewed the inner travails of the individual in the light of the Marxist analysis of society. The capacity for freedom and a meaningful life depended, in large part, on social conditions. "What robs men in general of a meaningful life" is a situation "where there is an unbearable consciousness that they are delivered over to a blind force."[58] A revolutionary attitude, a "spirit of denial and critique," is still necessary. Kolakowski reaffirmed the Marxist struggle to give history a "rational and humane form." What he now described as the "ontological strangeness" of reality could only be overcome by finding a way to "participate in the rhythm of history."[59] Indeed, "in proportion to the intensity" of this experience, even the existential anxieties would diminish.[60]

In his next major essay, "Responsibility and History," published in the summer of 1957, Kolakowski continued to explore the personal dilemmas arising out of the breakdown of his orthodox Marxist faith. He also renewed his attempt to account for the political quietism to which Stalinism had reduced the Polish people. How could one explain the moral impotence, the "ostentatious non-involvement of the individual in the vexatious changes taking place in this world?"[61]

Kolakowski approached the problem by presenting a dialogue between the "clerk," or moralist, and the "realist," or revolutionary. While the former, "the guardian of universal values," avoided social action out of a fear of contaminating his lofty moral principles, the latter, confident that he knew the direction of history, plunged into its "bloody swamps" in order to hasten the revolutionary process.[62] The clerk wished "to reserve to himself the right of moral judgment on social reality without assuming any responsibility," while the realist recognized the relativity of values and the inescapability of one's social involvement.

In the figure of the clerk Kolakowski explored the condition of dissenting intellectuals like himself who confronted the Stalinist attempt to impose "a single alternative on human reality in all spheres of social life."[63] But while his dialogue clearly favored the clerk, and the rational and moral views with which he was identified, he conceded that the debate could only lead, given the absence of common assumptions, to a dead end. It was necessary, therefore, to find a perspective in which "the arguments on both sides could be partially accepted."[64] Only in this way could the "long compromised revolutionary movement" be revitalized.

Kolakowski attempted to create that perspective by opposing his moral values to the orthodox Marxist view of history, or what he called the "opiate of the demiurge." Against the orthodox Marxist claim that "socialism is historical inevitability," that "what is morally right" can be identified with "what is economically progressive," he insisted on the independent status of the moral values underlying socialism.[65]

> Socialism is the sum total of social values whose implementation is incumbent on the individual as a moral duty. … To what extent these values can actually be implemented is a question altogether distinct from that of whether one

ought to work toward their realization. … If we were convinced that socialism was impossible, our duty to fight for it would not dwindle or weaken.[66]

To insist on the independent status of moral duty, and claim that "certain actions are ends in themselves," was not to deny the role of the social and economic determinants emphasized by Marx.[67] But the attempt to bridge the two realms—what Kolakowski referred to as the utopian and the realist—was a task that needed to "be tackled anew" by all those who sought to carry on the work of Marx.[68] For history, "like a skillful magician, daily startles us with fresh surprises."

In the remainder of the essay Kolakowski set out to reconcile his ethical individualism and social determinism. He argued that moral and cognitive judgments are logically independent, that knowledge of the social influences on one's decisions does not do away with moral responsibility. While he accepted the Hegelian, and Marxist, recognition that history could be understood only in terms of the "tendencies of human collectives," the individual still faced "at every step" basic moral choices.[69]

The essay "Responsibility and History" marked a further stage in Kolakowski's efforts to revise Marxism. In his attempt to combine his belief in the "total responsibility of the individual for his deeds" with a Marxist understanding of history, he had diverged further from the orthodox viewpoint.[70] And yet, despite his determination to free morality from the "nightmare of historiosophy," he denied that it could be eliminated entirely.[71] Utopianism, or the "artificial and mythological inflation of expected results," was an "indispensable factor in social progress."[72]

> Achieving even the simplest improvement in social conditions demands the mobilization of such a huge amount of collective energy that if the full extent of the disproportion between results and effort expended became public knowledge, the results would be so disheartening and would so paralyze men's courage and strivings, that any social progress would be impossible.

Kolakowski thus retained something of the utopian spirit that Marx had attempted to eliminate in his rationalistic and deterministic view of history.

Kolakowski's portrayal of the individual socialist, engaged in the struggle for a new society, now stood in clear contrast to that of Marx. While the uniqueness of the individual largely disappeared in Marx's description of the proletariat and the class struggle, Kolakowski emphasized the insecurities, even despair, of those taking part in the movement. Kolakowski's socialist, unlike the orthodox Marxist, faced a reality that was "ambiguous and misty."[73] The "torment of doubt" was a "constant companion," for the individual was "compelled to make morally binding decisions in total ignorance of their consequences." Not only did his choices entail risks, but a tragic outcome was a "permanent possibility."

Kolakowski's essays in the summer of 1957 established him as the "chief revisionist" in Poland.[74] And he was again the main target of the defenders of orthodox Marxism. Not only was he the object of a new attack by Gomulka, but he was also subjected to a sustained critique by his former mentor and the official theoretician of the Polish party, Schaff. By associating themselves with "the clerks," Schaff argued, the revisionists had cut themselves off "from life and politics," in favor of a sterile moralizing.[75] Schaff described the revisionism of Kolakowski as a spiritual offspring of existentialism and the Kantian "formulation of subjectivism in morals." His "reconstruction of Marxism amounts to the renunciation of the social revolution in favor of moral transformation of the individual and society" and implied the liquidation of Marxism as a distinct philosophical school.

Kolakowski was also subjected to harsh attacks from Moscow. Thus one of the spokesmen for the Russian Communist Party placed him in the "camp of the enemies of Communism."[76] "The disguised intent behind" Kolakowski's revisionism, he wrote, was "to erase the boundaries between Marxist-Leninist and bourgeois theory."

The fact that Kolakowski could remain a member of the Polish Communist Party in the face of these attacks indicated the changes in the cultural climate following the October Revolution. Nevertheless, while the old, blind acceptance of the party's dictates no longer operated, the retreat by Gomulka's government from its initial openness continued. During the summer of 1957 the government shut down the main literary vehicle for the young dissenting intellectuals, *Po Prostu,* or *Speaking Frankly.*[77] A shift in the public atmosphere was evident, too, in the decline of the discussion clubs that had sprung up during the "thaw" and provided gathering places for young intellectuals who were calling into question the communist order.[78] By the fall of 1957 they faced a crisis as membership declined and the enthusiasm of earlier years gave way to apathy and pessimism.

Kolakowski pressed on with his efforts to revise Marxism. One who heard him speak at a Warsaw club about this time described him—"lean and ascetic"—presenting his views by means of vivid metaphors.[79] Here again he attacked the Stalinists for transforming Marxism into a "kind of religion" and abandoning the scientific search after objective truths. In an interview shortly after the talk Kolakowski suggested that the current "mood of disillusionment and apathy" was the outcome of exaggerated hopes.[80] He conceded that the expectations aroused a year earlier had been unrealistic. Poland was not yet ready for a multiparty system; the movement toward political democracy could only be a slow process.

Kolakowski's realization that the reform movement in Poland had come to a halt probably influenced his decision to return to the study of Spinoza and spend much of 1958 abroad. In his dissertation on Spinoza five years earlier he had examined the philosopher through an orthodox Marxist lens. But in the new study, published late in 1958, he presented a congenial thinker.[81] He found in Spinoza searching inquiries into the fundamental questions of human existence—particularly the problems of freedom and mortality—that had occupied Kolakowski as he moved out of the Marxist framework. He was attracted as well to Spinoza's unflinching criticism of dogmas and his espousal of tolerance in a world being torn apart by religious conflict.

Kolakowski's study of Spinoza seems to have made him more aware of the inconsistencies in his own thought resulting from his efforts to revise Marxism. But this was not necessarily a fault. Hence his essay shortly after his return to Poland, "In Praise of Inconsistency."[82] Here he questioned any attempt to impose a completely consistent set of principles or values on social life. He cited cases of thinkers—for example, the Catholic philosopher Joseph De Maistre—who had tried "to carry their assumptions to their logical conclusions" and reached positions that could only be regarded as fanatical and inhuman.

Kolakowski's praise of inconsistency expressed his conviction that history is a much less tidy affair than that envisioned by orthodox Marxists. He now saw the world as full of contradictions and antagonistic forces that had given rise to incompatible values. The principle of inconsistency reflected a "clear awareness of the eternal and incurable antinomy in the world of values."[83] This was not a "temporary derangement" that could be "removed with the advent of a new era" but a condition that will "always be with us." It demanded, therefore, "a consciously sustained attitude of uncertainty" and a "feeling of possible personal error."

The principle of inconsistency had practical implications; it was applicable to communist policies in Poland. Kolakowski noted, for example, the dilemma facing communists like himself who believed that the "continuing influence of religious institutions on public life is damaging."[84] But since this influence expressed the will of the majority of the Polish people, it could be destroyed only by force. To avoid the evil of force, Kolakowski concluded, it was necessary to be inconsistent, tolerant of the existing situation while striving to educate the people to a higher "level of maturity."

Even the principle of inconsistency, Kolakowski argued, could not be carried out consistently. For there were "elementary situations" that demanded fixed moral principles.[85] In the face of "open aggression, genocide, torture, mistreatment of the defenseless," he observed, the principle of inconsistency "ceased to play a role." Here one had to be faithful to one's basic moral convictions.

As he continued his struggle to formulate a Marxism that made room for his commitment to individual freedom and moral responsibility, Kolakowski discovered support in the "Economic and Philosophical Manuscripts" of the young Marx. He was the first Marxist thinker in Poland to deal seriously with the Manuscripts. He did so in a lecture, "Karl Marx and the Classical Definition of Truth," delivered at the University of Tübingen in December 1958.[86]

In the writings of the young Marx Kolakowski found an approach to human knowledge that confirmed his skepticism toward the deterministic and mechanistic epistemology that Lenin, following Engels, had made the foundation of orthodox Marxism. In contrast to their "classical definition of truth"—the belief that knowledge consists of an ever closer approximation, or a copy, of an independent outer reality—the early Marx had viewed understanding as an outcome of man's practical struggles. "Man's practical activities," his attempts to satisfy his needs through the conquest of the chaos of reality, defined him as a "cognitive being."[87] The concepts and categories by means of which he made sense of the world were "created by a spontaneous endeavor to conquer the opposition of things."[88]

Although Kolakowski had found in the Manuscripts the "embryo of an epistemology" and a "philosophy worthy of continuation," he diverged from the young Marx.[89] The latter went on, through his analysis of capitalism, to develop an objective and unilinear view of history in which the proletariat would emerge as the agent of a radical transformation of society. But Kolakowski denied that an "absolute definitive interpretation [of history] can be established once and for all."[90] For "countless different pictures of the same collection of facts" were possible, and equally "compatible with accepted technical rules of scholarly work." The choice among them could be made only by means of "a certain view of the world," for this constituted "an integral part of historical interpretation."

While Marx, confident that he had gained an exhaustive interpretation of human development, dismissed metaphysical questions, or any suggestion that there was a "second enigmatic world," Kolakowski was increasingly open to such questions.[91] Having concluded that it was impossible to deduce "sound value judgments from so-called descriptive judgments,"[92] that there was a gap between "the world of values and the world of things in human cognition," he began to reconsider traditional philosophical and religious claims to grasp a non-empirical reality. Kolakowski was again raising issues that could not be addressed within the Marxist framework.

Some years later, looking back at the Revisionist movement in Poland, Kolakowski observed that it "had a certain inner logic that, before long, carried it beyond the frontiers of Marxism."[93] The common aim of the revisionists, he recalled, had been that of "restoring the role of the subject in the historical and cognitive process." Their attempt to bring humanistic values and the "rules of reason" to bear on the Leninist-Stalinist form of Marxism had, however, been devastating to such a "primitive structure of thought." Even more important, according to Kolakowski, was the inability of Marxism to "provide answers to questions that philosophy and the social sciences had raised since Marx's day," or to assimilate important concepts developed by "twentieth century humanistic culture." Hence the growing recognition that Marxism had been reduced to the ideology of "a powerful and self-contained sect" whose doctrines, "suddenly exposed to air … collapsed like mummified remains."

III

Revisionism lived on in Poland into the 1960s, but Kolakowski moved in a different direction. The critical bent of his thought now became more pronounced. In two major essays during 1959, "Rationalism as an Ideology" and the "Priest and the Jester," he expressed his growing skepticism, not only toward Marxism but also toward all absolutist or systematic claims.[94]

In the first of these essays Kolakowski re-examined the human capacity that had been central in his early Marxism and his subsequent effort to recover a meaning in life—reason. The essay was mainly a critique of the positivist form of rationalism, its rejection of any claim to knowledge that did not pass the test of verifiability as defined in the natural sciences.[95] Such an outlook, Kolakowski observed, was simply an ideology, blind to its own assumptions. But he extended his critique of rationalism to all attempts to provide a universal rational justification for a belief system. In the history of Christian thought, for example, logic had often served to make orthodoxies impervious to criticism.

Kolakowski also pointed to the limitations of a purely rational approach to human existence—its lack of correlation with happiness or "success in daily life."[96] In politics, for example, decisions could be made only in a context marked by ignorance, uncertainties, and risk. He cited episodes in history where seemingly irrational decisions had proved to be more progressive than those governed by logic. Not only was Kolakowski calling attention to the broad areas of social life that were dominated by "nondiscursive forms of knowledge" but he also concluded that irrational or mythical notions were indispensable to society.[97] Those who believed in the "possibility of the demystification of social consciousness" through the spread of reason were naive.[98]

Kolakowski had begun to develop a new philosophical anthropology to replace that which underlay Marxism. Although he simply sketched its main features in the essay on rationalism, it centered on the efforts of human beings, having lost the instinctual capacity to adapt to nature possessed by other creatures, to orient themselves to reality by constructing a world view.[99] At this point, however, Kolakowski still regarded such constructions as pathological, as attempts to "return to childhood," and as refusals to accept "unconditional responsibility" for human actions. Instead, he advanced his own conception of a "radical rationalism" that abandoned any attempt to build a systematic world view in favor of a provisional attitude toward the world.[100] Since there was no "God-like standpoint," the radical rationalist accepted the "chronic incompleteness of the world" and adopted a position of "provocative unrest." As a symbol for this outlook Kolakowski offered the Greek tragic hero, Orestes, who, having murdered his mother, had left the "shelter of the gods" and, indeed, broken with all moral and social conventions.[101] Orestes had, however, gained a new consciousness of freedom and autonomy, and a life marked by an "unceasing overcoming" of the human propensity to rest in absolutes. In the figure of Orestes Kolakowski seems to have found a symbol not only for his sense of liberation from the constraints of Marxism but also for his own social estrangement and growing isolation.

He continued to explore the human yearning for absolute belief systems in the essay "The Priest and the Jester." But as the subtitle of the essay—"Reflections on the Theological Heritage of Contemporary Thinking"—indicated, he was searching into the hidden religious sources of modern thought. From this perspective Kolakowski presented a new critique of Marxism, focusing on its underlying "secular eschatology"—the "belief in the future elimination of the disparity between man's essence and his existence."[102] Marxism had provided, in fact, new answers to such traditional religious problems as theodicy, the relationship between nature and grace, and faith and reason. It had satisfied the "nostalgia for revelation," for a "cognitive absolute" that explained "every cranny of the universe."[103]

> This obsession with monism, this stubborn desire to arrange the world according to some uniform principle, this search for a single magic spell to make reality transparent and decipherable ... proves to be more lasting than any other vicissitude in our intellectual development.[104]

Alongside this quest Kolakowski now saw a countertendency, exemplified by skeptics through the ages, to question any "unifying interpretation of the world." The individual human being, he declared, was caught up in an ongoing "clash between two universal and primal tendencies"—between the yearning for an "absolute reality" and a refusal to allow oneself to be captured by that reality.[105]

In the figure of the Jester, Kolakowski presented a new symbol for the ceaseless criticism of belief systems and institutions. In contrast to the Priest, the guardian of tradition, the Jester "must stand outside good society and observe it from the sidelines in order to unveil the non-obvious behind the obvious."[106] When Kolakowski described the Jester as one who "must frequent society so as to know what it holds sacred and to have the opportunity to address it impertinently," he may have been referring to his own new role in Poland. For he remained into the 1960s, even after the failure of his attempt to revise Marxism, a member of the Communist Party, criticizing it from within.

As a new chill settled over Polish political life in the 1960s, Kolakowski found in literary work other ways of exercising his role as a Jester. His play "Entrance and Exit," performed several nights in Warsaw during 1962, before it was shut down by the authorities, was a thinly disguised treatment of governmental incompetence.[107] He also portrayed, in his "Tales from the Kingdom of Lailonia," a world of absurdities, fantasies, and contradictions that implicitly called into question any attempt to order life rationally or ideologically.[108] In one of the Tales he described the way in which a "hump" that had grown on the back of a man gradually assumed a fully human form, then took over the body of its host, and in time was duplicated in all individuals within the society.[109] The hump was a metaphor, employed in several of Kolakowski's essays, to indicate the destructive power of ideologies.

Kolakowski also sought to reground the moral intuitions that had been the driving force of his thought. "Nothing is as deeply rooted in us," he declared in "The Priest and the Jester," as "the belief in a moral law."[110] And in his next essay, "Ethics without a Moral Code," he looked more closely at the moral responsibility of the individual.[111] Although he had never doubted that responsibility, he now introduced a new argument to support it. The individual, he argued, accepted "the debts of the world" as his own simply by virtue of his decision "to remain alive."[112] "We realized too," he added, "that we are obliged to care for the world's development and must refuse to accept it in its present state."

The discussion that followed focused on the complexities of moral decisions and the danger of any moral code that claimed to provide answers to all situations. Such a code represented a "flight from moral choice" and a "desire for security."[113] In real life, according to Kolakowski, there was rarely a neat fit between the obligations imposed by a code and the moral choices presented in a concrete situation. For each situation demanded a "cogito factor," a personal judgment based on a careful appraisal and often requiring as well a choice between conflicting values.[114] To disregard the "point of view of the individual," Kolakowski observed, would offend "our most basic moral intuitions." How does one decide, for example, between loyalty to a principle and kindness to a fellow human being in a situation where they are incompatible?

To recognize the inescapably personal nature of the individual's moral decisions was also to become aware of "the dark side of our moral choices."[115] "Often any choice we make" is likely to be harmful. Kolakowski drew on the Christian notion of sin to suggest that even the best of intentions might have bad outcomes. In "our twisted human existence," he observed, it was difficult to know, for example, whether a given social problem might be abolished or even "ameliorated ... by practical reforms."[116] Through his examination of "the reality comprehended by our moral experience" Kolakowski was developing a picture of the world quite different from that seen by Marxism. It was a "world with holes," a "world which is not yet finished."[117]

Kolakowski continued to re-examine the human condition in a second essay, also published in 1962, in which he considered contemporary views of the human personality.[118] He criticized conceptions of personality that he saw as either one-sidedly subjective or objective. The former could be found in the existentialists, in the "personalism" of recent Catholic thinkers, and in the solipsistic views derived from the anarchist tradition. The latter was expressed in the tendency of the bourgeois individual to adapt completely to "outer things" and seek a life of comfort.[119] What was missing from both perspectives, according to Kolakowski, was a conception of personality that was dynamic and expressive, engaged in a "permanent dialogue" with the outer world but destined to remain unfinished.[120] His notion of an authentic personality owed much to the writings of the young Marx and Marx's view that the capacity of the individual for a free and creative life was thwarted by the reified world of capitalism. But Marx, according to Kolakowski, had made the individual an "exemplar of a social class."[121] In his reaffirmation of the uniqueness of the individual, Kolakowski was also attentive to qualities that had been largely ignored in orthodox Marxism—love and friendship, or what he referred to as the "unexchangeable others."[122]

Amid the ruins of his Marxism, Kolakowski had been formulating his own philosophical anthropology. He developed it more fully in the next essay, "Philosophy as Discipline and Function."[123] Philosophy, he argued, was not simply a quest for knowledge in the usual sense. It arose out of the "disruption of the homeostasis" of man's relationship to nature.[124] For human beings, unlike other creatures, lacked the biological equipment that made for a perfect adaptation to nature. Hence the need for the special self-consciousness provided by philosophy. Kolakowski described it as a "prosthesis," an artificial tool that compensated for the loss of the equilibrium resulting from "enfeebled instincts."

Philosophy then was the way in which human beings became aware of the "strangeness of the world" and of their special infirmity.[125] Philosophy was part of the process through which mankind fashioned a second world, made up of social institutions and culture, that enabled it to cope with its crippled condition. But philosophy, along with religion, also raised questions for which there were no clear answers: "How to live" in a situation where judgments about meaning or values were required?[126] For the natural world in itself was "indifferent to all values" and made "no sense unless we provide answers." Meaning, therefore, could only "be our product," a condition that affirmed the "peculiarity of human beings over against the rest of things."

In returning to the problem of meaning Kolakowski posed the question of the relationship between philosophy and religion. Although he discussed the attempt of philosophers to find metaphysical or cosmological

sanctions for social behavior, as well as the efforts of modern thinkers—
Nietzsche and Ludwig Klages, for example—to find the way back to a
natural spontaneity, Kolakowski still emphasized the critical function of
philosophy. It functioned mainly to shatter the various forms of reification,
the tendency for belief systems and institutions to petrify and stand over
human beings as foreign objects. What was left then as a source of meaning
was religion, and the concept that would become central to Kolakowski's
thought—myth.

IV

Kolakowski had been reconsidering the place of religion in human existence for several years. In an earlier essay he had recognized the tenacity of
Catholicism in Polish life and the foolishness of any attempt to suppress it
by force.[127] During 1960 he took part in friendly discussions with Catholic
intellectuals.[128] The influence of these talks was evident in his essay "Minor
Theses of the Sacred and the Profane," published in 1962.[129] Here he took
issue with Marxists and others who held that religion would fade away as
society became more secularized and urbanized. There was no correlation,
Kolakowski argued, between these forces and "the degree of religiosity."
He realized, too, that some Catholics, unlike their Marxist opponents,
were "breaking out of their frozen condition and creating new life."[130] He
saw in this new "open Catholicism" a willingness to coexist with socialists
and, indeed, to accept much of the Marxist critique of capitalism. Kolakowski's essay attempted to soften the old antagonisms between "fanatical
atheists" like himself and the more extreme "integralist" or exclusive forms
of Catholicism.[131] After all, he concluded, "believers and non-believers belong to the same society and share its cultural tradition."

Kolakowski's shift toward a positive view of religion—a dominant
theme in his writings during the years ahead—reflected a major difficulty
in his philosophical anthropology. He had become convinced that the human need for a meaningful orientation to the world could not be satisfied
within a strictly natural or historical framework.[132] The meanings and values necessary for social life could only be legitimized by "unconditional" or
transcendental beliefs. Although he was still skeptical of particular religious or metaphysical ideas, he was increasingly concerned with the function of religious symbols and myths.[133] Why, he asked, are symbols required as binding forces in "community life?" Why is "reality complicated
in this way?"[134] He then discussed the ways in which anthropologists and

others had explained religion in instrumental terms. Religion had been viewed both as a means of filling the "gaps in human knowledge" and as a means of social control, taming or sublimating the instincts.[135]

Influenced by modern thinkers who had identified the religious, or the "holy," as a distinctive element in human experience—Rudolf Otto, Max Scheler, Mircea Eliade—Kolakowski now defended the view that religious symbols were sui generis, not derivable from other factors.[136] "Specifically religious values," he maintained, "cannot be dismantled or broken down." Although they often serve instrumental functions in social life, they do so only by being "to some extent non-instrumental." One must assume, therefore, that "there is an area of life or human needs" that corresponds to religious symbols and is "exclusively accessible to them." Religious symbols can not be judged by rational or scientific criteria, or be "represented in empirical terms or even verbally."

Kolakowski's view of the religious was closely related to his conception of human estrangement from nature. Notwithstanding their increasing power over nature by means of technology, human beings still experienced, in the face of the realities of suffering and death, the need for another form of integration.[137] Religious symbols came into play out of the desire to recover a lost harmony. Hence the crucial question—were contemporary forms of religious life condemned to a "slow death" in the face of the challenge presented by science or were they capable of new vitality?[138]

Kolakowski was still reluctant to accept the claim that "religion is an eternal form of human spiritual life" or the view that religious symbols were irreplaceable.[139] But he had become skeptical toward those schools of thought—Marxists, existentialists, positivists, and psychoanalysts—who held that "man can depend on nothing outside himself." Given the tendency in "our Civilization" to flee from "the basic questions of life," an authentic religious consciousness provided the only "genuine recognition of the human situation in the world and the impossibility of returning to the integration of the animal world." In the light of this conclusion it is not surprising that a number of Kolakowski's essays in the mid-1960s explored aspects of the Christian tradition and the reasons for its continuing vitality.

Kolakowski's exodus from Marxism had been accompanied by a growing sense of human limitations and of the darker aspects of life. In his "press conference" with the Devil, dated late in 1963, he confronted the problem of evil.[140] The "conference" was, in fact, a monologue in which the Devil criticized contemporary Christians for denying, or at least playing down, his role in their tradition. In their eagerness to be "modern, progressive, hygienic, utilitarian," and scientific, the churches had come to see evil as merely contingent.[141] Kolakowski's Devil urged them to "give back to his name its primitive function."

> Satan appears in his full glory where destruction has no end but itself, where cruelty is inflicted for its own sake, humiliation only for the sake of humiliation, death for death, suffering without any purpose, or where purpose is only a superimposed mask rationalizing the destructive hunger.[142]

Several of the essays in these years dealt sympathetically with Christian thinkers. In Pascal, for example, Kolakowski discovered a figure who shared his own conviction that human beings lived in two heterogeneous worlds—the temporal and an "eternal ... or unknown reality"—which no common language could bridge.[143] Pascal too, had recognized the limits of reason as well as the paradoxes and contradictions that marked the human condition. "One did not need ... to believe in God," Kolakowski observed, to hold these views.

Erasmus also exemplified qualities with which Kolakowski could identify.[144] The continuing importance of Erasmus lay in his affirmation of those values in Christianity—love, mercy, tolerance—that stood in sharp contrast to the legalism of the Old Testament and the rigidities of the major Protestant reformers. "All who struggle against the exclusive and sclerotic condition of the church," Kolakowski wrote, "are indebted to him." And even "those who stand outside the church but are not indifferent to its fate" could appreciate the contribution of Erasmus to European culture.

In the contemporary Catholic philosopher Teilhard de Chardin, Kolakowski saw an especially interesting attempt to overcome the divide between "the empirical and the other world."[145] Teilhard, facing the deepening crisis of Christianity in a world more and more dominated by science and secular forms of thought, had boldly affirmed "worldly life as the genuine place for the fulfillment of Christian values."[146] His theory of "creative evolution" eliminated the old boundaries between the secular and the holy and viewed "all areas of life, including technology and politics," as expressions of "divine energy." But Teilhard's pantheistic solution failed, according to Kolakowski, to deal with the crucial problems of sin and evil. Kolakowski thought it unlikely that a Christianity based on "the belief in the essential goodness of being" could survive.[147]

Kolakowski's new sympathy for Christianity inevitably settled on the figure of Jesus. In earlier writings he had questioned the historical exis-

tence of Jesus. But in a lecture, "Jesus Christ, Prophet and Reformer," delivered in Warsaw in October 1965, he attempted to answer the question—
In what way did the mission that Jesus ascribed to himself "become a component of the complicated weaving which forms our inherited cultural
treasure?"[148]

Kolakowski approached the question as a philosopher. He distinguished between those philosophers, particularly Hegel and Nietzsche,
who had viewed Jesus in the light of their broad interpretations of European history, on the one hand, and those thinkers like Pascal and Kierke-
gaard, on the other, for whom Jesus was a "counter element permanently
alive in every existence."[149] "In some limited sense," Kolakowski added, the
latter view "is also acceptable to people" who are not committed to "the
dogmatic contents of Christianity."

Kolakowski's Jesus did not claim to be divine. It was Paul who started
the process of divinization. The real Jesus, according to Kolakowski, was
"a Jewish reformer charged with a supernatural mission," persuaded that
"the end of the world was imminent."[150] Given the nearness of the apoca-
lypse, "all earthly realities" had lost their meaning and independent value.

What mattered most to Kolakowski was the moral teaching of Jesus, at
the center of which was the gospel of love. Even though this teaching, and
the new emphasis on the inner life of the spirit, were born of apocalyptic
prophesies, they remained alive in the European tradition. To the New
Testament's abolition of contract, or law, "in favor of love" one could trace
"all the utopias of universal brotherhood," including Marxism, even
though "often they are indifferent to their own remote beginnings."[151]
Other elements crucial to the spiritual development of Europe followed
from the central doctrine of love. Kolakowski included the "hope of elimi-
nating violence from the relations among people," "the abolition of the
ideas of a chosen people" in favor of the universalization of fundamental
human values, and the recognition that "spiritual creation" could not be
measured by its contribution to "material productivity." Yet Jesus had also
shown people how "they hide from themselves their own misery." And
while this teaching had often been used to discourage efforts to improve
the world, it pointed to the limitations of human existence, to its
"essentially crippled" condition.

How then to rescue the "historical meaning of the existence of Jesus"
from what Kolakowski saw as two dangers—the clerical dogmatism
which, "for the last four centuries has oppressed and sterilized our national
culture," on the one hand, and, on the other, "a crudely formulated athe-

ism" bent on taking from "the cultural tradition ... its most vital sap."[152] Convinced that European culture required the "person and the teachings of Jesus Christ," Kolakowski expressed his "uncertain hope" that Christianity would be able to renew its spiritual origins. Hence his conclusion:

> The stature of the man, who for centuries was not just a teacher of dogmas but a model of the most illustrious human values, cannot fall into non-existence without an essential disruption of the continuity of spiritual life. For he incarnated, personally, the ability to express his truth in full voice, the ability to defend it to the end without evasions, and the ability to absolutely resist the established reality which did not accept him. ... He was a model of that radical authenticity, only in which, every human being can give real life to his values.

No wonder Kolakowski could describe himself as an "inconsistent atheist."[153] His reinterpretation of the human condition had brought him close to Christianity. He recognized, moreover, parallels between his own struggles against the communist order and that of earlier religious dissenters. For the religious dissenters, like their communist counterparts, had fought to preserve the inner spiritual meaning of their faith against the legalistic and coercive tendencies present in its organized form.

This was the subject of Kolakowski's book *Christians without Church*, published in France in 1965.[154] It dealt with dissenting religious groups in Holland during the seventeenth century who, in their reaction against the theological and institutional apparatus of the church, and its compromises with the world, attempted to live strictly according to the gospel. In the face of the church's "religion of law" they affirmed a "religion of grace."

Kolakowski found much that appealed to him in this "confessionless Christianity." In its radical individualism he saw a response to institutionalized religion that resembled his own protest against the communist order. The intense feelings of love and the close relationship to God expressed by these believers seemed to him to be the most authentic form of the Christian faith. He recognized, too, in the mysticism that was an important feature of this development a continuing source of Christian vitality through the centuries. His growing skepticism toward the claims of rationalists had made him much more sympathetic toward human yearnings for contact with a transcendental reality.

Kolakowski's changing outlook found systematic expression in the *Presence of Myth*, completed in 1966.[155] This book has been described as the "central axis" of his work.[156] For he placed the mythic, in earlier years a primary target for his critical rationalism, at the center of his philosophical anthropology. Here again his starting point was his belief that the empirical world was, for human beings, a "place of exile."[157] They suffered from an "amnesia of Being" and experienced a yearning for contact with an "unconditional reality distinct" from the rational and utilitarian activities that characterized much of life. "We all carry within us," he wrote, "a need to refer ourselves to a mythic reality," a need to make sense out of empirical realities and to become convinced of the permanence of human values.[158] "We cannot imagine a culture totally bereft of mythological element."[159]

In the process through which culture replaced instincts as the means of human adaptation and survival, philosophy played a special role. It served as an instrument that enabled human beings, in their alienated state, to see themselves as objects and, at the same time, as "incomprehensible." The task of philosophy, he wrote, was to awaken the mythical consciousness. But it could do no more. Philosophy simply pointed to the need to "move beyond" itself into the realm of faith.[160]

Kolakowski was not content simply to mark off the mythic as an autonomous sphere of human experience. He attempted to demonstrate its decisive role in all areas of human activity—the artistic, technological, historical, and the sexual. Even science and logic, he maintained, presupposed mythic notions of "reason" or the "truth."[161] What mattered most, however, was the capacity of myths to provide the values and meanings that enabled human beings to counter the indifference of the natural world and live together in harmony. To mythological sources he traced what was fundamental to the Western moral tradition—the freedom and dignity of the individual.[162]

The mythic also made unconditional demands on the individual; it was the source of moral obligation.[163] It required "surrender not understanding," participation rather than reflection. In short, it called for faith. Kolakowski illustrated this by means of the Christian gospel of love.[164] In the "total entrusting acceptance" of "another person" he saw the most authentic expression of the mythic.

From this perspective Kolakowski presented a new critique of contemporary society. He noted the ways in which human beings sought to escape from the "mythic project"; the attempt to tame nature through technology, the effort to find personal identity by means of material possessions, or through erotic encounters.[165] His critique centered, however, on what he called the "culture of analgesics."[166] One of the distinctive features of modern society was the resort to drugs or other narcotics to escape from the realities of suffering and death. But the absence or weakening of a compelling myth also led to a passive attitude toward life. This diminished sense of responsibility was reinforced by mass culture and the feeling that "we are determined totally by our place in the social fabric."

The absence of a mythic consciousness could also be seen in the belief, expressed particularly by intellectuals, that human beings were "totally responsible for the world" around them. This made for "a world of complete predictability" and a tendency to be "swallowed up totally in everyday immediacies." Here, too, according to Kolakowski, was a refusal to consider ultimate questions and "face life."[167]

The mythic answer to human dilemmas held, to be sure, its own hazards. Kolakowski discussed the ways in which the various mythological traditions—Christian, rationalist, socialist—had "contained their own poison" and, indeed, the seeds of totalitarianism.[168] A myth might "grow like a tumor" and, by taking "over most areas of culture ... drain away freedom and responsibility." Myths did not provide absolute security.[169]

> What we know for certain is that in maintaining any kind of human fellowship we need a faith in ... non-arbitrary values, and that, at the same time, it is dangerous to believe that these values are at any time fixed and completed. ... A mythology can be socially fruitful only when it is unceasingly suspect, constantly subject to vigilance which would frustrate its natural tendency to turn into a narcotic.

Art and philosophy, Kolakowski suggested, might serve as "antibodies to neutralize" this process.

There were, as he recognized, fundamental difficulties in his treatment of the mythic. Could one participate fully in the mythological if one understood its social function?[170] Would this not paralyze the trust required? Could one, for example, "hold a deep belief in divine care over the world and at the same time be deeply convinced" that such a faith grew out of life's frustrations and social needs?

Kolakowski dealt with this difficulty by distinguishing the instrumental from the mythical levels of human experience: "the genetic interpretation of myth belongs to a different order of spiritual life than participation in myth."[171] The mythic was not subject to instrumental or scientific reasoning; indeed, insofar as it succumbed to a "technological consciousness" and the "cult of science," it "loses its vitality." Although the "clash of myth with knowledge about myths is real" and inevitable, Kolakowski believed that the "mutual suspicion of these two layers of culture" was salutary.

How, he asked, does one settle disputes "regarding the truth of conflicting myths?" Are we "condemned to total arbitrariness ... since there are no generally obligating criteria" for adopting a mythology?[172] Kolakowski rejected the claims of the relativist, that all views are "equally justified," as well as the belief of the moral nihilist that "everything is permitted." He held that it is possible to "distinguish in mythical speech what is the deposit of a real concentration of feeling and imagination from what is causal whim."

Again Kolakowski insisted that there was no final security in the mythic. Human beings were condemned to move between two orders — the mythic and the phenomenal or contingent—with no hope for a lasting synthesis. Indeed, both the "achievement of synthesis," as well as the abandonment of the will to synthesis, would "mean death to culture."[173]

If human beings could only heal the wounds inflicted by their separation from nature by means of myth, what of the future?[174] Kolakowski was skeptical toward the possibility of a new mythology. And while he recognized the decline of religion in modern life, he believed that a revitalized Christianity offered the best hope for the renewal of mythological authority. "All significant religious developments" during the previous thirteen centuries, he observed, had appealed to the "existing mythological treasury." At a number of points in his study he criticized contemporary Christian thinkers for what he saw as their tendency to weaken their own tradition.

The Presence of Myth marked a new stage in Kolakowski's journey away from Marxism. Even in his earlier years he had been largely concerned with what orthodox Marxists viewed as the "superstructure." In re-examining the human condition he had, in fact, turned the Marxist system upside down and placed the free individual and his moral responsibility at the apex of his thought. The extent of his defection from Marxism had not been lost on the communist authorities in Poland. They refused to allow the publication of *The Presence of Myth*. Their decision was probably influenced by Kolakowski's return to the public arena a few weeks before his study was completed.

In October 1966, Kolakowski accepted an invitation from students at the University of Warsaw to take part in a Jubilee marking the tenth anniversary of the October Revolution. Speaking before an overflow crowd made up of students and faculty, he asked, "What do we have to celebrate today?" He answered, "Nothing at all."[175] And he went on to restate many of the criticisms he had made of the communist regime earlier and concluded that it had left the country with a sick economy, a deeply wounded working class, a hostility toward intellectual life, and an unwillingness to tolerate opposition. The meeting ended with the adoption of a resolution calling for more freedom. For his role in the affair Kolakowski was expelled from the party.

The Jubilee opened a new period of unrest in Poland.[176] Over the next several years tensions grew as students, intellectuals, and artists pressed for more freedom while the government responded with increased censorship. Discontent among the students, some of whom were sons and daughters of high-ranking party officials, spread to other university cities, culminating in massive demonstrations in March 1968.

Kolakowski, who was viewed by the government as a chief instigator of the student protests, was now dismissed from his chair of philosophy. He was again subjected to harsh criticism from Gomulka and party intellectuals. They attacked him for his efforts to open a dialogue with non-Marxist thinkers, for his indifference to the social and economic developments emphasized by Marx, and, particularly, for his views of religion. One critic charged that he was seeking a "synthesis between Marx and Christ."[177]

Kolakowski was only one among a number of prominent intellectuals who felt the wrath of the party at this time.[178] They included leading sociologists, political economists, and scientists. Even Schaff, who during the 1960s had been following Kolakowski's path toward a more humanistic Marxism, lost his position as the party's chief ideologist.[179] The treatment of Schaff also reflected a resurgence of anti-Semitism in Poland, directed in part against the sympathy that Jewish intellectuals had shown for the Zionist cause. For Polish cultural life in general the damage was severe. The only recourse for many of the country's intellectuals and artists was inner or outer migration. Kolakowski chose the latter. He left Poland in 1969.

V

His criticism of Stalinism had won for Kolakowski admiration within the wider European world. To one of the most important communist dissenters, Milovan Djilas, who had read Kolakowski in his Yugoslavian prison cell, he seemed an especially "vital and relevant figure."[180] Kolakowski had passed, according to Djilas, "through all the phases" typical of the heretics of Communism—from the "emotional dizziness induced by 'Stalinism' to the search for fresh inspiration" in the writings of the young Marx. And having subjected Marxism to the "fires of creative criticism," he had gained the moral force granted only to a "free and creative spirit."

Kolakowski's courageous dissent had ensured him a warm reception in the West, and academic opportunities as well. After a period of travel and lecturing, he found a permanent academic home at All Souls College, Oxford. There he continued to reflect on the questions that arose during the dissolution of his Marxist faith.

Some elements within Europe's political left, however, viewed Kolakowski with suspicion. The hostility of the students in Frankfurt, when he was considered for the Adorno chair, was noted earlier. Elsewhere his ever sharper criticism of Marxism evoked a sense of dismay, even betrayal. Hence the long "Open Letter to Leszek Kolakowski" by the British Marxist historian E. P. Thompson, published in 1973.[181]

Thompson felt a close "kinship" with Kolakowski.[182] While he did not claim to match the heroism of the Polish dissenter, Thompson noted his own break with the Communist Party in 1956 and his search for an independent course as a Marxist. "We were both voices of Communist revisionism," he declared, seeking to "rehabilitate the utopian energies within the socialist tradition." Thompson recalled his admiration for Kolakowski's essays of the mid-1950s, particularly "Responsibility and History."[183] Like Kolakowski, he had deplored and condemned the ossified priestly forms of Marxism developed by the communists.

But then, citing Kolakowski's recent essays and interviews, published in *Encounter* and *Daedalus* and presented at a conference at Reading in April of 1973, Thompson expressed his "sense of injury and betrayal."[184] He was uncertain as to just where Kolakowski would place himself in the Marxist tradition. He was perplexed by Kolakowski's claim that "religious consciousness" was an "irreplaceable feature of human life."[185] Since "we are still in the youth of man's secular self-knowledge," Thompson observed, it was too soon to predict the outcome. Thompson was troubled, too, by what he saw as Kolakowski's one-sided treatment of the New Left in the West, his dismissal of the student radicals as "blind enthusiasts."[186] And he objected to Kolakowski's willingness to appear in a journal, *Encounter*, that was receiving subsidies from the American Central Intelligence Agency. Even Kolakowski's appearance at the conference in Reading seemed to Thompson to mean compromises with the bourgeois enemy.

Thompson was most upset by Kolakowski's abandonment of the Marxist vision of a radical transformation of society. "I do not find the idea of a formidable revolution in men's minds as absurd as you do."[187] The struggle of the working class still held a "potentia," according to Thompson, a capacity to "enter an age in which human wills and aspirations can take charge and are no longer subservient to economic necessity and the law bounded inevitability of the past."[188]

Thompson suggested that Kolakowski had been soured by his experiences under communism. His criticisms of the system, therefore, had moved from irony to caricature, and then to a gross exaggeration of its failings. Along the way he had lost the Marxist understanding of capitalism as a total system. And once he arrived in the West Kolakowski could no longer recognize the pervasive and insidious nature of the hegemony of the "bitch of consumer capitalism."[189] "The beast has not changed," Thompson declared. He cited the experience of Britain after 1945, when the promising reforms of the Labor Party had soon been stripped of their genuinely socialist elements and reabsorbed into the capitalistic order.

Thompson was not ready to give up on Kolakowski. Although the latter had made little effort, since coming to the West, to enter into a "dialogue with those who thought themselves to be your friends," Thompson invited him to rejoin the common struggle.[190] "We need your skills," he wrote, to combat both the "closed Marxism" of the East and the reactionary tendencies in the West.

Kolakowski's reply made it clear that he no longer considered himself a Marxist.[191] While he acknowledged his intellectual debts to that tradition, he had concluded that many of its doctrines were "false or meaningless, or else true only in a very restricted sense."[192] Most of Marx's predictions had "proved to be erroneous," for his theory of class consciousness was false. Nor could he share Thompson's readiness to "think about society in categories of global systems." As for the attempt to reform communism, which still engaged Thompson, it was for Kolakowski a "dead option."[193] And so, he concluded, "the gulf between us is likely unbridgeable."

Kolakowski did not abandon the socialist cause. But he had come to see it in a "deep crisis," requiring, therefore, a re-examination of "its very roots."[194] During the years after leaving Poland he pursued that task in two ways. He resumed the inquiry, expressed in his philosophical anthropology, and developed further his view of religion and the mythological, into the human condition. And he continued his critique of Marxism, together with the aim of explaining its relationship to Stalinism.

In his first major essay after leaving Poland, "Hope and Hopelessness," he reflected on the possibility of reform in his homeland.[195] The essay was prompted in part by the riots of industrial workers in the northern cities of Gdansk and Stettin in December 1970, which led to the fall of Gomulka.[196] Kolakowski was struck by what he saw as the "regrettable passivity" characteristic of "a large part of the Polish intelligentsia" during "the dramatic action of the workers."[197] He attributed it to the view, widely held by intellectuals at this time, that the communist system "in its present form is unreformable."[198] All the "hopes for its partial, gradual 'humanization' … must be in vain," so the argument went, since "we are dealing with a totally inflexible mechanism, lacking self-regulating devices" and hence "capable of change only in the face of violent catastrophes." Although Kolakowski developed this argument, providing along the way an acute and, in the light of the future, a prescient diagnosis of the ruinous tendencies in the communist system, he rejected it as an "ideology of defeatism." This way of thinking, embedded in the Marxist tradition, blinded men and women to the possibilities for reform.

To support his belief that reform was possible Kolakowski recalled the ways in which the capitalist order in the West had been modified, despite the Marxist forecasts, by the working-class struggle. There were, he insisted, "ineradicable internal contradictions"[199] in the communist system that could be exploited by those who resisted. He noted, for example, the conflict between the system's need for a centralized power and the desire of ruling groups for security against the kind of terrorism exercised by Stalin. Kolakowski emphasized, too, the ways in which "despotic socialism" placed "powerful brakes on technical and productive progress."[200]

He focused mainly, however, on the growing ideological failure of the system. For the "grotesque creature called Marxism-Leninism still hangs at the neck of the rulers like a hopeless tumor, limiting their freedom of movement."[201] Although the Marxist ideology still provided the only legitimation for communism, it was "dying a slow death … sinking into an inert boredom and numbness." Hence the growing reliance on repression.[202] In Poland, Kolakowski maintained, the system had long since lost its legitimacy. The "breaking down of rigid orthodoxies," he argued, provided an opportunity for the intelligentsia in Poland, which had preserved its cultural past, to renew, with the working class, the struggle for a genuine socialism. But a new socialism, given the end of the international communist movement, could only be achieved within a sovereign nation. Such a socialism, he insisted, would have to be pluralistic, both economically and politically; it would tolerate "a multiplicity of forms of social ownership" as well as competing political parties. What really mattered, he concluded, was the belief that change was possible. He insisted that "instruments of pressure" were available for "nearly everyone."[203]

Kolakowski's appeal to his fellow countrymen did not go unheeded.

According to one observer, the essay "had a tremendous impact inside Poland."[204] It was "no exaggeration," he added, to call it "the fundamental text of the Polish democratic opposition in the 1970's."

But Kolakowski was, as he put it in an essay published in 1971, stranded.[205] The dream of a "world wide revolutionary movement ... which would unite all the values of a revolutionary humanism" was dead.[206] Soviet communism had taken the Marxist left captive and come to exercise a kind of blackmail on "the whole world of the Left." For attempts by Marxist intellectuals outside of Russia to criticize the brutal workings of communism could be viewed as a betrayal of the larger cause and, indeed, as an apology for capitalism.

Nor did Kolakowski see any hope in the new "Post Stalinist Left" in the West. Here was a movement, drawn in large part from the younger generation of the affluent middle classes, that had given up on the workers and looked to the newly liberated peoples of the former colonial areas as the bearers of historical progress. But having abandoned the values of "reason, tolerance, conscience, and persuasion," and having lost any strong support among intellectuals and workers, the New Left was more likely to lead to fascism. It was, Kolakowski concluded, simply "a pathological excrescence of capitalism."[207]

Kolakowski denied that it was possible any longer to clarify the problems of social injustice by means of "artificial ideological constructions." Given the diversity of social and political conditions in the modern world, the task of establishing clear standards for dealing with all of the victims of oppression had become extremely difficult.[208] Ideological solutions were more likely to rely on disguises, gross lies, or demagoguery.

Although Kolakowski had retreated to a particularistic and limited conception of the Left, he had not abandoned his quest for social justice, freedom, and equality. But how, given his rejection of the Marxist account of the struggle, to reground the socialist cause? In a number of essays during the 1970s he attempted to reconnect socialism with the traditional ideas and values of Western civilization. The conservative turn in his thought was evident in an essay, "The Meaning of Tradition," published in the year he left Poland.[209]

The essay focused on a theme that had emerged as a central feature of Kolakowski's thought—the necessary tension between rebellion and tradition in any healthy society. A society in which tradition becomes a cult condemns itself to stagnation but a society which seeks to live simply out of a revolt against tradition "destroys itself."[210]

The essay was mainly a defense of tradition and authority. Kolakowski denied that these elements, indispensable features of any society, could be judged simply in rational or utilitarian terms. Like the mythic constructions which they presupposed, tradition and authority could function as sources of values and human solidarity only if they were matters of faith. Criticism, while essential, was only valid within a given tradition.

Kolakowski was convinced that Western civilization had entered a time of profound cultural and spiritual crisis. "Never," he wrote, "has the attack on tradition been as violent as today."[211] He attributed this in part to the dislocations associated with urbanization and industrialization. But he was especially troubled by the attitudes of the younger generation. It was no longer equipped, whether in the Western capitalistic societies or in the communist systems, with the stock of values required for a life of meaningful confrontation with the world.

> The children, whose father had acquired property by the sweat of his brow, feel the meaninglessness of an unending hunt after ever more and ever newer and therefore ever more rapidly consumed goods. The child whose father had risked his life in the revolutionary struggle for a just world, now experiences the world formed by its alleged ideals as a fearful world under the dictate of an Ideology which is repeated unceasingly and which no one believes any longer.[212]

Although Kolakowski conceded that the inherited stock of values and meanings had lost much of its force, he still looked to Christianity and to socialism for inspiration and guidance.

> The Gospel does not cease to be the chief source of our morality because it has served unscrupulous fanatics. Socialism does not cease to be a guiding idea of earthly society because tyrannical powers have appropriated its name.[213]

The problem then was to understand why ideals that once appeared to be the hope of the world now seemed bankrupt. "We must investigate" the ways in which the original meanings of Christianity and socialism have degenerated into caricatures. How was the "shadow of Mr. Hyde concealed behind the silhouette of Dr. Jekyll?"[214]

Kolakowski explored this problem—the weakening of tradition and the cultural crisis—in an essay, "The Revenge of the Sacred in Secular Culture," published in 1973.[215] Here he focused on that aspect of religious life which set limits to human understanding and ambition—the sense of the sacred. Again he marked off the religious as autonomous to some extent, not to be reduced to mankind's desire to control the world, or to particular social functions.

Kolakowski acknowledged that "there are no infallible methods for penetrating the concealed, underground layers of culture." But he suggested that it was possible, in "times of social crisis," to see developments not normally visible.[216] He was convinced that the deeper meanings which a sacred sensibility bestowed on "the main areas of human activity"—birth and death, marriage and sexuality: the disparities of age and generation; work and art, vocations and professions—were disappearing. He cited, as examples, the loss or blurring of form in the arts and analogous trends in fashions and even in sexual behavior. "We have entered another world," he declared, "in which our system of ... classification, even its most vital and basic elements, has ceased to apply."[217]

Kolakowski granted that the sense of the sacred and the "spirit of conservatism" that it encouraged had often served to reinforce "irrational privilege." But he was mainly concerned with the consequence of losing such an outlook. For a totally secular culture was prone to "the most dangerous illusions"—the belief in man's total autonomy and perfectibility.[218] These attitudes, he observed, "may be the most efficient instruments of suicide ever to have been invented by human culture." Hence the need for the restraints induced by sacred feelings. By pointing to a meaning "beyond that which is inherent in human history," the sense of the sacred also enables human beings to accept the fact of "life as an inevitable defeat."

Kolakowski developed this argument in his next essay, "Can the Devil be Saved?"[219] Here he examined the denial of human limitation implicit in those views of history, both secular and religious, that envisioned human redemption or "the ultimate reconciliation of all things." Against such millennialist or utopian expectations, Kolakowski defended the traditional Christian and Jewish understanding of human imperfection, expressed in the idea of original sin. It was, he maintained, "a penetrating insight into human destiny."[220] Much of his discussion, as in a number of essays in these years, was directed against those Christian thinkers—Teilhard de Chardin, and others—who had compromised with the optimism and rationalism of the Enlightenment, and reduced evil and sin to mere contingencies in human development. They expressed, according to Kolakowski, a "great fear" of being "out-distanced and isolated" in a "basically un-Christian society."

During the 1970s Kolakowski assumed a paradoxical role—that of a nonbeliever who defended the basic Christian teachings. He had now repudiated the Marxist belief that "the Communist future will encompass the perfect reconciliation of man's empirical existence with his genuine essence."[221] The "myth of Prometheus," which had dominated his Marxist years, and the figure of Orestes, who had symbolized the skeptical aftermath, had now been displaced by Nebuchadnezzar, the biblical king who, having tried to "exalt himself to the dignity of God" was "degraded to the condition of a beast."[222]

Kolakowski had not left "the living tradition of socialist thought."[223] But only a socialism that "understood the complexity of the brutal forces acting in human history" could carry on the "fight against social oppression and human misery." Moreover, he had found in Christianity a corrective to the Marxist indifference to the inner life, and the capacity to look beyond the "external pressures" on human existence.

In the face of his "vague feeling" that "all components of our civilization are afflicted with a sickness for which nobody knows the cure,"[224] Kolakowski envisioned a new relationship between socialism and Christianity. He did not seek a "grand synthesis" of the two traditions. For his conception of Christianity was essentially spiritual and private. He denied, in fact, that Christianity could "resolve the sorry dilemmas that arise at every step of life" or deal directly with social or political problems. Its primary function was "to build a barrier against hatred in the consciousness of individuals."[225] Its relationship to the socialist quest for a just order was that of a fruitful tension.

In 1978 Kolakowski drew together his reflections of the previous two decades into a credo entitled "How to Be a Conservative-Liberal-Socialist."[226] It was a synthesis, albeit dynamic, in which he reconciled his socialist values with the broader traditions of Western thought. Along with the conservative emphasis on human limitation and the need for authority, and the liberal affirmation of individual freedom, he restated the socialist challenge to the unchecked workings of the market and the profit motive under capitalism.

VI

During the 1970s Kolakowski also settled his accounts with Marxism. Begun about the time he left Poland, his three-volume study, *Main Currents of Marxism*, was published in 1977. He described the work as a handbook—as a straightforward exposition of the origins and development of Marxist thought.[227] It was, in fact, an interpretation of that development and one which reflected, particularly in the final volume, "The Breakdown," his own changing relationship to Marxism. No wonder several re-

viewers have seen the *Main Currents* as the story of ideological disenchantment, as a version of "the God that failed."[228]

Kolakowski announced his approach to Marxism in the opening sentence of the first volume—"Karl Marx was a German philosopher."[229] Central to Marxist thought, he declared, was its "answer to certain fundamental questions that philosophers had posed for centuries in one form or another."[230] The questions arose out of an "awareness of human imperfection": Was there "a remedy for the contingent state of man?" Could human
beings discover a connection to a "non-accidental and non-contingent
Being?" Could they overcome the "unbearable disjunction" between their
"empirical, temporal, factual existence" and their sense of an essential self?
The Marxist answers to these questions, Kolakowski argued, could be understood only within "the setting of European cultural history as a whole."

In European history the Neo-Platonists, particularly Plotinus, had, according to Kolakowski, expressed most clearly the "mythopoeic longing
for a lost paradise."[231] This longing for a self-sufficient and authentic life
had "never disappeared from our culture." In the "Christian version of Pla-
tonism," however, that of Augustine, man was viewed as a fallen creature,
"a helpless, miserable being, incapable of self-liberation" and hence dependent on the grace of God. Kolakowski went on to discuss the ways in
which Christian thinkers—Eriugena, Meister Eckhart, Nicholas of Cusa,
Jacob Boehme, and others—viewed man's "final reconciliation with himself through reconciliation with Absolute Being." Here lay the "historical
background of the Hegelian dialectic and, therefore, of Marxian historiography."[232]

Kolakowski examined the process through which the human aspiration
for perfection discarded the Christian interpretation and entered a "radically anti-religious framework." [233] Thinkers during the Enlightenment
came to believe that mankind could recover its "lost identity" within a
strictly immanental or natural process. Once human beings discovered the
workings of "benevolent natural harmony," all of life's conflicts and misfor-
tunes would disappear.

Kant opened "a new chapter" in the philosophical attempt to realize an
"essential humanity" by conceiving of the task as that of emancipation
from nature by means of an "autonomous reason and will."[234] Fichte and
Hegel then brought the Kantian ego or self into close relationship to contemporary, particularly German, history. For Hegel, history itself became
the locus of the reconciliation of the individual will and the "divine idea,"
or what he viewed as "Universal Reason." The "divided state" with which

the older religious and philosophical systems had struggled was being overcome through the mediations of social institutions, particularly the state.[235]

Hegel's dialectical understanding of history made no sense, according to Kolakowski, in the absence of the older "eschatological perspective," the vision of man's recovery of a true or an essential self.[236] And yet, while Hegel viewed the historical process as creative, as leading to the fulfillment of humanity, he remained firmly fixed on the historical process itself. He thought it "vain and foolish to imagine ideals independently of the actual state of history." "His anti-utopianism," Kolakowski insisted, "is emphatic and unambiguous."

Hence the radical nature of the leap taken by Marx during the disintegration of the Hegelian synthesis. For he emerged with a "new eschatology" — a "vision of a new world" in the future in which "all sources of conflict, aggression, and evil" had been removed.[237] Marx's discovery of the proletariat as the force which would realize that world was, Kolakowski observed, simply a "philosophical deduction." But the vision, first formulated clearly in the *Economic and Philosophical Manuscripts* of 1844, entailed the "full and perfect reconciliation of man with himself and nature, the complete identification of human essence and existence, the harmonization of man's ultimate destiny and his empirical being." This eschatology continued to underlie Marx's thought as he developed his analysis of capitalism and his conception of the coming revolution. The "whole of his work down to the last page of *Capital* was a confirmation and elaboration" of the basic ideas formed in his early years.[238]

Society, viewed from Marx's eschatological perspective, could only be understood holistically, as a "conceptually linked system," rather than as a "chaotic mass of direct perceptions."[239] And the social process, driven, according to Marx, by technology and the class struggle, could only be understood in the light of its future outcome. That future, communism, would mean an overcoming of man's self-estrangement, the process through which human beings under capitalism had become enslaved by their own creations. The proletariat would gain, through its practical struggles, an awareness of this development. For the proletariat grasped reality in the very act of transforming it. In Marx's dialectical conception of that process, knowledge and action, theory and practice, coincided. There was no "separate perception of what is and what ought to be."[240]

Throughout his account of Marx's thought Kolakowski continued to hear "the exhortation of a prophet."[241] Alongside the conviction that the historical process was "helping on the revolution" ran a current of "moral indignation at the cruelty and villainy" of capitalistic exploitation.[242] Along with Marx's emphasis on the economic determinants went a call for human action, for "the conscious rational participation of the masses."[243]

Kolakowski attempted, as he put it, to interpret the Marxist doctrines "as sympathetically as possible."[244] But toward the end of the first volume he ventured a critique. He questioned Marx's claim to "explain all historical change" in terms of the class struggle and technological progress.[245] The fundamental flaw in Marxist theory lay, however, in his conviction that he could predict the future. The vision of communism was, in fact, the decisive element in the system. But that vision, like the "proletarian's historic mission," had been the outcome of "philosophical deduction." "Empirical evidence for it" came only later.

Marx had, in short, expressed in new terms the older eschatological aspiration. His view of history culminated in "the complete unity of man, the identification of existence with essence, and the abolition of contingency in human life."[246] He had also assimilated, according to Kolakowski, three emerging motifs in Western thought—the romantic reaction to capitalism, the "Faustian-Promethean faith in man's unlimited powers as self-creator," and the rationalistic and deterministic outlook of the Enlightenment. The "whole of Marx's thought," Kolakowski maintained, could be "interpreted in terms of these three motifs and their interrelation."[247]

As he continued his account of Marxist development in the second volume, the "Golden Age," dealing with the period from 1889 to 1914, Kolakowski introduced a major paradox.[248] For the form of Marxism that dominated those years was an aberration; it deviated markedly from the system of thought developed earlier by Marx. Engels was largely responsible for the deviation. Strongly influenced by contemporary natural science, he translated Marxism into a "naturalistic evolutionism," an objective "dialectic of nature," which completely altered Marx's dialectic by turning it into a deterministic doctrine.[249] The "revolutionary eschatology" of Marx, together with the concept of alienation that underlay it, largely disappeared.

In his discussion of the "Golden Age," during which he devoted chapters to the most significant Marxist thinkers in the early years of the century, Kolakowski paid special attention to Polish Marxists. For Poland had been "an important center of the Marxist movement."[250] "It was here," according to Kolakowski, "that socialism for the first time split up in accordance, more or less, with the principles which subsequently divided social democracy from communism" in Europe.

Kolakowski discovered in one of the earlier Polish Marxist thinkers, Stanislav Brzozowski, a figure whose "spiritual evolution" anticipated much of his own development.[251] Brzozowski, too, had turned to Marxism in search of meaning in life and for answers to moral concerns. And once inside the Marxist framework, he had, like Kolakowski later, rebelled against the positivistic and deterministic outlook of its orthodox interpreters and insisted that the individual was "unconditionally responsible for himself and for external reality."[252] Brzozowski had also recovered a true understanding of Marx's conception of "praxis," as a "form of social activity" through which human beings comprehend "the historical process from the inside." He was, Kolakowski observed, "one of the first to contrast Marx and Engels as minds of a completely opposite stamp."[253] But in the end Brzozowski, like Kolakowski, became disenchanted with Marxism and turned back to Christianity as a source of values and meaning.[254]

The "Golden Age" also held the answer to the question that had, at least in part, motivated the study—how had Marxism led to the tyranny of Stalinism? Kolakowski traced the origins of the totalitarian form of socialism to the work of Lenin. Having dismissed democratic institutions and civil liberties as techniques of bourgeois oppression, Lenin had used terroristic methods, in the context of civil war, to establish the dictatorship of the Communist Party. The dialectical materialism of Engels became, at the same time, a total philosophy of life; Lenin denied the "possibility of impartiality or neutrality in any sphere of life."[255] The way was thus prepared for Stalin, whose totalitarianism was the "natural outcome of the system" established by Lenin. "Any crack in the ideological monolith" was a "threat to its existence."[256]

The unfolding of the logic of Leninism was the main theme of the third volume of the *Main Currents*. For the "breakdown" of orthodox Marxism stifled creativity in all realms of life and made it increasingly difficult for the communist bureaucracy to adjust to a changing world. The system was condemned to "inevitable dissolution."[257]

The process of dissolution was hastened, paradoxically, by the recovery of what Kolakowski viewed as the essential character of Marxism—its eschatological vision. This was mainly the work of Georg Lukács. Moved by the ethical concerns and the quest for meaning evident among many young intellectual converts to Marxism in the early years of the century,

Lukács rediscovered elements in Marxism that had been buried during its later development. By reinstating the concepts of "totality" and "alienation," expressed in his account of reification, Lukács had reaffirmed the belief that the historical process, embodied in the proletariat, was "ripening toward the final transformation of society."[258] He had, unwittingly, disclosed the "mythological, prophetic, and utopian" features of Marxism that had eluded its more scientific adherents.[259] By restoring to Marx's disciples the quality of mythic conviction, however, Lukács had made Marxism invulnerable to "rational or empirical criticism." It was, Kolakowski observed, "perhaps the most striking example in the twentieth century of what may be called the betrayal of reason by those whose profession is to use and defend it."[260]

In reviewing the new currents of Marxist thought in the twentieth century, including the Frankfurt school, Kolakowski concluded that they were all doomed to sterility. His harshest judgment was directed against Herbert Marcuse, who seemed to him not a genuine Marxist at all but "a prophet of semi-romantic anarchism in its most irrational form."[261] Critical theorists, in general, expressed a "nostalgia for the pre-capitalistic culture of an elite."[262]

The scorn with which Kolakowski treated the later development of Marxism—an attitude almost completely absent from his earlier discussions of the tradition—reflected his personal involvement in the recent ideological struggles. His account of the humanistic Marxist challenge to Stalinism can be read as autobiography, as a record of his own efforts to save Marxism from its institutionalized corruption. "Like other heretics in history," he recalled, the revisionists had "appealed for a return to the sources" of an "authentic marxism."[263] Increasingly, however, they had fixed on the task of restoring "the role of the subject in the historical and cognitive process." But there had been an "inner logic" in revisionism, he concluded, "which, before long, carried it beyond the frontiers of Marxism."[264]

Marxism, Kolakowski declared in an "Epilogue," has been "the greatest fantasy of our century ... a dream offering the prospect of a society of perfect unity, in which all human aspirations would be fulfilled and all values reconciled."[265] As such it had functioned like a religion, but "a bogus form of religion, since it presents its temporal eschatology as a scientific system, which religious mythologies do not purport to be."[266] To that fallacy one could trace the disastrous outcome of the Marxist tradition—the "monstrous edifice of lies, exploitation, and oppression" found in communism.

Not that communism was an inevitable outcome of Marxism; it was, however, "a plausible conclusion."[267] As an "explanatory system" and a method for changing society, Kolakowski concluded, Marxism "is dead," leaving behind a "depressing air of sterility and helplessness."[268]

VII

Following the completion of the *Main Currents* Kolakowski continued to reflect on the course of Marxism while developing further a different interpretation of modern history. Although he claimed that we are "incurably ignorant of our own spiritual foundation," his essays in the years ahead were occupied in large part with the spiritual condition of Western civilization.[269] "Why," he asked, "is the malaise associated with the experience of modernity so widely felt," and what are its sources?[270] He remained convinced that the answer lay in the "apparently progressive evaporation of our religious legacy and the sad spectacle of a godless world," or what Max Weber had described as "disenchantment."

Kolakowski continued to believe that the fate of Western civilization, the survival of its core values, was inextricably tied to Christianity. It had been, he maintained, the "seminary of the European spirit."[271] In his distinctive understanding of that spirit he again emphasized its recognition of human incompleteness and spiritual uncertainty. Christianity, he argued, "has neither found nor promised any lasting solution to man's temporal lot." Indeed, it was the continuing capacity for self-doubt and self-criticism that gave Europeans the unique ability, expressed in the discipline of anthropology, to enter sympathetically into other cultures. This sense of uncertainty and human limitation, despite the periodic failure of Christians to be faithful to its spirit, enabled Christianity to provide a needed equilibrium or "homeostasis."

Kolakowski's sense of the loss of this spiritual equilibrium offers a key to his reinterpretation of European history. He traced the origins of that process back to the eleventh century when, with the development of scholastic philosophy, secular reason began to be separated from faith.[272] This marked the rise of "modernity," during which the various areas of human culture—art, philosophy, science, and politics—became increasingly autonomous. Having cut themselves off from the normative framework provided by Christianity, each of these activities looked within for "its own criteria of validity."[273] Thus the artist came to affirm the free play of his imagination, while the politician, as Machiavelli recognized, was concerned simply with the pursuit of power or domination. Kolakowski placed special emphasis on the growing autonomy of science, or rather its philosophical form, "scientistic rationalism," which became, with the Enlightenment, the main ideological rival of Christianity.

To this process of secularization and the loss of the Christian sense of self-doubt and human limitation, Kolakowski attributed the various attempts in Western history to envision ultimate solutions to all human problems. From this perspective he renewed, in several of the later essays, his criticism of Marxism, emphasizing, in particular, its abandonment of the spiritual ground of Western culture.[274] Thus despite his own "disguised moralism," Marx had set aside traditional moral claims and disregarded as well the fundamental premise of Christianity, the "inherent dignity of being human." Indeed, Marx's holistic conception of society made it possible to view the individual, as Lenin and Stalin would demonstrate, as no more than a replaceable part, as a "lifeless robot," in a great social machine.

Marxism was only one form of the widespread effort in modern Western life to find security in ideologies, in "all embracing world views" that imposed an "a priori meaning on all aspects of human life."[275] They represented, in their expectations of a "New Man," and a "New Time," which would follow the obliteration of the "inherited stock of culture" and institutions, "degenerate forms of religious messianism." For in contrast to genuine religious faith, ideologies claimed to be rational or scientific. They were, therefore, fundamentally dishonest; they suffered from a "bad conscience."

Kolakowski was not content simply to repudiate apocalyptic yearnings and utopian aspirations. They were "a permanent form of human spiritual life."[276] Despite their dangers—the disastrous political outcomes of attempts to realize dreams of a perfect human fraternity—they might advance human well-being. "Only an infinite hope," Kolakowski observed, could generate, at times, "the energy needed to achieve finite results." A utopia might serve, moreover, as a "regulative idea," enabling people to judge existing social arrangements in the light of an ideal order.[277] Restating the special dialectic found in so much of his writing, Kolakowski insisted on the need for both the skeptical and the utopian outlook. Without their unceasing conflict life would stagnate.

In his post-Marxist view of the human condition Kolakowski had moved far from the clear sense of causal connections and the rational ordering of social life found in Marxist theory. Instead, he now saw a bewildering multiplicity of more or less independent forces, often working at cross purposes. He wrote, too, of the "inherently self-opaque" nature of human consciousness. [278] Not only were the motives of most individuals hidden from themselves, but they often pursued goals that were incompatible. Attempts to explain human action in rational terms were useless. Indeed, consistency itself was a danger in social life. To follow out the logic of a single principle, such as liberty or equality, was likely to produce its opposite. Even the values of tolerance and pluralism, to which Kolakowski was firmly committed, held dangers. For they might lead to a reluctance to distinguish between good and evil or to a failure to defend essential values. [279]

History, viewed from Kolakowski's new perspective, presented little more than "a garbage heap of discontinuous events." [280] And while he denied once more that there was any reliable method for penetrating into the deeper levels of cultural development, he insisted on the human need to "do away with the haphazardness of individual events" and "endow them with meaning." Only by means of our "little holy histories," he wrote, do we find out "who we are." In one of his late essays, "Politics and the Devil," Kolakowski offered an interpretation of Western history in the form of a dialectical relationship between God and the Devil. [281] It was a story of the ways in which the stratagems of the Devil, designed to draw individuals away from the path of righteousness, were resisted and countered by those human beings, endowed with free will, who remained faithful to divine guidance.

Kolakowski's emphasis on the irrationalities and unmanageable complexities of life was especially evident in his later political essays. Here was a realm in which the unknown and the unpredictable were inescapable. Political leaders usually faced, in Kolakowski's words, "package deals" in which they were asked to satisfy incompatible interests and values. [282] Even "our best choices," he observed, might lead to "unpleasant consequences." In the modern world, moreover, the political held a special menace. Having gained a large measure of autonomy, it was in danger of losing the moral and religious values without which it would degenerate into a mere play of power. [283]

Given his growing skepticism toward the possibility of a rational ordering of life, it is hardly surprising that Kolakowski now viewed intellectuals ambivalently. While he continued to affirm their critical function in society as well their efforts to create "new worlds," he also pointed to their role as "destroyers of tradition," as "enemies of stability." [284] They had, after all, been guilty of "horrible mistakes" in the twentieth century and contributed to its destructive ideologies. Insofar as intellectuals had assumed a "special mission" to the "oppressed and the poor," moreover, they had often developed—he cited the Frankfurt school—a "contempt for ordinary people."

Philosophy, however, still occupied a special place in Kolakowski's view of social development.

> The cultural role of philosophy is not to deliver the truth but to build the spirit of truth, and this means never to let the inquisitive energy of mind go to sleep, never to stop questioning what appears to be obvious and definitive ... and always to suspect that there might be "another side" in what we take for granted, and never to allow us to forget that there are questions that lie beyond the legitimate horizon of science and are nevertheless crucially important to the survival of humanity as we know it.[285]

Since philosophy was incapable of reaching ultimate truth, or what Kolakowski called the "underground," he was critical of those modern thinkers—Henri Bergson, Heidegger, Edmund Husserl—who claimed that they had discovered an unconditional basis for knowledge.[286] Among contemporary philosophers Karl Jaspers was of special interest to Kolakowski.[287] He had shown, in his diagnosis of the "spiritual crisis," that myth was "an indispensable part of culture"; he had hurled us "out of our empirical thinking."[288] But Jasper's attempt to translate the Christian mythology into philosophical terms was mistaken. Not only did it strip Christianity of its distinctive doctrines, but it negated "one of [its] great accomplishments," the presentation of "its doctrine in such a way that no space remained for a distinction between the faith of the common man and that of the learned or enlightened."[289]

It was to Christianity then that Western societies must look in order to regain their "sought after equilibrium."[290] Although contemporary Christianity and its main competitor for "spiritual domination," the Enlightenment, were both "gripped by a sentiment of helplessness and confusion," only the latter, according to Kolakowski, was exhausted.[291] After a "century of Enlightenment," he wrote, "we suddenly woke up in mental and cultural disarray."[292] Not only had thinkers in that tradition lost the capacity to "distinguish between good and evil," but its "scientistic philosophy" had reached the "intellectual impasse" foreshadowed in the "epistemological nihilism" of Hume.[293] The outcome was a utilitarian view of life and a tendency to "treat human beings as instruments to be manipulated." The form of humanism that had proclaimed the complete autonomy of the individual had turned on itself and "reached a suicidal stage."[294]

To explain the erosion of religious faith in Western civilization, Kolakowski pointed to "moral rather than intellectual changes."[295] The "desire to dominate nature" had replaced the belief that "there is a realm of reality that is [only] definable in moral" rather than in merely biological or even social terms. His moral belief in the "irreducible and unique core" of the human personality anchored Kolakowski's thought.[296] He traced the source of this belief to the Bible and found it developed most fully in the teachings of Jesus. From those teachings he drew the principle that became in the late essays his guiding precept for personal and social life—not to hate.[297]

Kolakowski's insistence on the inescapability of the moral sense in human beings suggests that he had, in his quest for meaning, come full circle—back to that time in his life when his moral aspirations had led him to Marxism. After the breakdown of his Marxist faith he had sought, through his philosophical anthropology, another way of grounding his values. But in the later essays he moved beyond a strictly anthropocentric perspective and affirmed a "realm of 'ratio' which precedes any actual civilization" and includes distinctions "between good and evil."[298] In Christian mythology he had come to see, for the West at least, a compelling disclosure of a transcendent reality. Indeed he was critical of those Christian theologians, particularly Rudolph Bultmann, who were bent on cleansing Christianity of its mythological elements in order to make it more palatable to a common sense shaped by modern science.[299] And despite his great sympathy for Kant's attempt to justify the dignity, freedom, and rationality of the individual on secular grounds, he did not find it convincing.[300]

Religion, and the sense of the sacred, remained for Kolakowski an indispensable part of human experience and a necessary basis for the taboos without which a society would have to fall back on mere coercion. In his fullest discussion of the religious he distinguished it once more from a rational or scientific understanding of reality.[301] Religion did not refer to "a set of propositions" but to a "special kind of perception" in which "understanding, knowledge, a feeling of participation in an ultimate reality, and moral commitment," came together in a "single act" of faith.[302] As such the religious could only be understood, apart from rare experiences of the mystics, through "real participation in a religious community."

Kolakowski's late essays expressed his conviction that the Christian account of the human condition had proven to be more realistic than that of the Marxists or any strictly secular or humanistic interpretation. What then of his own relationship to Christianity? How did he differ from those intellectuals he criticized, who lacking any "religious attachment, faith, or loyalty proper," insisted on the "irreplaceable educational and moral role of religion in our world?"[303] Several commentators have described Kolakowski as a Christian outside the church.[304] In view of his insistence that a genuine religious faith required participation in the ritual acts of a believing community, however, his outsidedness would seem to disqualify him as a believer. When asked on one occasion, he simply replied, "I do not wish to speak of my personal religious convictions."[305]

Perhaps one can apply to Kolakowski himself the attitude of self-doubt and the sense of human incompleteness that, he believed, distinguished Western culture. For he was convinced that this culture had reached a new time of fundamental uncertainty. "All the words and signs that make up our conceptual framework are dissolving before our eyes," and "we have entered another world."[306] No wonder one reviewer of his late essays has found there a "post modern sensibility."[307] Kolakowski, however, was unwilling to enter those "unchartered waters" of postmodernism without the ballast of traditional moral and religious values. It was one more inconsistency—a treasured word in Kolakowski's vocabulary—in an outlook that accepted inconsistencies as an inescapable part of living.

Conclusion

De Man, Horkheimer, and Kolakowski turned to Marxism to fulfill hopes that arose out of their bourgeois backgrounds. Marxism seemed to offer a way of realizing moral and cultural aspirations which, they believed, had been thwarted, indeed, betrayed, by bourgeois institutions and practices. In their efforts to advance those aspirations by means of orthodox Marxist theory, however, they soon encountered difficulties—ethical, psychological, and sociological—that they could not resolve. The process of ideological dissolution followed.

Political institutions presented the initial difficulty, for attempts to achieve revolutionary changes through the political process—parliamentary in Belgium and Germany, communist in Poland—demonstrated their futility. De Man could only experience frustrations in his efforts, first as a Marxist and then as an ethical socialist, to apply his ideas in the Belgium political system. Horkheimer, in contrast, quickly dismissed the political process in Weimar Germany, convinced that neither the Social Democratic nor the Communist Party represented an effective vehicle for his Marxism. Kolakowski, confronting a political order frozen into the authoritarian form imposed by Stalinist Russia, could only remain outside, as a critic, pointing to the contradictions between that order and the Marxist goals.

To encounter the resistances that existing political institutions presented to the Marxist program for radical change was also to confront the crucial problem facing Marxist thinkers in Europe after World War I—the aberrant course of the proletariat. Where working-class parties had entered the parliamentary process, as in Belgium and Germany, their leaders had set aside distinctively socialist goals in order to pursue the immediate interests that a representative political system was designed to accommodate. De Man responded to the dilemma by developing new approaches to the education of working-class leaders. Horkheimer attempted to find out why the workers were not developing the revolutionary consciousness necessary for them to play the historical role forecast by Marx. Kolakowski, too, recognizing that the Polish workers were still captive to old ways of thinking, called on his fellow Marxist intellectuals to take up the unfinished task of nurturing a new socialist consciousness.

Each of the intellectuals set out to recover Marx's revolutionary subject. Each recognized that orthodox Marxists, confident in the objective laws of history, had failed to provide a satisfactory account of human agency. All three of the intellectuals turned to the realm of consciousness in search of solutions to the problem of motivation. As long as they remained Marxists, they acknowledged, to be sure, the decisive role of economic and social determinants. But they were, in effect, giving priority to what orthodox Marxists regarded as the superstructure, or epiphenomena, in social life. It was a stage in the dissolution of the Marxist ideology.

The shift in emphasis, from considering objective social forces to examining the inner lives of socialists, was evident in De Man's *Psychology*, where he stressed the role of moral and religious sentiments in the movement. Horkheimer reinstated a strong sense of human agency in his reformulation of dialectical materialism. But he also sought to identify "psychical linkages," mediating ideas and feelings capable of translating the practical struggles of the workers into revolutionary action. Kolakowski followed another path, paying special attention to the moral responsibility of the individual as the key to the revitalization of Marxism.

The focus on consciousness also indicated the continuing force of the ethical and cultural aspirations that had initially moved each of the intellectuals to adopt Marxism. Unwilling to identify socialism simply with the pursuit of material interests, each expressed from time to time the need to instill into the workers what Horkheimer described as the "higher values." Each, in fact, carried into the movement the attitudes and tastes he had acquired during his bourgeois upbringing.

Committed to their visions of socialism, the intellectuals experienced a growing distance from the working class. De Man, in fact, gave up on the workers as the main bearer of the socialist cause and moved steadily toward an elitist and authoritarian point of view. Horkheimer, cut off from any effective contact with the workers by the Nazi conquest of Germany, concluded by the late 1930s that the European working class as a whole was hopelessly trapped in false ways of thinking. Only Kolakowski, among the three, retained a more optimistic view of the workers, seeing in their practical struggles correctives both to the failings of intellectuals and the rigidities of official Marxism in Poland.

Insofar as they questioned the socially transforming role of the proletariat, the intellectuals were surrendering a crucial part of the mythical underpinning of Marxism. Committed as intellectuals to developing the theoretical or rational content of the ideology, moreover, they inevitably weakened those qualities from which it gained much of its popular appeal. No wonder De Man, Horkheimer, and Kolakowski all looked to intellectuals like themselves to carry forward the revolutionary mission.

But reason alone, as each of these intellectuals came to recognize, could not sustain the socialist vision. Hence De Man's attempt, in his pageant, "Wir," to recover the mythical features of the movement. Horkheimer's break with Marxist rationalism was expressed in his essay "The End of Reason." And after discovering, with Adorno, that Marxism was simply one version of the instrumental reason that had been so destructive in Western history, he sought in his later years to recover a more adequate and value-laden conception of reason. Kolakowski, too, concluded that reason can not answer the questions that matter most in life. Having dismantled the Marxist mythology, he went on to defend the indispensable place of the mythic, or the religious, in social and cultural life.

The foundation of Marxism was the belief that human beings could take complete control of their world—not only the natural environment but history as well. This Promethean confidence in human autonomy was another casualty of the process through which Marxism, at least that of Horkheimer and Kolakowski, disintegrated.[1] The journey of these two intellectuals was marked by a growing sense of human limitation and, indeed, a recovery of traditional religious notions of sin and evil. De Man, however, continued until the end of his life to explain the eclipse of his socialist hopes in terms of human mistakes and lost opportunities.

As they lost confidence in the objective claims and rationalistic structure of Marxism, each of the intellectuals reconsidered the personal basis for his continuing commitment to socialism. Thus De Man, at the end of his *Psychology*, acknowledged that his socialism was, in the last analysis, simply a private "Credo." And he reaffirmed the ethical drive that had moved him to join the socialist cause. Horkheimer, too, faced with the intellectual and historical uncertainties of the late 1930s, confessed that his continuing faith in Marxism rested ultimately on an "existential judgment." He recognized, moreover, that his ties to the working class could only be explained in terms of his moral feelings. After his Marxist faith collapsed he listened once more to the "inner voice" that had moved him during his pre-Marxist years. The personal turn can also be seen in Kolakowski, who, after giving up his attempt to revise Marxism, looked for new foundations for his belief in a socialist society. Having explored, with the aid of Western existential thinkers, the inescapably individual nature of one's choices, he went on to reground his faith in the moral and religious traditions he had challenged earlier.

To leave Marxism behind was to confront a world no longer intelligible in ideological terms. De Man's conclusion, that history in any meaningful sense had come to an end, was a stark expression of the collapse of the ideology. But this did not prevent him from offering an alternative narrative of what had gone wrong in European history. Horkheimer, however, discovered in the development of instrumental reason another way of explaining modern history. Only his lingering faith in the capacity of isolated intellectuals qualified his gloomy forecast of a coming authoritarianism. Kolakowski, reflecting perhaps a later, more prosperous and secure time in Europe, did not share the deep pessimism of his predecessors. Not only had he become skeptical of the claims by intellectuals that they could grasp the social whole and, indeed, identify the deeper forces at work in history, but his reconciliation with liberal and conservative traditions in European life had led to a more hopeful view of the future than that found in De Man or Horkheimer.

Kolakowski presented in his later writings a view of the world in which ideology had lost its power to enchant. Having abandoned Marxism he concluded that our lives are "in large degree unpredictable and governed by chance."[2] This was not a cause for despair. For it restored a sense of the "infinite complexity of human affairs" and reawakened the "feeling of fathomless mystery" that we encounter, even in the "apparently simplest things and beings," in our daily lives.[3]

With this more modest view of human understanding Kolakowski went on to reinstate much of what the Marxist ideology had set aside. He reaffirmed "truth in the traditional sense" as well as the core value of Western civilization—the basic dignity and equality of all persons.[4] He reaffirmed as well the traditional virtues, personal and civil, noting, however, that they could only be acquired "from living among people who practise them."[5] To ground these values and the belief that "we really are free agents" Kolakowski relied on his views of God and the sacred.[6] Lacking these beliefs, he was convinced, "our civilization" would surrender to a "spirit of rationalism and scientism" in which "each person is reducible to his function" and hence "replaceable."[7] Such an outcome "would mean the end of humanity as we know it."

Kolakowski did not expect such an ending or, indeed, a "world without conceivable alternatives to existing political institutions."[8] He rejected the views of those who announced the "end of history." His faith in what he referred to as the "human instinct for curiosity"—his new term for the critical spirit that was part of his view of human development—was too strong. But he joined those contemporary social thinkers who believed that Western societies had reached a major impasse. And like a number of philosophers and theologians, he traced the present cultural crisis and the threat of nihilism back to the time in European history when reason had broken away from religious foundations.[9]

The intellectual journeys of De Man, Horkheimer, and Kolakowski illuminate the fate of Marxism in modern history. Each of these intellectuals came to recognize, like Sorel before them, that the source of Marxist vitality lay in its mythical underpinnings, the eschatological, religious-like faith in a transformed world. Without the "mythical inflation" of the socialist goal, in Kolakowski's words, Marxism was incapable of moving large numbers of men and women.

But Marxism, as the lives of the three intellectuals indicated, was subject to its own form of demythologizing. Through their efforts to develop the rational or theoretical component of the ideology they weakened its mythical elements and hence its popular appeal.[10] Reduced to theory, Marxism became more and more the affair of intellectuals. The Marxist ideology also became increasingly vulnerable to the test of history and to the criticisms of intellectuals inside and outside the movement.

The Marxist union of the mythical and the theoretical was the product of a special time in European history, when the decline of traditional religious beliefs made the older millennial and eschatological yearnings available for secular "reoccupations."[11] But the dangers associated with that union were evident in the later development of Marxism. For insofar as Marxists viewed their yearnings as realizable inside of history, indeed, as the natural and rational outcome of existing social forces, they became susceptible to the "totalitarian seduction."[12] No wonder then, some Marxists concluded that it was necessary to abandon their eschatological hopes.[13]

What then remains of Marxism? A great deal. It continues to offer a powerful critique of a capitalistic society whose inner workings seem necessarily to result in extreme disparities of wealth and well-being. Marxism survives, too, as a method of social inquiry, as a way of exploring the complex relationships between the economic, political, and cultural realms. Detached from its extravagant mythic claims, Marxism can contribute to the ongoing attempt to understand the development of capitalism and contribute as well to the quest for a more just and humane society.[14]

Is anything left of the eschatological hope? Has this distinctive feature of Western civilization disappeared? Not entirely. Christian thinkers have, in recent years, sought to take back that hope from the Marxists and reestablish it on sacred ground.[15] Even "Post-Marxists," most notably Jacques Derrida, have attempted to preserve something of the "messianic eschatology" in Marxism in the form of "specters" or spirit.[16]

And what of the other secular forms of the eschatological—the non-Marxist utopian dreams of the future?[17] Has the utopian imagination, as some have argued, dried up?[18] Does the present poverty of that imagination support the claims of those who, viewing the recent triumphs of neoliberal capitalism, announce the end of viable alternatives?

If, as a number of social thinkers have maintained, the utopian disposition has been an essential element in a vital Western culture, efforts to envision radically new ways of living will likely continue.[19] But the future makers of utopias will need to struggle with the underlying question posed by the efforts of De Man, Horkheimer, and Kolakowski to realize the promise in the Marxist ideology. What are the limits to the attempts of human beings to achieve autonomy and gain total control over their history?

Notes

Notes

Introduction

1. "Foreword" to Marx's doctoral dissertation, Karl Marx, Friedrich Engels, *Collected Works*, I (New York, International Publishers, 1975), p. 31. Also see W. Johnson, "Marx's Verse of 1836–37," *Journal of the History of Ideas* (Apr. 1967): 259–68.

2. See the discussion in Agnes Heller and Ferenc Fehér, *The Grandeur and Twilight of Radical Universalism* (New Brunswick, N.J., Transaction Publishers, 1991), pp. 120–26, 207–8.

3. Hans Blumenberg, *The Work of Myth*, tr. by Robert Wallace (Cambridge, Mass., M.I.T. Press, 1985), p. 591.

4. See, for example, Robert Tucker, *Philosophy and Myth in Karl Marx* (New York, Cambridge University Press, 1961); Heller and Fehér, *Grandeur and Twilight*, pp. 203–5; and J. L. Talmon, *Political Messianism: The Romantic Phase* (London, Secker and Warburg, 1960), esp. pp. 216–25, 505–11.

5. See Jules Monnerot, *Sociology of Communism*, tr. by Jane Degras and Richard Rees (Westport, Conn., Greenwood Press, 1976). Originally published in France in 1949. Monnerot likens Marxism, in its communist form, to the challenge that Islam once presented to European civilization.

6. My earlier studies include *Marxism and the Origins of British Socialism* (Ithaca, N.Y., Cornell University Press, 1973); *British Socialists: The Journey from Fantasy to Politics* (Cambridge, Mass., Harvard University Press, 1979); and *Marxist Intellectuals and the Working-Class Mentality in Germany: 1887–1912* (Cambridge, Mass., Harvard University Press, 1993).

Chapter 1: The Nietzschean Presence

1. Ernst Gystrow, "Etwas über Nietzsche und uns sozialisten," *Sozialistische Monatshefte* (Oct. 1900): 637–40. Gystrow was a pseudonym for Willy Hellpach.

For his relationship to the movement, see Hellpach, *Wirken in Wirren. Lebenserinnerungen*, I (Hamburg, C. Wegner, 1949), pp. 213–36.

2. For discussions of the relationship between Nietzsche's ideas and the socialist intellectuals in Germany, see the following: R. Hinton Thomas, *Nietzsche in German Politics and Society: 1890–1918* (Manchester, Manchester University Press, 1983), pp. 1–63; Kurt Sollmann, "Literarische Intelligenz. Nietzsche und die Sozialdemokratie," in Sollmann, *Literarische Intelligenz vor 1900* (Köln, Pahl-Regenstein, 1982), pp. 220–73; Helmut Scheuer, "Zwischen Sozialismus und Individualismus—Zwischen Marx und Nietzsche," in Scheuer, ed., *Naturalismus. Bürgerliche Dichtung und soziales Engagement* (Stuttgart, W. Kohlmanner, 1974), pp. 150–74; Steven Aschheim, "Nietzschean Socialism—Left and Right, 1890–1933," *Journal of Contemporary History* (Apr. 1988): 147–68, and Aschheim, *The Nietzschean Legacy in Germany, 1890–1990* (Berkeley, University of California Press, 1994), pp. 17–50. A later stage in this development is discussed in David Bathrick and Paul Breines, "Marx und oder Nietzsche. Anmerkungen zur Krise des Marxismus," in Reinhold Grimm and Jost Hermand, eds., *Karl Marx und Friedrich Nietzsche* (Königstein Ts., Athenaeum, 1978), pp. 119–35.

3. The differences within the social strata making up the German bourgeoisie are discussed in James Sheehan, *German Liberalism in the Nineteenth Century* (Chicago, University of Chicago Press, 1978), pp. 239–57. The new "Mittelstand" is examined in David Blackbourn, "The 'Mittelstand' in German Society and Politics: 1871–1914," *Social History* 2 (1977): 409–33.

4. For the impact of the economic changes on the lower middle class, see Robert Gellately, *The Politics of Economic Despair* (London, Sage, 1974), and Shulamit Volkov, *The Rise of Popular Anti-modernism in Germany* (Princeton, Princeton University Press, 1976).

5. See Hartmut Titze, "Enrollment Expansion and Academic Overcrowding in Germany," in Konrad Jarausch, ed., *The Transformation of Higher Learning: 1860–1930* (Chicago, University of Chicago Press, 1983), pp. 57–99; and John Craig, "Higher Education and Social Mobility in Germany," ibid., pp. 219–44.

6. Nietzsche's place in the German tradition of "Bildung" is discussed in W. H. Bruford, *The German Tradition of Self-Cultivation* (London, Cambridge University Press, 1975), pp. 165–89.

7. The most important of these circles, the "Friedrichshagen" group, is discussed in Herbert Scheuer, *Bürgerlich-oppositionelle Literaten und sozialdemokratische Arbeiterbewegung nach 1890* (Stuttgart, Metzler, 1974).

8. *Neue Zeit* 13, no. 19 (1894–95): 588.

9. Hermann Conradi, *Adam Mensch* (Leipzig, W. Friedrich, 1888), pp. 41, 122.

10. Ibid., pp. 101, 350.

11. Ibid., p. 445.

12. Ibid., p. 350.

13. Ibid., p. 362.

14. Ibid., p. 96

15. Ibid., p. 58.

16. Ibid., p. 221.

17. Ibid., p. 102.

18. Ibid., pp. 232–35.

19. Gothard Wunberg, "Utopie und fin de siecle. Zur deutschen Literatur-kritik vor der Jahrhundertwende," *Deutsche Vierteljahrschrift für Literaturwissen-schaft und Geistesgeschichte* (Dec. 1969): 685–706. For the argument that a "crisis of consciousness," resulting from the fear of "modernity," characterized the Wilhelm-ian era, see Martin Doerry, *Übergangsmenschen* (München, Weinheim, 1986).

20. Hermann Conradi, "Ein Kandidat der Zukunft—Übergangsmensch," in Conradi, *Gesammelte Schriften*, I, ed. by Paul Sysmank und Werner Peters (München, G. Muller, 1911), p. 450.

21. The debt of the two thinkers to the Enlightenment is discussed in Peter Heller, "Marx und Nietzsche in ihren Verhaltnis zur Aufklarung," in Grimm and Hermand, *Karl Marx und Friedrich Nietzsche*, pp. 3–17. Their common features as well as their differences are viewed from the standpoint of "modernization" in Nancy Love, *Marx, Nietzsche and Modernity* (New York, Columbia University Press, 1966). See also James Miller, "Some Implications of Nietzsche's Thought for Marxism," *Telos* 37 (fall 1978): 22–41.

22. For the romantic roots of their thought, see Ernst Behlr, "Nietzsche, Marx und die deutsch Frühromantik," in Grimm and Hermand, *Karl Marx und Friedrich Nietzsche*, pp. 38–62. The romantic sources of Marxism are emphasized in Leonard P. Wessell, Jr., *Karl Marx, Romantic Irony and the Proletariat: The Mythopoetic Origins of Marxism* (Baton Rouge, Louisiana State University Press, 1979).

23. See M. H. Abrams, *Natural Supernaturalism* (New York, Norton, 1971). The "secularization" thesis developed by Abrams is challenged by Bernard Yack, *The Longing for Total Revolution* (Berkeley, University of California Press, 1992). Both Nietzsche and Marx, according to Yack, expressed a "longing for total revolu-tion" that arose out of the conviction of a number of late-eighteenth-century thinkers that contemporary social and economic changes were dehumanizing. For a utopian reading of Nietzsche, see H. Baier, "Das Paradies unter dem Schatten der Schwerter. Der Utopie des Zarathustra jenseits des Nihilismus," *Nietzsche-Studien* 13 (1984): 46–88; and Kurt Mueller-Vollmer, "Unzeitgemassheit. Die Struktur der Utopie bei Fichte, Marx, und Nietzsche," in Grimm and Hermand, *Karl Marx und Friedrich Nietzsche*, pp. 78–96.

24. For an account of the party's development at this time, see Vernon Lidtke, *The Outlawed Party* (Princeton, Princeton University Press, 1969).

25. For details, see Dirk H. Müller, *Idealismus und Revolution, Zur Opposition der jungen gegen den Sozialdemokratischen Parteivorstand, 1890 bis 1894* (Berlin, Colo-quium, 1975), pp. 46–109.

26. For Wille's role, see Kurt Sollmann, "Bruno Wille und die Sozialdemok-ratie. Zur politischeideologische Dimension," in Sollmann, *Literarsche Intelligenz*, pp. 85–127, and Sollmann, "Zur Ideologie intellectueller Opposition im begin-nenden Imperialismus am Beispiel Bruno Willes," in Gert Mattenklott und Klaus R. Scherpe, eds., *Positionen der literarischen Intelligenz zwischen bürgerlicher Reak-tion und Imperialismus* (Kronberg Ta., Scriptor, 1973), pp. 179–209.

27. Paul Ernst, "Gefahren des Marxismus," *Berliner Volks-Tribüne* (Aug. 9, 1890).

28. Conrad Schmidt to Friedrich Engels. June 25, 1890. Engels Correspondence, L5575, International Institute of Social History, Amsterdam.

29. Joseph Bloch to Friedrich Engels, Sept. 3, 1890. Ibid., L577.

30. The meeting is described in Müller, *Idealismus und Revolution*, pp. 61–64.

31. See Sollmann, "Bruno Wille," pp. 118–20.

32. The "Manifesto" is reprinted in Hans Müller, *Der Klassenkampf und die Sozialdemokratie. Zur Geschichte der 'Jungen,' der linken Opposition in der frühen SPD (1870–1890)* (Berlin, Druck und Verlagskooperative, 1969), p. 118. Reprint of the 1892 edition.

33. Paul Ernst, "Das Gebildete Proletariat in Deutschland," *Sozialistische Akademiker* (Apr. 1896): 238.

34. Franz Mehring, "Zur Philosophie und Poesie des Kapitalismus." This is the last chapter of Mehring's *Kapital und Presse* (Berlin, 1891). It is reprinted in Franz Mehring, *Werkauswahl*, III, ed. by Fritz J. Raddatz (Darmstadt, Sammlung Luchterhand, 1975), pp. 119–35.

35. Franz Mehring, "Nietzsche gegen den Sozialismus," *Neue Zeit* 15, no. 18 (1896–97): 545–49.

36. Franz Mehring, "Aesthetische Streifzuge," IX, "Friedrich Nietzsche," in Mehring, *Werkauswahl* III, p. 130. The essay was published in the *Neue Zeit* early in 1899.

37. Wolfgang Heine, "Erinnerungen." Unpublished manuscript in the Bundesarchiv. Coblenz.

38. Lily Braun, *Memorien einer Sozialistin*, I, Lehrjahr (Berlin, A. Langen, 1911). For her return to Nietzsche, see ibid., II, Kampfjahr, pp. 634–53.

39. The two articles appeared in *Die Gesellschaft* during 1891 and were published in book form, *Psychopathia Spiritualis. Friedrich Nietzsche und die Apostel der Zukunft* (Leipzig, W. Friedrich, 1892). Citations are from the book.

40. Ibid., pp. 86, 91–94.

41. See his essay "Aus dem Nachlass eines Lebenden," in Kurt Eisner, *Taggeist* (Berlin, J. Edelheim, 1901).

42. Frank Servaes, "Nietzsche und der Sozialismus," *Frei Bühne* 3 (1892): 85–82, 101–211.

43. Ibid., p. 88.

44. Ibid., p. 211.

45. Hermann Duncker, "Eine Philosophie für das Proletariat," *Sozialistische Monatshefte* I (July 1897): 405–7.

46. Gystrow, "Etwas über Nietzsche," and Hellpach, *Wirken in Wirren*, pp. 245–93.

47. Paul Ernst, "Das Moderne Drama," in Ernst, *Der Weg zur Form* (München, G. Muller, 1928), p. 64. The essay was published in 1898.

48. See Paul Ernst, *Friedrich Nietzsche* (Berlin, Gotz und Tetlaff, 1900).

49. Ernst's later sympathy for National Socialism is discussed in George L. Mosse, *Masses and Man* (New York, H. Fertig, 1980), pp. 80–83.

50. See Thomas, *Nietzsche in German Politics*, ch. 3; and Roger Fletcher, *Revisionism and Empire* (London, George Allen and Unwin, 1984), pp. 52–54, 83–84, 96–97.

51. Max Maurenbrecher, *Die Gebildeten und die Sozialdemokratie* (Leipzig, 1904), p. 18.

52. Ibid., pp. 19–21.

53. Max Maurenbrecher, *Das Leid. Eine Auseinandersetzung mit der Religion. Dem Ineinanderstromer in Karl Marx und Friderich Nietzsche gewidnet* (Jena, E. Dietrichs, 1912), pp. 136–37.

54. For Maurenbrecher's later development, see Thomas, *Nietzsche in German Politics*, pp. 46–47; and Stephen E. Anschheim, "After the Death of God: Varieties of Nietzschean Religion," *Nietzsche-Studien* 17 (1988): pp. 236–39.

55. For Nietzsche's influence in Britain, see David S. Thatcher, *Nietzsche in England, 1890–1914* (Toronto, University of Toronto Press, 1970); and Patrick Bridgwater, *Nietzsche in Anglosaxony* (Leicester, Leicester University Press, 1972).

56. See Stanley Pierson, *Marxism and the Origins of British Socialism* (Ithaca, N.Y., Cornell University Press, 1973), ch. 4.

57. See Stanley Pierson, *British Socialists* (Cambridge, Mass., Harvard University Press, 1979), pp. 102–6.

58. Dan Laurence, ed., *Collected Letters of George Bernard Shaw*, II (London, Dodd and Mead, 1972), p. 162.

59. Quoted in Thatcher, *Nietzsche in England*, p. 200.

60. *The Collected Works of George Bernard Shaw*, X, *Man and Superman* (New York, H. H. Wise, 1930), p. 198.

61. Thatcher, *Nietzsche in England*, p. 200.

62. George Bernard Shaw, *Major Barbara* (New York, Crofts Classics, 1971), pp. 5–7.

63. See Pierson, *British Socialists*, pp. 325–30.

64. Ibid., pp. 193–96. See also the discussion of Orage in Thatcher, *Nietzsche in England*, pp. 219–68.

65. Orage, *Nietzsche in Outline and Aphorism* (London, T. N. Foulis, 1907), pp. 20, 47, 89, 44.

66. Edwin Muir, *An Autobiography* (London, W. Sloane Associates, 1954), p. 26.

67. See the account of Sorel's early years in John Stanley, *The Sociology of Virtue* (Berkeley, University of California Press, 1981), pp. 1–75.

68. Sorel cites Nietzsche in his preface to S. Merlino, *Formes et essence du socialsme*, published in 1898. Much of the preface has been translated and reprinted in Richard Vernon, *Commitment and Change: Georges Sorel and the Idea of Revolution* (Toronto, University of Toronto Press, 1978), pp. 81–92.

69. Several of the relevant essays, written at the turn of the century, can be found in John Stanley, *From Georges Sorel: Essays in Socialism and Philosophy*, tr. by John and Charlotte Stanley (New York, Oxford University Press, 1976), pp. 7–75. Sorel discusses Marx's failure to deal with religion and the resulting gaps in his theory in "Betrachtungen über die materialistische Geschichtsauffassung," *Sozialistische Monatshefte* 2 (July 1898): 316–22.

70. Edward Shils, "Introduction" to Georges Sorel, *Reflections on Violence*, tr. by T. E. Hume and J. Roth (New York, Collier Books, 1961), p. 15.

71. Ibid., pp. 230–33. For a comparison of the views of Nietzsche and Sorel of

the mythic, see Hans Barth, *Masse und Mythos. Die Theorie der Gewalt: Georges Sorel* (Hamburg, Rowohlt, 1959), pp. 84–86. See also David Gross, "Myth and Symbol in Georges Sorel," in Seymour Drescher, David Sabean, and Allan Sharlin, eds., *Political Symbolism in Modern Europe: Essays in Honor of George L. Mosse* (London, Transaction Books, 1982), pp. 100–117.

72. See the discussion in J. R. Jennings, *Georges Sorel* (London, Macmillan, 1985), pp. 154–55.

73. Sorel, *Reflections*, p. 127.

74. This point is made in F. F. Ridley, *Revolutionary Syndicalism in France* (Cambridge, Cambridge University Press, 1970), pp. 159–63.

75. Jennings, *Sorel*, pp. 143–46, 155–58.

76. The relationship between Sorel and Berth is discussed in Paul Mazgaj, *The Action Francaise and Revolutionary Syndicalism* (Chapel Hill, University of North Carolina Press, 1979), pp. 123–24. Also see Zeev Sternhell, *Neither Right nor Left: Fascist Ideology in France*, tr. by David Maisel (Berkeley, University of California Press, 1986), pp. 86–90.

77. Edourd Berth, *Les Méfaits des Intellectuals* (Paris, Riviera, 1914), p. 13.

78. Ibid., pp. 54–56, 182, 265.

79. Ibid., p. 54.

80. Sorel's development after 1908 is discussed in Stanley, *Sociology of Virtue*, ch. 10; and Mazgaj, *Action Francaise*, pp. 115–27. The new emphasis on leadership is noted in Jack J. Roth, *The Cult of Violence: Sorel and the Sorelians* (Berkeley, University of California Press, 1980), p. 110.

81. Sorel's relationship to the nationalistic movement in Italy, and to Mussolini, is discussed most fully in ibid., pp. 92–94, 128–39, 183. For Sorel's view of Lenin and the Bolsheviks, see ibid., chs. 8, 9, and 10.

82. See Jennings, *Sorel*, pp. 164–67.

83. Sorel's tribute, "In Defense of Lenin," was written in 1918 and is included as an appendix in the fourth edition of *Reflections on Violence*, published in 1919. See the edition cited above, pp. 277–86.

84. Roth, *Cult of Violence*, p. 161.

85. Ernst Nolte, "Marx und Nietzsche in Sozialismus des Jungen Mussolini," *Historische Zeitschrift* 191 (Oct. 1960): 249–335. The quotation can be found on p. 335.

86. Ibid., p. 310.

87. See, for example, Dennis Mack Smith, *Mussolini* (New York, Knopf, 1982), p. 3.

88. Mussolini's early essay on Nietzsche is discussed in Walter Adamson, "Modernism and Fascism: The Politics of Culture in Italy. 1903–1922," *American Historical Review* 95 (Apr. 1980): 385–86.

89. The strength of Mussolini's Marxist convictions is emphasized in the Nolte essay. See also A. James Gregor, *Young Mussolini and the Intellectual Origins of Fascism* (Berkeley, University of California Press, 1979), pp. 37–43.

90. Ibid., ch. 3.

91. This aspect of Mussolini's thought and its relationship to the intellectuals gathered around the journal *La Voce* is emphasized in articles by Walter Adamson:

"Modernism and Fascism," noted above; "The Language of Opposition in Early Twentieth Century Italy: Rhetorical Continuities between Pre-war Florentine Avant-gardism and Mussolini's Fascism," *Journal of Modern History* 34 (Mar. 1992): 22–51, and "Fascism and Culture: Avant-Gardes and Secular Religion in the Italian Case," *Journal of Contemporary History* 24 (July 1989): 411–35.

92. Mussolini's borrowings from such thinkers as Bergson, Peguy, and James are discussed in Nolte, "Marx und Nietzsche," pp. 278, 324–25.

93. See James Edward Miller, *From Elite to Mass Politics, Italian Socialism in the Giolittian Era: 1900–1914* (Kent, Ohio, Kent State University Press, 1990).

94. See Richard Bosworth, *Italy and the Approach of the First World War* (London, St. Martin's Press, 1983), pp. 26–27. See also Adrian Lyttelton, *The Seizure of Power: Fascism in Italy, 1919–1929* (Princeton, Princeton University Press, 1987), pp. 1–44.

95. For details, see Gregor, *Young Mussolini*, pp. 129–34.

96. His letter to Giuseppi Prezzolini, editor of *La Voce*, in July 1912, is quoted at length in Emilio Gentile, *Il mito dello stato nuovo* (Bari, Laterza, 1982), p. 114.

97. His leadership in these years is discussed in Paul Piccone, *Italian Marxism* (Berkeley, University of California Press, 1983), pp. 114–17.

98. Quoted in Domenico Settembrini, "Mussolini and the Legacy of Revolutionary Socialism," *Journal of Contemporary History* 11 (Oct. 1976): 247.

99. The fullest account in English is Gregor, *Young Mussolini*, chs. 7, 8, 9, and 10.

100. See Piero Melograni, "The Cult of the Duce in Mussolini's Italy," *Journal of Contemporary History* 11 (Oct. 1976): 223; and Emilio Gentile, "Fascism as Political Religion," *Journal of Contemporary History* 25 (May–June 1990): 229–52.

101. See Michael Ledeen, *Universal Fascism* (New York, H. Fertig, 1972), pp. 157–68. Ledeen develops the view, advanced by Renzo De Felice, that the Fascist regime should be distinguished from the Fascist movement, which carried over elements of revolutionary socialism. For the controversy generated by De Felice's views, see Borden W. Painter, Jr., "Renzio De Felice and the Historiography of Italian Fascism," *American Historical Review* 95 (Apr. 1990): 390–406.

102. Settembrini, "Mussolini and the Legacy of Revolutionary Socialism," p. 240. For a comparison of Mussolini and Lenin, see pp. 247–57.

103. Nicolas Berdyaev, *Dream and Reality: An Essay in Autobiography*, tr. by Katharine Lampert (New York, Macmillan, 1962), pp. 119–20. See also his *Origins of Russian Communism*, tr. by R. M. French (Ann Arbor, University of Michigan Press, 1948), pp. 84–92.

104. Berdyaev, *Dream and Reality*, p. 124.

105. See Christopher Read, *Religion, Revolution, and the Russian Intelligentsia: 1900–1912* (Totowa, N.J., Barnes and Noble, 1979), pp. 2–39.

106. The term "Nietzschean Marxists" is employed by George L. Kline in his book, *Religion and Anti-Religious Thought in Russia* (Chicago, Chicago University Press, 1968), pp. 4–6. See also his essay "Nietzschean Marxists in Russia," in Frederick Adelmann, *Demythologizing Marxism* (Chestnut Hill, Mass., Boston College Press, 1969), pp. 166–83.

107. Quoted in Kline, *Religious and Anti-Religious Thought*, pp. 106–7, 122. See

also A. L. Tait, "Lunacharsky: A 'Nietzschean Marxist'?" in Bernice Glatzen Rosenthal, ed., *Nietzsche in Russia* (Princeton, Princeton University Press, 1986), pp. 276–310; and Jutta Scherrer, "La Crise de L'Intelligentsia Marxists avant 1914: A. V. Lunacarskij et le Bogostroitel'stvo," *Revue des Etudes Slaves* 51, nos. 1–2 (1978): 297–315.

108. See Mary Louise Loe, "Gorky and Nietzsche: The Quest for a Russian Superman"; and Zenovia A. Sochor, "A. A. Bogdanov: In Search of Cultural Liberation," in Rosenthal, *Nietzsche in Russia*, chs. 11, 13.

109. See the account in Bertram D. Wolfe, *Three Who Made a Revolution* (Boston, Beacon Press, 1948), pp. 500–508.

110. Adam Ulam, *Lenin and the Bolsheviks* (London, Seeker and Warburg, 1966), pp. 271–74.

111. Lenin, "Materialism and Empiro-criticism," in *Collected Works*, 14 (Moscow, Foreign Language Publishing House, 1962), p. 329.

112. Ibid., pp. 126, 187.

113. Only Bogdanov was expelled from the Bolsheviks. For his continuing efforts on behalf of the cultural hegemony of the proletariat, see Jutta Scherrer, "Pour l'hegemonie culturelle du proletariat aux origines historiques du concept et de la vision de la culture proletarienne," in Marc Ferro and Sheila Fitzpatrik, eds., *Culture and Revolution* (Paris, Ecole des hautes études en sciences sociales, 1989), pp. 11–23.

114. See Bernice Rosenthal's introduction to *Nietzsche in Russia*, pp. 16–17.

115. Read, *Religion, Revolution*, p. 56.

116. The roles of the two men are discussed in Nina Tumarkin, *Lenin Lives: The Lenin Cult in Russia* (Cambridge, Mass., Harvard University Press, 1983), pp. 180–83, 200–203.

Chapter 2: Henri De Man

1. First published in Germany in 1926, *Zur Psychologie des Sozialismus* (Jena, Dietrichs) was soon translated into French and English and a number of other languages. I will cite from the English edition, translated by Eden and Cedar Paul (London, George Allen and Unwin, 1928). It has been reprinted under the title *The Psychology of Marxist Socialism* (New Brunswick, N.J., Transaction, 1985) with a critical introduction by Peter J. Steinburger.

2. The first book-length study of De Man, by Adriaan M. Van Peski, was completed in 1960. It did not find a publisher until 1969, but Van Peski summarized his interpretation in an article, "Hendrik De Man. Ein Wille zum Sozialismus," in the *Hamburger Jahrbuch für Wirtschafts-und Gesellschaftspolitik* (1963), which also appeared in pamphlet form. In 1966, two studies of De Man were published: Peter Dodge, *Beyond Marxism: The Faith and Works of Hendrik De Man* (The Hague, Martinus Nijhoff, 1966); and Pierette Rongere, "L'Apport de Henri De Man au socialisme Contemporain," in Robert Reibel et Pierrette Rongere, *Socialisme et Éthique* (Paris, Presses Universitaires de France, 1966). Both present favorable accounts of De Man's socialist career. The sharpest criticism came from Zeev Sternhell, *Neither Right nor Left: Fascist Ideology in France*, tr. by David Maisel (Berkeley, University of California Press, 1986), who includes De Man among those Euro-

pean thinkers who, having given an idealistic and ethical turn to socialism, became fascists. The book was published in France in 1983. The studies by Michel Brelaz, *Henri De Man. Une autre idée du socialisme* (Geneva, Éditions des Antipodes, 1985), and *Léopold III et Henri De Man* (Geneva, Éditions des Antipodes, 1988), reject Sternhell's interpretation, as does Dan White in his *Lost Comrades: Socialism of the Front Generation* (Cambridge, Mass., Harvard University Press, 1992). De Man is also treated favorably in Karsten Oschmann, *Über Hendrik De Man. Marxismus, Plansozialismus und Kollaboration. Ein Grenzganger in der Zwischenkriegzeit* (Dissertation, Albert Ludwigs Universität zu Freiburg, 1987). I have not read Mieke Claeys-Van Haegendoren, *Hendrik de Man: Een Biographic* (Antwerp, De Nederlandische Boekhandel, 1972). See also the important collection of essays, Ivo Rens, ed., *Sur l'oeuvre d'Henri De Man. Rapports. Revue européenne des sciences et Cahiers Vilfredo Pareto*, 12, no. 31 (1974); Peter Dodge's anthology, *A Documentary Study of Henri De Man, Socialist Critic of Marxism* (Princeton, Princeton University Press, 1979); and the *Bulletin de l'Associations pour l'Étude de l'Oeuvre d'Henri De Man*, published almost annually from 1974 (Geneva, Switzerland).

3. See Henry De Man, *The Remaking of a Mind* (New York, Scribner's, 1919), De Man, *Après Coup* (Brussels, Toison d'Or, 1941), De Man, *Cavalier Seul* (Geneva, Cheval Aile, 1948), and De Man, *Gegen den Strom* (Stuttgart, Deutsche Verlags-Anstalt, 1953).

4. Thus Dodge writes of De Man's "life long dedication to a radical cause in the name of bourgeois values." Dodge, *Beyond Marxism*, p. 7.

5. The concept of the "bourgeoisie" has become so amorphous and fluid in modern historical writing as to raise questions about its usefulness. But no term conveys so well, as I will demonstrate, De Man's character and his values. Moreover, he would increasingly acknowledge the "bourgeois" sources and the bourgeois nature of his socialist vision.

6. De Man, *Gegen den Strom*, p. 7.

7. Serge Noiret, "Political Parties and the Political system in Belgium before Federalism, 1830–1980," *European History Quarterly* (Jan. 1994): 103.

8. Recent studies of the European bourgeoisie have emphasized its diversity, its internal tensions, and its regional and national variations. See Jurgen Kocka and Allen Mitchell, eds. *Bourgeois Society in Nineteenth Century Europe* (Oxford, Berg, 1993); Pamela M. Pilbean, *The Middle Class in Europe: 1789–1914* (London, Macmillan, 1990); and David Blackbourn and Richard Evans, eds., *The German Bourgeoisie* (London, Routledge, 1991). For a full discussion of the concept of the bourgeois, see Peter Gay, *The Bourgeois Experience: Victoria to Freud—Education of the Senses* (New York, Oxford University Press, 1984), pp. 17–44, 469–76.

9. The rejection of the established bourgeois way of life by many of "the best, the most articulate, the most creative members" of its affluent sections was a feature of Belgium society during the 1880s. They were moved not by social or political feelings; their opposition to the "vulgarity of the bourgeoisie" was "individualistic and aesthetic." But a few were converted to socialism during the 1890s. E. H. Kossmann, *The Low Countries, 1780–1940* (Oxford, Clarendon Press, 1978), pp. 330–31. For an overview of this phenomenon, see Roland Nitsche, *Der Hässliche Bürger* (Gutersloh, Bertelsmann, 1969).

10. For the development of the notion of the self-sufficient individual, the "modern ideology" of the West, together with its national refractions and reactions, see Louis Dumont, *Essays on Individualism: Modern Ideology in Anthropological Perspective* (Chicago, University of Chicago Press, 1986). For a discussion of the idea of autonomy as "a central component of the modern European bourgeois code of ethics," see Joel Whitebook, "Saving the Subject: Modernity and the Problem of the Autonomous Individual," *Telos* 50 (winter 1981–82): 79–102. Writing from a psychoanalytical perspective, in which Freud is seen as developing the Kantian ideals of autonomy and maturity, Whitebook defends those ideals against the contemporary demolitions of the subject by postmodernists. Through his attempt to reconcile psychoanalysis and critical theory, he points to a postbourgeois and "post conventional" notion of the subject. See Joel Whitebook, *Perversion and Utopia: A Study in Psychoanalysis and Critical Theory* (Cambridge, M.I.T. Press, 1995), esp. pp. 118–21; 257–62. For a strictly philosophical treatment of the subject, see J. B. Schneewind, *The Invention of Autonomy* (New York, Cambridge University Press, 1998).

11. De Man, *Cavalier seul*, p. 14.

12. De Man, *Gegen den Strom*, p. 11.

13. See Maxine Sztejnberg, "La Fondation du parti ouvrier belge et les ralliement de la classe ouvriére l'action politique, 1882–1886," *International Review of Social History* (1963): 198–215.

14. Robert Wuthrow, *Communities of Discourse* (Cambridge, Mass., Harvard University Press, 1989), has argued that strong socialist parties arose in Belgium and Germany because the liberal parties were weak and incapable of appealing effectively to the working class. See esp. pp. 446–56. A similar "structuralist argument" is presented in Gregory M. Luebbart, *Liberalism, Fascism, or Social Democracy* (New York, Oxford University Press, 1991), see pp. 140–42, and 305–9.

15. Kossmann, *Low Countries*, pp. 476–77.

16. De Man, *Gegen den Strom*, p. 55.

17. Ibid., p. 56.

18. Ibid., p. 57.

19. Ibid., p. 59.

20. Ibid.

21. Ibid., p. 62.

22. Ibid., pp. 64–65.

23. Ibid., p. 67.

24. Ibid., p. 73.

25. Ibid., pp. 83–84.

26. De Man, *Cavalier Seul*, p. 77. For a contemporary assessment of the movement, see Henri Charriaut, *La Belgique moderne* (Paris, Biblioteque de Philosophie Scientifique, 1910), pp. 242–51.

27. De Man, *Cavalier Seul*, p. 83.

28. De Man, *Remaking of a Mind*, p. 76.

29. Ibid., pp. 271–89.

30. De Man, *Psychology of Socialism*, p. 112.

31. De Man, *Cavalier Seul*, p. 123.

32. Ibid., pp. 130–31.

33. Ibid., pp. 133–34. The regimen at the school is described by Jules Roland, "Quelques souvenirs sur Henri De Man," *Bulletin* 6 (June 1977): 18–25.

34. Oschmann, *Über Hendrik De Man*, p. 116.

35. See the essay on "Workers Control," translated and reprinted in Dodge, *A Documentary Study*, pp. 100–134.

36. The development of the Academy is discussed in Otto Antrick, *Die Akademie der Arbeit in der Universität Frankfurt A.M.* (Darnstadt, Edmund Roether, 1966).

37. De Man, *Psychology of Socialism*, p. 11.

38. Ibid., p. 329.

39. Madeleine Grawicz, "Henri De Man et La Psychologie Social," in Rens, *Sur l'Oeuvre d'Henri de Man*, p. 76.

40. De Man, *Psychology*, p. 469.

41. Ibid., pp. 26–27.

42. Ibid., p. 186.

43. Ibid., p. 30.

44. Ibid., p. 334.

45. Ibid., p. 49.

46. Ibid., p. 39.

47. Ibid., p. 45.

48. Ibid., pp. 133–36.

49. Ibid., p. 142

50. Ibid., p. 118.

51. Ibid., p. 477.

52. Ibid., p. 35.

53. Developed at length in chs. 12, 13, and 14 of the *Psychology*.

54. Ibid., pp. 13–16.

55. Ibid., p. 20.

56. See esp. ch. 7, "Intellectuals and the State," pp. 195–218.

57. Ibid., p. 222.

58. Ibid., p. 224.

59. Ibid., p. 490.

60. Ibid., p. 172.

61. Ibid., p. 465.

62. Ibid., p. 267.

63. Ibid., p. 500.

64. Ibid., p. 228.

65. See Brelaz, *Henri De Man*, p. 160. The fullest assessment and critique of the *Psychology* can be found in Oschmann, *Über Hendrik De Man*, pp. 133–223. See also Grawicz, "Henri De Man," pp. 75–102, and Pierre Naville, *Psychologie, Marxisme, Materialisme* (Paris, M. Riviere, 1946).

66. De Man, *Psychology*, p. 469.

67. For a critique of De Man's treatment of motives, see Oschmann, *Über Hendrik De Man*, pp. 303–17.

68. De Man, *Psychology*, p. 160.

69. Ibid., p. 508.

70. Ibid., p. 478.

71. Ibid., p. 501. Nevertheless, De Man undertook a vigorous campaign by means of advertising and lectures to promote the book. See Oschmann, *Über Hendrik De Man*, pp. 144–47.

72. De Man, *Psychology*, p. 8.

73. For the history of the organization, see Franz Walter, *Sozialistische Akademiker und Intellektuellen in der Weimar Republik* (Bonn, Dietz, 1990), pp. 89–130. See also Gustav Auernheimer, *"Genosse Herr Doktor": Zur Rolle von Akademikern in der deutschen Sozialdemokratie, 1892–1933* (Giessen, Focus, 1985), pp. 99–156.

74. De Man, *Gegen den Strom*, p. 194.

75. See Hugo Marx, *Werdegang eine jüdischer Staatsanwalt und Richters in Baden. 1892–1933* (Villigen, Neckar, 1965), pp. 191–97.

76. De Man, *Gegen den Strom*, p. 194.

77. Hendrik De Man, *Die Intellektuellen und des Sozialismus* (Jena 1926).

78. For an account of the Dresden conference and the problem of the intellectuals, see Stanley Pierson, *Marxist Intellectuals and the Working Class Mentality in Germany, 1887–1912* (Cambridge, Mass., Harvard University Press, 1993), pp. 162–76.

79. De Man, *Die Intellektuellen*, p. 6.

80. Ibid., p. 23.

81. De Man, *Gegen den Strom*, p. 195.

82. For an account of the conference, see Walter, *Sozialistische Akademiker*, pp. 94–98.

83. De Man, *Gegen den Strom*, p. 195.

84. Walter, *Sozialistische Akademiker*, pp. 102–4.

85. See Hugo Marx, "Ist eine Organisation der Intellektuellen in der Sozialdemokratie möglich?" in *Neue Blätter für den Sozialismus* (Oct. 1931): 512–17. See also the judgment of August Winkler, *Der Schein der Normalität. Arbeiter und Arbeiterbewegung in der Weimarer Republik. 1924 bis 1920* (Berlin, Dietz, 1985), pp. 709–11.

86. Brelaz, *Henri De Man*, p. 407.

87. See Ulrich Linse, "Hochschulrevolution Zur Ideologie und Praxis sozialistischer deutscher Studengruppen während der deutschen Revolutionzeit 1918–1919," *Archiv für Sozialgeschichte* (1974): 1–114.

88. See Henri De Man, *L'Idée Socialiste*, tr. from the German by H. Corbin and A. Kojevnikov (Paris, Bernard Grasset, 1935), pp. 269–74.

89. Walter, *Sozialistische Akademiker*, p. 27.

90. Franz Osterroth, "Der Hofgeismarkreis der Jung sozialisten," *Archiv für Sozialgeschichte* (1964): 525–69.

91. Ibid., p. 549. See also De Man's criticism of the "romantic nationalism" of the Hofgeismar group in *Die Tat* (Mar. 1924): 287–93.

92. August Rathmann, *Ein Arbeiterleben. Erinnerungen an Weimar und danach* (Wupertal, Peter Hammer, 1983), pp. 118–21.

93. See De Man's memorandum, reprinted in Martin Martiny, "Die Ent-

stehung und Politische Bedeutung der 'Neue Blätter für den Sozialismus' und ihren Freudeskreisen," *Vierteljahrsheft für Zeitgeschichte* 3 (1977): 391–96.

94. For an overview of the religious socialists in Germany, see Renate Breipahl, *Religiösen Sozialismus und bürgerliches Geschichtsbewussentsein zur Zeit der Weimarer Republik* (Zurich, Theologischer Verlag, 1971), pp. 113–64; and Johannes Kandel, "Schwarzes Kreuz auf roten Grund: Amerkungen zum Religiösen Sozialismus in der Weimerer Republik," in Horst Heimann and Thomas Meyer, eds., *Reformsozialismus und Sozialdemokratie* (Bonn, Dietz, 1982), pp. 59–74.

95. See Breipahl, *Religiösen Sozialismus*, pp. 59–64, 167–224; and the introduction by Jean Richard in Paul Tillich, *Christianisme et Socialisme. Ecrits Socialistes allemands* (1919–31), tr. by Nicole Grondin and Lucien Pelletier (Paris, Les Presses de l'Universite Laval, 1992), pp. xi–xc.

96. See Tillich's autobiographical reflections in Charles Kegley and Robert Bretall, eds., *The Theology of Paul Tillich* (New York, Macmillan, 1952), pp. 1–21.

97. Several of the essays from this period are reprinted in Paul Tillich, *The Protestant Era* (Chicago, University of Chicago Press, 1948) and *Political Expectations* (New York, Harper and Row, 1971).

98. Adrian Thatcher, *The Ontology of Paul Tillich* (Oxford, Oxford University Press, 1978).

99. Tillich's review of De Man's *Psychology* appeared in the *Blätter für religiösen Sozialismus* in 1927. It is translated and reprinted in Tillich, *Christianisme et Socialisme*, pp. 281–85.

100. Paul Tillich, "Les Principes fondamentaux du Socialisme Religioux," ibid., p. 209.

101. Ibid.

102. Paul Tillich, "Kairos," in *Protestant Era*, p. 46.

103. Hugo Sinzheimer, "Eröffung," in *Sozialismus aus den Glauben. Verhandlungen der sozialistischen Tagung in Heppenheim a.b. Pfingstwoche 1928* (Leipzig, Hotapfel, 1929), pp. 9–12.

104. Ibid., pp. 13–63.

105. Ibid., pp. 37–38.

106. Ibid., p. 43.

107. Ibid., p. 47.

108. Ibid., p. 46.

109. Ibid., pp. 64–89.

110. Ibid., pp. 90–94, 217–19.

111. Ibid., pp. 110–15.

112. Ibid., pp. 147–48.

113. Quoted in Brelaz, *Henri De Man*, pp. 431–32.

114. De Man, *Cavalier seul*, p. 154.

115. Ibid., p. 140.

116. Mary Gilbert, quoted in Brelaz, *Henri De Man*, p. 517.

117. See Franz Grosse, "Henri De Man et Les Sociaux-Democrats Allemands Avant 1933," in Rens, *Sur l'oeuvre d'Henri De Man*, pp. 121–30.

118. In a letter to Vandervelde in 1928 De Man confessed that he was still "at

heart an anarchist, enamoured with freedom and self-determination." Quoted by Michel Brelaz, "Pacifisme et Internationalisme dans Le Premiere Partie de L'Oeuvre D'Henri De Man (1902–1941)," ibid., p. 218.

119. For details, see Martiny, "Die Entstehung," pp. 391–96.

120. See Woodruff D. Smith, "The Mierendorff Group and the Modernization of German Social Democratic Politics 1928–1933," *Politics and Society* 1 (1973): 109–29.

121. See Hendrik De Man, "Verbürgerliche des Proletariats," *Neue Blätter für den Sozialismus* (Mar. 1930): 106–18. The essay is translated and reprinted in Dodge, *Documentary Study*, pp. 220–37.

122. See Wolfgang Schivelbusch, *Intellektuellendämmerung. Zur Lage der Frankfurter Intelligenz in den zwanziger Jahren* (Frankfurt A.M., Insel, 1982); and Almut Todorow, "Die 'Frankfurter Zeitung' als intellektuelles Forum der Weimarer Republik," in Manfred Gangl and Helene Roussel, eds., *Les Intellectuels et L'état sous La Republique De Weimar* (Paris, Éditions de la Maison des Sciences de L'Homme, 1993), pp. 147–58.

123. See Martin Jay, *The Dialectical Imagination. A History of the Frankfurt School and the Institute of Social Research, 1923–1950* (Boston, Little, Brown and Co., 1973), pp. 3–25; and Rolf Wiggershaus, *The Frankfurt School, Its History, Theories, and Political Significance*, tr. by Michael Robertson (Cambridge, Mass., Polity Press, 1994), pp. 9–36.

124. De Man's relationship to the Institute is discussed in Brelaz, *Henri De Man*, pp. 557–70. See also Gerd-Rainer Horn, *European Socialists Respond to Fascism, Ideology, Activism, and Contingency in the 1920s* (New York, Oxford University Press, 1996), p. 77.

125. De Man, *Gegen den Strom*, pp. 197–98.

126. Quoted in De Man, *Cavalier seul*, p. 144.

127. Hendrik De Man, *Der Kampf um die Arbeitsfreude* (Jena, Dietrichs, 1927). The English edition, *Joy in Work*, tr. by Eden and Cedar Paul, was published by Allen and Unwin in 1929. A selection from the book has been reprinted in Dodge, *Documentary Study*, pp. 180–229.

128. See the discussion in Joan Campbell, *Joy in Work: German Work. The National Debate, 1800–1945* (Princeton, Princeton University Press, 1989), pp. 178–85.

129. De Man, "Joy in Work," in Dodge, *Documentary Study*, p. 185.

130. Ibid., p. 218.

131. Ibid., p. 198.

132. Gladys Meyer, *The Magic Circle* (New York, Knopf, 1944), p. 93.

133. See the essay, "Le Socialisme et la Cultur," in Henri De Man, *Le Socialisme Costructif*, tr. from the German by L. G. Herbert (Paris, Librairie Felix Alcan, 1933), pp. 101–54.

134. Ibid., p. 149.

135. De Man's rationalistic bent is emphasized in Oschmann, *Über Hendrik De Man*, pp. 222–23. In a radio symposium in 1932, which included Paul Tillich and Gustav Radbruch, De Man criticized the "superficial rationalism" of the Enlightenment in favor of an older rationalism wedded to traditional moral beliefs. See

"Der Sozialismus und die geistige Lage der Gegenwart," in *Neue Blätter für den Sozialismus* (Jan. 1932): 8–18.

136. De Man, "Socialisme et la Capitalisme," in *Socialisme Constructif*, pp. 154–98.

137. Franz Borkenau, quoted by Manfred Gangl, "Mythos der Gewalt und Gewalt des Mythos. Georges Sorels Einfluss auf rechte und linke Intellektuelle der Weimarer Republik," in Manfred Gangl and Gerard Raulet, eds., *Intellektuellendiskurse in der Weimarer Republik* (Frankfurt, Campus, 1994), p. 189.

138. De Man, "Le Socialisme et le Nationalisme-fasciste," in *Socialisme Constructif*, pp. 199–248.

139. Ibid., pp. 208–9.

140. Ibid., p. 212.

141. The text is reprinted in Brelaz, *Henri De Man*, pp. 592–95.

142. For the background, see Wilfried van der Will and Rob Burns, eds., *Arbeiterkulturbewegung in der Weimarer Republik. Texte-Dokuments-Bilder* (Frankfurt, A.M., Ulstein, 1982) pp. 176–270. A pageant held in Frankfurt two years earlier centered on Marx and his teachings. For an account, see W. L. Guttsman, *Worker's Culture in Weimar Germany: Between Tradition and Commitment* (New York, Berg, 1990), p. 249. See also George L. Mosse, *The Nationalization of the Masses: Political Symbolism and Mass Movements in Germany from the Napoleonic Wars through the Third Reich* (Ithaca, N.Y., Cornell University Press, 1991), pp. 161–82.

143. See the description in Brelaz, *Henri De Man*, pp. 583–96; and Meyer, *Magic Circle*, pp. 168–70.

144. Quoted in Brelaz, *Henri De Man*, pp. 591–92.

145. Quoted in Meyer, *Magic Circle*, p. 179.

146. For an excellent account of the development of the Social Democratic Party in these years, see Donna Harsch, *German Social Democracy and the Rise of Nazism* (Chapel Hill, University of North Carolina Press, 1993).

147. De Man, *L'Idée Socialiste*, p. 57. The extent to which De Man idealized Flemish society during the Middle Ages can be seen by comparing his account with that in the recent study by David Nicholas, *Medieval Flanders* (London, Longmans, 1992). See esp. pp. 110–23, 132–39, and 180–86.

148. De Man, *L'Idée Socialiste*, p. 239.

149. See his review of the Manuscripts in *Das Kampf* (May, June, 1933). The *Bulletin* 8 (Dec. 1978), is largely devoted to De Man's treatment of the Manuscripts.

150. De Man, *L'Idée Socialiste*, p. 445. Denis de Rougement noted his surprise at finding that De Man's view of happiness was still essentially bourgeois. See Denis de Rougement, *Journal d'une époque, 1926–1946* (Paris, Gallimard, 1968), p. 228.

151. De Man, *L'Idée Socialiste*, p. 228.

152. Ibid., p. 491.

153. Ibid., p. 493.

154. Ibid., p. 505.

155. Ibid., p. 500.

156. The Plan and its sources are discussed most fully in Brelaz, *Henri De Man*,

chs. 21, 22. See also Mietke Claeys van Haegendoren, "La Pratique du Planisme en Belgique," in Rens, *Sur l'oeuvre d'Henri De Man*, pp. 131–42; Erik Hansen, "Hendrik De Man and the Theoretical Foundations of Economic Planning: The Belgium Experience, 1933–1940," *European Studies Review* (Apr. 1978): 234–58; Dick Pels, "Hendrik De Man and the Ideology of Planisme," *Bulletin* 14 (May 1987): 31–51; and Horn, *European Socialists*, pp. 80–82.

157. Pels, "Hendrik De Man," p. 38.

158. Ibid., p. 41.

159. De Man, *L'Idée Socialiste*, pp. 523–25.

160. Conditions in Belgium at this time are described in Kossmann, *Low Countries*, p. 658.

161. Brelaz, *Henri De Man*, p. 640.

162. Quoted in Meyer, *Magic Circle*, p. 178.

163. The Office is described by G. Le Franc, "Une heure avec Henri De Man," *Bulletin* 2 (Dec. 1974): 3–19.

164. The program that was adopted is reprinted in Dodge, *Documentary Study*, pp. 289–99. The excitement generated by De Man is described in Pels, "Hendrik De Man."

165. Oschmann, *Über Hendrik De Man*, p. 386.

166. For an account of the strategy and the campaign, see ibid., pp. 410–62; and Horn, *European Socialists*, pp. 82–84.

167. Oschmann, *Über Hendrik De Man*, pp. 408–9.

168. De Man presented his corporatist views at a conference in France in the summer of 1934. See the "Theses of Potigny," reprinted in Dodge, *Documentary Study*, pp. 300–305.

169. Oschmann, *Über Henri De Man*, p. 420.

170. See Reibel and Rongere, *Socialisme et Éthique*, pp. 96–97.

171. Paul-Henri Spaak, *Combats Inachevés* (Paris, Fayard, 1969), pp. 25–26.

172. Dodge, *Beyond Marxism*, p. 1170. See also the negative assessment in Oschmann, *Über Hendrik De Man*, pp. 403–9. Claeys van Haegendoren writes: "He never asked whether his intransigence and his feeling of superiority had not contributed to the hostility he aroused ... even, and especially, among his socialist colleagues." "La Pratique du Planisme," p. 242.

173. Henri De Man, *Aprés Coup*, pp. 280–81.

174. Ibid., pp. 252–56.

175. Ibid., pp. 293–94.

176. De Man, *Cavalier seul*, p. 298.

177. De Man, *Aprés Coup*, pp. 299–310.

178. For comparisons of Spaak and De Man as politicians, see Brelaz, *Leopold III et Henri De Man* (Geneve, Éditions des Antipodes, 1988), pp. 186–89; and Oschmann, *Über Hendrik De Man*, p. 429.

179. See the discussion in Dodge, *Beyond Marxism*, pp. 175–88.

180. See D. O. Kieft, *Belgium Returns to Neutrality* (London, Oxford University Press, 1972), pp. 102–14.

181. See Brelaz, *Leopold III et Henri De Man*, p. 21; and De Man's "Reflexions sur la monarchie constitutionelle," written in 1938 and reprinted in Michel Brelaz,

ed., *Henri De Man. Le 'Dossier Leopold III' et Autres Documents sur La Period de la Seconde Guerre Mondiale* (Geneva, Éditions des Antipodes, 1987), pp. 42–50.

182. For a balanced account of the dispute, see Jean Vanwelkenhuyzen, *Quand Les Cheminse Separaent. Aux sources de la question royale* (Paris, Éditions Duculot, 1988).

183. De Man's "Programme du 19 Juin, 1940," is reprinted in Brelaz, *Henri De Man, Le 'Dossier,'* pp. 173–80. De Man's response to the German conquest is examined against the background of the later controversy surrounding his nephew, Paul De Man, in Dick Pels, "Treason of the Intellectuals: Paul De Man and Hendrik De Man," *Theory, Culture, and Society* (Feb. 1981): 21–56.

184. The "Manifesto" is reprinted in Dodge, *Documentary Study*, pp. 324–28. The authoritarian turn in De Man's thought is emphasized in Herman Balthazar, "Henri De Man dans La 'Revolution Avorte,'" in Rens, *Sur l'Oeuvre d'Henri De Man*, pp. 197–215. See esp. pp. 206–8. Oschmann sees a fundamental break in De Man's development at this point. "His writings at that time had little to do with his previous socialist thought." *Über Hendrik de Man*, p. 583.

185. See Brelaz, *Leopold III et Henri De Man*, pp. 161–248; and Oschmann, *Über Hendrik De Man*, pp. 530–40.

186. See De Man's account in *Cavalier seul*, pp. 264–66, and *Gegen den Strom*, pp. 252–57.

187. Reprinted in Brelaz, *Henri De Man. Le 'Dossier,'* pp. 205–9.

188. Balthazar, "Henri De Man," p. 203.

189. Oschmann, *Über Hendrik De Man*, p. 532.

190. The eight articles are reprinted in Brelaz, *Henri De Man. Le 'Dossier,'* pp. 227–57. For a discussion, see ibid., pp. 210–18.

191. The text of the judgment is reprinted in ibid., pp. 350–57.

192. For a discussion of the verdict, see Oschmann, *Über Hendrik de Man*, pp. 556–63; and Brelaz, *Leopold III et Henri De Man*, pp. 52, 293.

193. De Man discusses his deteriorating relationship to the king and to his court in "Reflexions sur la question de l'entourage du Roi," written in 1941 and reprinted in Brelaz, *Henri De Man. Le 'Dossier.'* See also his wartime letters to the king, ibid., pp. 127–54, and the later correspondence, pp. 424–41.

194. Hendrik De Man, *Vermassung und Kultur verfall. Eine Diagnose Unsurer Zeit*. Dritte Auflage (Berlin, Franke, 1970). The concluding chapter, from an English version, "The Age of Doom," is reprinted in Dodge, *Documentary Study*, pp. 331–53.

195. De Man, *Vermassung*, p. 44.

196. Ibid., p. 52.

197. Ibid., p. 109.

198. Ibid., p. 118.

199. Ibid., p. 97.

200. Ibid., pp. 124–25.

201. Ibid., p. 24.

202. Ibid., p. 172.

203. Ibid., p. 126.

204. Ibid., p. 172.

205. Ibid., p. 184.

206. Ibid., p. 181.

207. Ibid., p. 187. De Man's "apocalyptic" outlook is discussed briefly in Klaus Vondung, *Die Apokalypse in Deutschland* (München, Deutscher Taschenbuch, 1988), p. 498.

208. The text of the Bad Godesberg statement in 1959 is reprinted in Susanne Miller and Heinrich Potthoff, eds., *A History of German Social Democracy from 1848 to the Present*, tr. from the German by J. A. Underwood (New York, Berg, 1986), pp. 274–76.

209. De Man's prescience is recognized in several of the essays in Rens, *Sur l'oeuvre d'Henri De Man*. See esp. A. Dauphin-Meunier, "Henri De Man et Walter Rathenau," pp. 118–20.

210. See Franz Grosse, "Henri De Man et Les Sociaux Democrats Allemands Avant 1933," ibid., p. 129.

211. De Man, *Vermassung*, pp. 166–67, and De Man, *Gegen den Strom*, p. 270.

212. De Man, *Gegen den Strom*, p. 58.

213. Ibid., p. 286.

214. Ibid., pp. 290–91.

215. Oschmann, *Über Hendrik de Man*, p. 106.

216. Peter Hofstatter includes De Man in the group of modern intellectuals who "no longer feel at home in their time" and blame the masses for their predicament. See his *Gruppendynamik. Kritik der Massenpsychologie* (Hamburg, Rowohlt, 1971), p. 10.

217. Lutz Niethammer, *Posthistoire, Has History Come to an End?* tr. by Patrick Camiller (London, Verso, 1944), pp. 82–85, 149. See also the discussion of De Man's *Vermassung*, pp. 82–85. For a general discussion of the "end of history" theme, see Perry Anderson, *A Zone of Engagement* (London, Verso, 1992), pp. 279–375.

Chapter 3: Max Horkheimer

1. Max Horkheimer, *Gesammelte Schriften*, 1, "Aus der Pubität. Novellen und Tagebuchblätter, 1914–1919," ed. by Alfred Schmidt (Frankfurt A.M., S. Fischer, 1988), pp. 107–8.

2. Ibid., p. 14.

3. See Schmidt's "Nachwort," ibid., p. 365. The ways in which "From Puberty" anticipated Horkheimer's later thought are also discussed in Schmidt's essay, "Die ursprüchliche Konzeption der Kritischen Theorie in frühen und mittleren Werk das Horkheimers," in Axel Honneth and Albrecht Wellmer, eds., *Die Frankfurten Schule und die folgen* (Berlin, Walter de Gruyter, 1986), pp. 89–112.

4. See Horkheimer's account of his family life in "Das Schlimme erwarten und doch das Gute versuchen," *GS*, 7, "Vorträge und Aufzeichungen, 1949–1973," ed. by Gunzelin Schmid Noerr (Frankfurt A.M., S. Fischer, 1985), pp. 442–44. The ambiguous relationship between the Jewish bourgeoisie and the wider German bourgeoisie is discussed in Noah Isenberg, *Between Redemption and Doom: The Strains of German-Jewish Modernism* (Lincoln, University of Nebraska Press, 1999), esp. pp. 1–17, 147–50.

5. *GS*, I, p. 114.
6. Ibid., pp. 71–72.
7. Ibid., pp. 159–60.
8. Ibid., pp. 107–13.
9. Ibid., p. 80.
10. Ibid., p. 73.
11. Ibid., p. 80.
12. Ibid., p. 31.
13. Ibid., p. 126.
14. Ibid., p. 24.
15. Ibid., pp. 29–30.
16. Ibid., p. 67.
17. Ibid., pp. 100–101.
18. Ibid., p. 96.
19. Ibid., p. 116.
20. Ibid., pp. 160–61.
21. *GS*, II, ed. by Gunzelin Schmid Noerr (Frankfurt A.M., S. Fischer, 1987), pp. 289–328.
22. Ibid., p. 304.
23. *GS*, I, pp. 140–41.
24. Ibid., p. 187.
25. Ibid., pp. 147–51.
26. Ibid., pp. 183–90.
27. Ibid., p. 112.
28. Ibid., p. 84.
29. Ibid., pp. 125–29.
30. Ibid., p. 33.
31. In one of his early letters Horkheimer expresses his own sense of guilt. Cited in Helmut Gumnior and Rudolf Ringguth, *Max Horkheimer in Selbstzeugnischen und Bilddokumenten* (Reinbek bei Hamburg, Rowohlt, 1973), pp. 7–9. The authors see this letter as marking "the beginning of his protest against suffering, injustice, exploitation and violence." The letter is quoted at length in Noerr's editorial afterword to the four volumes of Horkheimer's letters. See *GS*, 18, p. 828. Referring to the ways in which the rich feed off the labors of the poor, Horkheimer wrote: "We are cannibals who complain that the flesh of the slaughtered gives us a stomach ache."
32. *GS*, I, p. 119.
33. Ibid., pp. 172–73.
34. *GS*, 7, p. 452. His bonding with Pollock, which would last all his life, is discussed in Noerr's afterword to his letters. See *GS*, 18, pp. 827–28.
35. *GS*, I, p. 62.
36. Ibid., p. 36.
37. Ibid., p. 248.
38. Ibid., pp. 278–79.
39. Ibid., p. 255.
40. See the story "Gregor," ibid., pp. 286–97.

41. See the story "Jochai," ibid., pp. 164–72.

42. Ibid., pp. 266–67, 295.

43. Ibid., p. 304.

44. Ibid., p. 309.

45. Ibid., p. 336.

46. Ibid., p. 340.

47. Ibid., p. 350.

48. Ibid., p. 349. This theme, together with the other attitudes and values expressed in "From Puberty," runs through the letters to Rosa Riekher, or "Maidon," the young woman he would marry. See, for example, the letters in *GS*, 15, pp. 9–52.

49. *GS*, 1, p. 353.

50. Ibid., p. 354.

51. Ibid., p. 360.

52. For an exploration of this sensibility, see Michael Löwy, *George Lukács: From Romanticism to Bolshevism*, tr. by Patrick Camiller (London, New Left Books, 1979), esp. pp. 10–67; and Michael Löwy, *Redemption and Utopia*, tr. by Hope Heaney (Stanford, Stanford University Press, 1968), for a general treatment of Jewish messianism.

53. See his own account in *GS*, 7, pp. 446–48.

54. See the chapter on Horkheimer in Martin Jay, *Marxism and Totality: The Adventures of a Concept from Lukács to Habermas* (Berkeley, University of California Press, 1984), pp. 196–219.

55. Horkheimer to Rosa Riekher, 30 Nov. 1921, *GS*, 15, pp. 76–79. Many years later a fellow student in Frankfurt, Theodor Adorno, would recall his impressions of Horkheimer. "You seemed to me," he wrote his friend, "scarcely like a student" but rather a young gentleman from a wealthy family "who paid respect to science from a certain distance" and who remained undamaged by the "vocational deformations of academic life" where learning was so easily confused with reality. Adorno's long letter, celebrating Horkheimer's seventieth birthday, was published in *Die Zeit* (25 Mar. 1965). See Horkheimer, *GS*, 18, pp. 590–99. See also Susan Buck-Morss, *The Origin of Negative Dialectics: Theodor W. Adorno, Walter Benjamin, and the Frankfurt Institute* (New York, Free Press, 1977), pp. 7–10.

56. Horkheimer's early philosophical development is discussed by Noerr in his afterword to volume 2 of *GS*, pp. 455–60.

57. Horkheimer, "Das Schlimme erwarten," *GS*, 7, pp. 457–60.

58. *GS*, 1, p. 284.

59. Rolf Wiggershaus, *The Frankfurt School: Its History, Theories and Political Significance*, tr. by Michael Robertson (Cambridge, Mass., M.I.T. Press, 1995), p. 46.

60. See the introduction by Noerr to the diary entries in *GS*, 11, p. 237.

61. Ibid.

62. See Noerr's afterword in *GS*, 2, pp. 459–61.

63. An English edition was published much later. See Horkheimer, *Dawn and Decline, Notes 1926–1931 and 1950–1969*, tr. by Michael Shaw (New York, Seabury Press, 1978). The unpublished "Notizen" and diary entries, the "Philosophische Tagebuch," can be found in *GS*, 11, pp. 237–61 and 262–85.

64. *GS*, 2, pp. 248–49.
65. Ibid., pp. 254–55.
66. Ibid., pp. 276–78.
67. Ibid., p. 243.
68. Ibid., pp. 264–66.
69. Horkheimer, *Dawn and Decline*, p. 30.
70. Ibid., p. 37. In a note entitled "Marxism and Messianism," Horkheimer maintained that the "perfected society" was "not the goal of 'history' but the goal of definite men." Ibid., pp. 268–69.
71. Ibid., p. 251.
72. Ibid., p. 92.
73. Ibid., pp. 34–36.
74. Ibid., p. 74.
75. See Noerr's afterword in *GS*, 2, p. 462.
76. Horkheimer, *Dawn and Decline*, p. 65.
77. Ibid., p. 46.
78. Ibid., p. 44.
79. Ibid., p. 51.
80. Ibid., p. 37.
81. Ibid., p. 258.
82. Ibid., p. 261.
83. Lukács' influence on Horkheimer, as well as their differences, are discussed by Michael Korthals, "Die kritische Gesellschaftstheorie des frühen Horkheimer," *Zeitschrift für Soziologie* (Aug. 1985): 315–29.
84. Horkheimer, *Dawn and Decline*, p. 41.
85. Ibid., p. 88.
86. Ibid., pp. 61–65.
87. Ibid., p. 61.
88. Ibid., p. 63.
89. Ibid., pp. 64–65.
90. Ibid., p. 27.
91. Ibid., pp. 65–66.
92. Ibid., pp. 45–46.
93. Ibid., p. 58.
94. *GS*, 9, p. 22.
95. *GS*, 2, p. 257.
96. For discussions of Horkheimer's relationship to German philosophical idealism, see Alfred Schmidt, "Max Horkheimer's Intellectual Physiognomy," in Seyla Benhabib, Wolfgang Bonss, and John McCole, eds., *On Max Horkheimer* (Cambridge, Mass., M.I.T. Press, 1993), pp. 30–32; Anselm Skuhra, *Max Horkheimer. Eine Einführung in sein Denken* (Stuttgart, W. Kohlhammer, 1974), pp. 25–28; Erwin Rogler, "Horkheimer's materialistische 'Dechifferung' der transzendental-philosphischen Erkenntniskritik," in Alfred Schmidt and Norbert Altwicker, eds., *Max Horkheimer heute; Werk und Wirkung* (Frankfurt A.M., Fischer, 1986), pp. 79–80. The later stage of that relationship is discussed by Herbert Schnädelbach, "Max Horkheimer and the Moral Philosophy of German Idealism," in *On Max*

Horkheimer, pp. 281–308. However, the positivistic and empirical bent of Horkheimer in the late 1920s and early 1930s is emphasized in Korthals, "Die kritische Gesellschaftstheorie des frühen Horkheimer," pp. 320–21.

97. The continuing influence of Schopenhauer is emphasized in Gerard Raulet, "What Good Is Schopenhauer: Remarks on Horkheimer's Pessimism," *Telos* (winter 1979–80): 98–106.

98. Horkheimer, *Dawn and Decline*, p. 24.

99. Ibid., pp. 101–2.

100. The essay is reprinted in Max Horkheimer, *Between Philosophy and Social Science: Selected Early Writings*, tr. by G. Frederick Hunger, Mathew S. Kramer, and John Torpey (Cambridge, Mass., M.I.T. Press, 1993), pp. 313–88.

101. Ibid., p. 354.

102. Ibid., p. 383.

103. Ibid., pp. 370–72.

104. Ibid., pp. 378–79.

105. Ibid., p. 380.

106. Ibid., p. 388.

107. See "A New Concept of Ideology," in *Between Philosophy and Social Science*, pp. 129–50.

108. Ibid., p. 147.

109. For a criticism of Horkheimer's treatment of Mannheim, see Rüdiger Bubner, *Modern German Philosophy*, tr. by Eric Matthews (New York, Cambridge University Press, 1981), pp. 172–73.

110. Wiggershaus, *Frankfurt School*, p. 35. For a discussion of the earlier development of the Institute, see Manfred Gangl, "L'Institute de Recherches Sociales sous la Conduite de Karl Grunberg (1923–1930): La Recherche Pratique en Rêponse a La Crise," in Gérard Raulet, ed., *Weimar ou L'Explosion de la Modernité* (Paris, Éditions anthropos, 1984), pp. 151–65.

111. Wiggershaus, *Frankfurt School*, p. 37.

112. Horkheimer, "The Present Situation of Social Philosophy and the Tasks of an Institute for Social Research," in Max Horkheimer, *Between Philosophy and Social Science*, p. 6.

113. Ibid., p. 1.

114. Ibid., p. 11.

115. Ibid., p. 12.

116. Ibid., p. 3.

117. Ibid., pp. 9–10.

118. Ibid., p. 12.

119. See Wiggershaus, *Frankfurt School*, pp. 57, 113–16, 169–75. The study was published in Germany in 1980 and in an English translation in 1984. Erich Fromm, *The Working Class in Weimar Germany*, tr. by Barbara Weinberger (Cambridge, Mass., Harvard University Press, 1984). The introduction by Wolfgang Bonss discusses the relationship of Horkheimer to the project and to Fromm.

120. Fromm, *Working Class*, pp. 27–29.

121. The constraints, even embarrassment, which marked Horkheimer's references to Marxism are noted by Paul Connerton, *The Tragedy of Enlightenment: An*

Essay on the Frankfurt School (New York, Cambridge University Press, 1980), pp. 35–37.

122. Horkheimer, "History and Psychology," in *Between Philosophy and Social Science*, p. 119. The turn to Freud to overcome the deficiencies of the Marxist treatment of human subjectivity is discussed in Joel Whitebook, *Perversion and Utopia: A Study of Psychoanalysis and Critical Theory* (Cambridge, Mass., M.I.T. University Press, 1995), pp. 2–3.

123. "History and Psychology," pp. 120–21.

124. Ibid., pp. 124–25.

125. Ibid., p. 119.

126. Ibid., p. 123.

127. Ibid., p. 125.

128. Ibid., p. 123.

129. Ibid., p. 125.

130. Ibid., p. 128.

131. See Seyla Benhabib, *Critique, Norm, and Utopia: A Study of the Foundations of Critical Theory* (New York, Columbia University Press, 1986), p. xi. See also her essay "Zur Dialektik von Gluck und Vernunft," in Honneth and Wellmer, *Die Frankfurten Schule*, pp. 128–38.

132. See Alfred Schmidt, "Max Horkheimer's Intellectual Physiognomy," in *On Max Horkheimer*, pp. 35–36.

133. Horkheimer, "Materialism and Metaphysics," in Horkheimer, *Critical Theory, Selected Essays*, tr. by Matthew J. O'Connel et al. (New York, Seabury, 1972), pp. 10–46; and "Materialism and Morality," in *Between Philosophy and Social Science*, pp. 15–48. Horkheimer's "materialism" has also been interpreted as antiphilosophical or as a "deconstruction of philosophy." See Hauke Brunkhorst, "Dialectical Positivism of Happiness: Horkheimer's Materialist Deconstruction of Philosophy," in *On Max Horkheimer*, pp. 67–98.

134. See the accounts in Wiggershaus, *Frankfurt School*, pp. 127–48; and Jay, *Dialectical Imagination*, pp. 29–40.

135. "Materialism and Metaphysics," pp. 17–18.

136. Ibid., pp. 25–26.

137. Ibid., p. 23.

138. See Franz Lienert, *Theorie und Tradition. Zum Menschenbild in Werke Max Horkheimer* (Bern, Peter Lang, 1977), who argues that Horkheimer's intellectual development presupposed an image of a man as rational and free. See esp. pp. 13–19.

139. "Materialism and Metaphysics," p. 15.

140. Ibid., p. 44.

141. Ibid., p. 23. See also Lienert, *Theorie und Tradition*, pp. 63–64; and Herbert Schnädelbach, "Max Horkheimer and the Moral Philosophy of German Idealism," in *On Max Horkheimer*, p. 291.

142. "Materialism and Metaphysics," p. 26. Horkheimer's conception of the dialectic is discussed in Brunkhorst, "Dialectical Positivism," pp. 86–89; and David Held, *Introduction to Critical Theory* (Berkeley, University of California Press, 1980), pp. 175–95.

143. "Materialism and Metaphysics," p. 24.

144. Lienert sees in his dialectic the expectation of a "kairos," a calling forth of a just society through a "dialectical upswing." See Lienert, *Theorie und Tradition*, p. 50.

145. See the chapter on Horkheimer in Martin Jay, *Marxism and Totality*, where his development is seen as a "retreat from Hegelian Marxism." See also John Grumley, *History and Totality: Radical Historicism from Hegel to Foucault* (New York, Routledge, 1989), pp. 153–79.

146. For a critique of Horkheimer's conception of the dialectic, see Wolf Heydebrand and Beverly Burris, "The Limits of Praxis in Critical Theory," in Judith Marcks and Zoltan Tar, eds., *Foundations of the Frankfurt School of Social Research* (London, Transaction Books, 1988), pp. 401–15. See also the discussion by Bubner, *Modern German Philosophy*, pp. 173–77.

147. Lienert, *Theorie und Tradition*, p. 52.

148. See Anselm Skuhra, *Max Horkheimer*, pp. 44–46; and Therborn, "The Frankfurt School," in Marcks and Tar, *Foundations*, p. 348.

149. Joseph B. Maier, "Contribution to a Critique of Critical Theory," ibid., p. 31.

150. Michael Löwy, "Partisan Truth: Knowledge and Social Classes in Critical Theory," ibid., p. 303.

151. Horkheimer, "Materialism and Morality," p. 18.

152. Ibid., p. 15.

153. Ibid., p. 19.

154. Ibid., p. 20.

155. Ibid., p. 25.

156. Ibid., p. 36. Horkheimer's "moral philosophy" and the problems to which it gives rise is discussed in Schnädelbach, "Max Horkheimer," in *On Max Horkheimer*, pp. 281–314. See also the critique by Thomas McCarthy, "The Idea of Critical Theory and Its Relation to Philosophy," Ibid., pp. 146–47.

157. Horkheimer, "Materialism and Morality," p. 35.

158. Horkheimer, "The Rationalism Debate in Contemporary Philosophy," in *Between Philosophy and Social Science*, pp. 217–64, and "On the Problem of Truth," ibid., pp. 177–216.

159. Horkheimer, "Rationalism Debate," p. 217.

160. Ibid., p. 220.

161. Ibid., pp. 224–27.

162. Ibid., p. 254.

163. Ibid., p. 259.

164. Ibid., p. 251.

165. Ibid., p. 228.

166. "Problem of Truth," p. 193.

167. "Rationalism Debate," p. 230.

168. Ibid., p. 262.

169. Ibid., p. 261.

170. "Problem of Truth," pp. 198–99.

171.   See Therborn, "Frankfurt School," p. 346; and Skuhra, *Max Horkheimer*, pp. 41–43. See also Jay, *Dialectical Imagination*, p. 152.

172.   Connerton, *Tragedy of Enlightenment*, pp. 37–38.

173.   See Axel Honneth, "Max Horkheimer and the Sociological Deficit of Critical Theory," in *On Max Horkheimer*, pp. 187–214, and Honneth, *The Fragmented World of the Social: Essays in Social and Political Philosophy*, tr. by Charles Wright (Albany, N.Y., State University of New York Press, 1995), pp. 71–72.

174.   "Rationalism Debate," p. 241.

175.   Jay, *Dialectical Imagination*, pp. 291–92.

176.   See "Remarks on Philosophical Anthropology," and "Egoism and Freedom Movements: On the Anthropology of the Bourgeois Era," in *Between Philosophy and Social Science*, pp. 151–76, and pp. 49–110.

177.   "Remarks on Philosophical Anthropology," p. 159. For a comparison of Scheler's anthropology with that of Horkheimer, see Lienert, *Theorie und Tradition*, pp. 57–65.

178.   "Remarks on Philosophical Anthropology," p. 174.

179.   "Egoism and Freedom Movements," p. 52.

180.   Ibid., p. 74.

181.   Ibid., p. 84.

182.   Ibid., pp. 95–99.

183.   "Problem of Truth," p. 214.

184.   "Egoism and Freedom Movements," pp. 104–5.

185.   Ibid., p. 109.

186.   "Remarks on Philosophical Anthropology," pp. 152–53.

187.   Ibid., p. 154.

188.   "Egoism and Freedom Movements," p. 110.

189.   The essay is included in Horkheimer, *Critical Theory*, pp. 47–128. Franco Ferraritti maintains that "all the key elements in Critical Theory and its ambiguities are present" in this essay. See "The Struggle of Reason against Total Bureaucratization," in Marcks and Tar, *Foundations*, p. 235.

190.   For discussions of the project, see Wiggershaus, *Frankfurt School*, pp. 149–56; and Jay, *Dialectical Imagination*, pp. 113–42.

191.   "Authority and the Family," p. 52.

192.   Ibid., pp. 56–57.

193.   Ibid., p. 58.

194.   Ibid., p. 67.

195.   Ibid., p. 93.

196.   Ibid., p. 95.

197.   Ibid., p. 96.

198.   Ibid., p. 98.

199.   Ibid., p. 128.

200.   Ibid., p. 109.

201.   Ibid., p. 124.

202.   Ibid., p. 125.

203.   Ibid., p. 120. See the discussion in Mechthild Rumpf, "Mystical Aura:

Imagination and the Reality of the 'Maternal' in Horkheimer's Writings," in *On Max Horkheimer*, pp. 309–34.

204. "Authority and the Family," p. 124.

205. The essay is included in Horkheimer, *Critical Theory*, pp. 188–243. For commentaries, see Helmut Dubiel, *Theory and Politics: Studies in the Development of Critical Theory*, tr. by Benjamin Gregg (Cambridge, Mass., M.I.T. Press, 1985), p. 49; and Werner Post, *Kritische Theorie und metaphysicher Pessimismus. Zum Spätwerk Max Horkheimers* (München, Kosel, 1971), p. 29. Löwry argues, in contrast to my treatment, that Horkheimer adopts a position very much like that developed by Lukács in the early 1920s. See "Partisan Truth: Knowledge and Social Class in Critical Theory," in Marcks and Tar, *Foundations*, pp. 289–304.

206. "Traditional and Critical Theory," in Horkheimer, *Critical Theory*, p. 242.

207. Ibid., p. 210.

208. Ibid., p. 212.

209. Ibid., p. 214.

210. Ibid., pp. 214–16.

211. Ibid., p. 217.

212. Ibid., p. 220.

213. Ibid., pp. 237–38.

214. Ibid., p. 241.

215. Ibid., pp. 227–29.

216. See the "Postscript," *Critical Theory*, p. 251.

217. The Institute's relationship to Columbia University is discussed in Wiggershaus, *Frankfurt School*, pp. 144–46. See also Horkheimer's reports to President Butler, *GS*, 16, pp. 91–94, 419–23.

218. Horkheimer expresses his determination to remain faithful to the German philosophical tradition in letters to Adolph Lowe, 4 Jan. and 4 May 1938, *GS*, 16, pp. 351–59, and 444–47. See also his letter to Robert Maynard Hutchins, 7 Jan. 1939., ibid., pp. 536–39. Later he suggested that they had been mistaken in keeping so distant. See his letter to Pollock, 9 June 1943, *GS*, 17, pp. 352–53.

219. See Pollock's memoranda, Aug. 1935 and Aug. 1936, *GS*, 16, pp. 380–89, and 606–10.

220. See esp. Adorno's letter to Horkheimer, 13 May 1935, *GS*, 14, pp. 345–52. Volumes 15 and 16 of the correspondence contain more than twenty lengthy letters—eight pages or more—during the period between November 1934 and November 1937.

221. Benjamin died tragically in 1940. The reasons for the separations and estrangements are discussed by Noerr in his afterword to the four volumes of the correspondence. See *GS*, 18, pp. 853–56.

222. The first of the essays is included in *Between Philosophy and Social Science*, pp. 265–312. The second can be found in Stephen Eric Bronner and Douglas MacKay Kellner, *Critical Theory and Society: A Reader* (New York, Routledge, 1989), pp. 77–94.

223. "Montaigne and the Function of Scepticism," p. 299.

224. "The Jews and Europe," p. 78.

225. Ibid., pp. 88, 84.

226. Ibid., pp. 89–90. For a discussion of Horkheimer's treatment of anti-Semitism, see Dan Diner, "Reason and the 'Other': Horkheimer's Reflections on Anti-Semitism and Mass Annihilation," in *On Max Horkheimer*, pp. 335–63. See also Ehrhard Bahr, "The Anti-Semitism Studies of the Frankfurt School: The Failure of Critical Theory," Marcks and Tar, *Foundations*, pp. 312–18.

227. See Frederick Pollock, "State Capitalism: Its Possibilities and Limitations," in Bronner and Kellner, *Critical Theory*, pp. 95–118. Franz Neumann criticizes Pollock's views in letters to Horkheimer, 23 and 30 July 1941, *GS*, 17, pp. 103–11. The dispute is examined in Held, *Introduction to Critical Theory*, pp. 52–65; and Andrew Arato, *From Neo-Marxism to Democratic Theory* (London, M. L. Sharpe, 1993), pp. 10–18. Also see William David Jones, *The Lost Debate: German Socialist Intellectuals and Totalitarianism* (Urbana, University of Illinois Press, 1999), pp. 129–34, 137–43.

228. Reprinted in Andrew Arato and Eike Gebhardt, eds., *The Essential Frankfurt School Reader* (New York, Urizen Books, 1987), pp. 95–117.

229. Ibid., p. 103.

230. "Montaigne and the Function of Scepticism," p. 307.

231. "Authortarian State," p. 106.

232. Ibid., p. 116.

233. Ibid., p. 115.

234. Ibid., p. 117. For a more positive reading of "The Authoritarian State," see Dick Howard, *The Marxian Legacy*, 2d ed. (Minneapolis, University of Minnesota Press, 1988), pp. 7, 77. Howard acknowledges, however, that Horkheimer "leaves us as well with the uncertainty whether it is hope or despair that animates him." See also Gumnior and Ringguth, *Max Horkheimer*, pp. 70–76.

235. The essay is reprinted in Arato and Gebhardt, *Essential Frankfurt School Reader*, pp. 26–48.

236. Ibid., pp. 26–27.

237. Ibid., p. 28.

238. Ibid., p. 31.

239. Ibid., pp. 28–30.

240. Ibid., p. 34.

241. Ibid., p. 39.

242. Ibid., p. 36.

243. Ibid., p. 38.

244. Ibid., p. 40.

245. See his essay "The Social Function of Philosophy," *Critical Theory*, p. 265.

246. "End of Reason," p. 41.

247. Ibid., p. 43.

248. Ibid., pp. 44–46.

249. Ibid., pp. 36–37.

250. Ibid., pp. 47–48.

251. Several writers discuss the impact of these events on "left wing intellectuals." See Skuhra, *Max Horkheimer*, p. 57; and Therborn, "Frankfurt School," p. 356.

252. Moishe Postone traces the "pessimistic turn" in Horkheimer's thought to his failure to develop an adequate critique of the "limitations of traditional Marx-

ism." His subsequent development, together with that of Pollock, was, according to Postone, misconceived and sterile. See his *Time, Labor, and Social Domination: A Reinterpretation of Marx's Critical Theory* (New York, Cambridge University Press, 1993), ch. 3.

253. The impact of Benjamin's historical pessimism is noted in Wolin, *Terms of Cultural Criticism: The Frankfurt School, Existentialism, Poststructuralism* (New York: Columbia University Press, 1992), p. 61. See also Anson Rabinbach, *In the Shadow of Catastrophe* (Berkeley, University of California Press, 1997), pp. 174–75.

254. For Horkheimer's increasingly close relationship to Adorno, see Stefan Breuer, "The Long Friendship: On Theoretical Differences between Adorno and Horkheimer," in *On Max Horkheimer*, pp. 257–80. See also David Hoy, "A Deconstructive Reading of the Early Frankfurt School," in David Hoy and Thomas McCarthy, *Critical Theory* (Cambridge, Mass., Blackwell, 1994), p. 114; and Buck-Morss, *Origin of Negative Dialectic*, pp. 66–69.

255. Dubiel, *Theory and Politics*, pp. 26–27.

256. Max Horkheimer and Theodor Adorno, *Dialectic of Enlightenment*, tr. by John Cumming (New York, Continuum, 1994), p. xi.

257. The question of the primary authorship of the various essays is discussed in Noerr's afterword in *GS*, 5, pp. 425–30. See also Rabinbach, *Shadow of Catastrophe*, p. 166; and Jurgen Habermas, "Remarks on the Development of Horkheimer's Work," in *On Max Horkheimer*, pp. 55–58.

258. Horkheimer and Adorno, *Dialectic of Enlightenment*, p. 21.

259. Ibid., pp. 5–6.

260. Ibid., p. 12.

261. Ibid., p. xiii.

262. Ibid., p. 36.

263. Ibid., p. xiii.

264. Ibid., p. 36.

265. Ibid., p. 41.

266. Ibid., p. xvi.

267. Ibid., pp. 19–20.

268. Ibid., pp. 41–42.

269. Ibid., p. 85.

270. Ibid., pp. 92–93.

271. Ibid., p. 103.

272. Ibid., p. 100.

273. Ibid., pp. 98–99.

274. Ibid., p. 100.

275. Ibid., p. 101.

276. Ibid., p. 109.

277. Ibid., pp. 94–95.

278. Ibid., p. 97.

279. Ibid., pp. 100–101.

280. Ibid., pp. 114–15.

281. Ibid., pp. 118–19.

282. Lienert emphasizes the continuing presence of an "a priori" or "trans-

cendental motive" in Horkheimer's thought. See his *Theorie und Tradition*, pp. 54, 78.

283. Max Horkheimer, *The Eclipse of Reason* (New York, Oxford University Press, 1947).

284. Ibid., p. 9.

285. Ibid., p. 18.

286. Ibid., pp. 12–15.

287. Ibid., pp. 55, 36.

288. See "Conflicting Panaceas," ibid., pp. 58–91.

289. Ibid., pp. 82–83.

290. Ibid., p. 132.

291. For an understanding of this essay I have relied heavily on Georg Lohmann, "The Failure of Self-Realization: An Interpretation of Horkheimer's 'Eclipse of Reason,'" in *On Max Horkheimer*, pp. 387–412.

292. Horkheimer and Adorno, *Dialectic of Enlightenment*, p. 105.

293. Horkheimer, *Eclipse of Reason*, p. 113.

294. Lohmann, "Failure of Self-Realization," p. 392.

295. Horkheimer, *Eclipse of Reason*, p. 101.

296. Ibid., p. 126.

297. For a criticism of this notion, see Lohmann, "Failure of Self-Realization," p. 395.

298. Horkheimer, *Eclipse of Reason*, p. 92.

299. Ibid., p. 92.

300. Ibid., p. 97.

301. Horkheimer, *Eclipse of Reason*, p. 136.

302. Ibid., p. 146.

303. Ibid., p. 150.

304. Ibid., pp. 159–60.

305. Ibid., p. 141.

306. Ibid., p. 161.

307. Ibid., p. 162.

308. Lohmann, "Failure of Self-Realization," p. 405; and Horkheimer, *Eclipse of Reason*, p. 187.

309. Horkheimer, *Eclipse of Reason*, p. 186.

310. Ibid., p. 163.

311. Lohmann, "Failure of Self-Realization," p. 407.

312. For a discussion of this process, see Dubiel, *Theory and Politics*, pp. 92–93, 102–5.

313. The project is discussed in Wiggershaus, *Frankfurt School*, pp. 273–79; and Jay, *Dialectical Imagination*, pp. 219–52.

314. Jay, *Dialectical Imagination*, p. 221.

315. Wiggershaus, *Frankfurt School*, p. 396.

316. See, for example, Pollock's letter, 14 Jan. 1944, *GS*, 17, pp. 541–42.

317. Wiggershaus, *Frankfurt School*, p. 350.

318. See Diner, "Reason and the 'Other,'" pp. 348–56; and Rabinbach, *In the Shadow of Catastrophe*, pp. 184–91.

319. Horkheimer to Isaac Rosengarten, 12 Sept. 1944, *GS*, 17, p.199. Quoted in Rabinbach, *Shadow of Catastrophe*, p. 194.

320. Wiggershaus, *Frankfurt School*, p. 344.

321. Ibid., pp. 387–92.

322. Jay, *Dialectical Imagination*, p. 256.

323. Wiggershaus, *Frankfurt School*, p. 388.

324. Ibid., pp. 398–408.

325. See esp. Pollock's memoranda during March 1949 in *GS*, 18, pp. 16–22.

326. See Pollock's letter to Horkheimer, 12 July 1950, *GS*, 18, pp. 151–52.

327. See Horkheimer's letter to Felix Weil, 30 May 1949, *GS*, 18, pp. 39–40.

328. For details, see Wiggershaus, *Frankfurt School*, chs. 5 and 6, esp. pp. 397–408, 431–42.

329. Wiggershaus, *Frankfurt School*, pp. 442–46.

330. Ibid., pp. 435–42, 479–89. See also Held, *Introduction to Critical Theory*, p. 198.

331. Honneth, *Fragmented World*, p. 85.

332. Wiggershaus, *Frankfurt School*, p. 544. Horkheimer criticizes Habermas in a long letter to Adorno, 27 Sept. 1959, *GS*, 18, pp. 437–52. Although he conceded that Habermas had a "brilliant future," he feared that his attempt to renew the radical drive in critical theory would "ruin the Institute." Adorno noted his many disagreements with Horkheimer's views in the margins of the letter.

333. See Wiggershaus, *Frankfurt School*, p. 624, for examples of Horkheimer's conservatism.

334. In the "memoranda" and letters to Pollock during the 1950s Horkheimer expressed his yearning to rekindle their passion for "pure theoretical work" and lamented the "external distractions" associated with the rebuilding of the Institute. See, for example, the "Memorandum" of 8 Sept. 1951, *GS*, 18, pp. 218–21, and the letter to Pollock 11 Nov. 1956, *GS*, 18, pp. 365–69.

335. Horkheimer's "Notes" can be found in volumes 6, 7, 8, and 14 of the *GS*. The "shavings" recorded by Pollock are in volume 14, pp. 172–547. A number of the items in volumes 7 and 8 are reprinted in Max Horkheimer, *Critique of Instrumental Reason*, ed. by Matthew J. O'Connel et al. (New York, Seabury Press, 1974). Many of the items in volume 6, drawn from the years 1950–69, make up the second part of *Dawn and Decline*, published after Horkheimer's death.

336. See Schmidt's "Afterword" in *GS*, 6, p. 438.

337. Wiggershaus, *Frankfurt School*, pp. 384–85. See also Dubiel, *Theory and Politics*, pp. 71, 92.

338. Wiggershaus, *Frankfurt School*, pp. 388–89.

339. *GS*, 6, p. 318.

340. Ibid., p. 304.

341. Ibid., p. 314. See also his letter to Wilhelm Weischedel, 25 Aug. 1958, *GS*, 18, pp. 433–37.

342. *GS*, 6, pp. 205, 267.

343. Ibid., p. 241.

344. *GS*, 14, p. 113.

345. Ibid.

346. *GS*, 6, p. 301, and *GS*, 14, pp. 208–9. Nevertheless, he continued to feel great affection and gratitude to the country that had given him shelter. He still hoped, during the 1960s, to recover the American citizenship that he had lost after returning to Germany. See his letter to John J. McCloy, 8 May 1962, in *GS*, 18, pp. 525–27.

347. *GS*, 6, p. 308.

348. *GS*, 14, p. 113.

349. Ibid., pp. 128, 137, 217. See also Skuhra, *Max Horkheimer*, pp. 85–96.

350. *GS*, 6, pp. 236–37, 212.

351. *GS*, 14, pp. 137, 141.

352. Ibid., p. 124.

353. *GS*, 6, pp. 308–11.

354. Ibid., p. 267.

355. Ibid., p. 392.

356. Ibid., p. 410, and *GS*, 14, p. 322.

357. *GS*, 6, p. 270.

358. See the "Afterword" by Eike Gebhardt in *Dawn and Decline*, p. 250.

359. *GS*, 14, p. 204.

360. *GS*, 6, p. 204.

361. Ibid., p. 410.

362. *GS*, 14, p. 351.

363. Ibid., p. 240.

364. *GS*, 6, pp. 287–88. See the essay "The Concept of Man," in *GS*, 7, pp. 54–80. See also *GS*, 14, p. 125.

365. See the essay "The Relevance of Schopenhauer," in *GS*, 7, pp. 122–42. See also Gérard Raulet, "Kritik der Vernunft und kritischer Gebrauch des Pessimismus," in Schmidt and Altwicker, *Max Horkheimer heute*, p. 41; and Gérard Raulet, "What Good Is Schopenhauer?" *Telos* (winter 1979–80): 98–106.

366. *GS*, 14, 99, 228–32.

367. Ibid.

368. See Wiggershaus, *Frankfurt School*, pp. 502–4.

369. *GS*, 6, p. 314.

370. Ibid., p. 253.

371. Ibid., p. 322.

372. Ibid., p. 304.

373. Ibid., p. 228.

374. *GS*, 14, p. 215.

375. See esp. the interviews with Helmut Gumnior, Otmar Hersche, and Gerhard Rein in *GS*, 7, pp. 385–484.

376. *GS*, 14, p. 129.

377. For an overview of Horkheimer's views on religion and Christianity, see Matthias Lutz-Bachmann, "Humanität und Religion. Zu Max Horkheimers Deutung des Christentum," in Schmidt and Altwicker, *Max Horkheimer heute*, pp. 108–28. The subliminal "religious dimension" in critical theory and the way it "erupts into view" in the late interviews is discussed in J. A. Colombo, *An Essay on Theology and History: Studies in Pannenberg, Metz, and the Frankfurt School* (Atlanta, Ga.,

Scholars Press, 1990), pp. 150–54. See also Rudolf J. Siebert, *The Critical Theory of Religion: The Frankfurt School* (New York, Mouton, 1985), ch. 2; and Julius Carlsbach, *Karl Marx and the Radical Criticism of Judaism* (London, Routledge and Kegan Paul, 1978), pp. 234–57.

378. See the discussions of Machiavelli and Hobbes in "Beginnings of the Bourgeois Philosophy of History," in Horkheimer, *Between Philosophy and Social Science* pp. 314–63.

379. *GS*, 6, p. 365.

380. Included in Horkheimer, *Critical Theory*, pp. 129–31.

381. *GS*, 6, p. 393.

382. *GS*, 14, p. 321.

383. Ibid., p. 215.

384. *GS*, 8, p. 272.

385. *GS*, 6, p. 225.

386. See Wiebrecht Ries, "Die Rettung des Hoffnungslosen. Zur 'theologia occulta' in d. Spätphilosophie Horkheimers u. Adorno," *Zeitschrift für Philosophische Forschung* (1966): 69–81.

387. See the interview with Helmut Gumnior, "The Yearning for the Wholly Other," in *GS*, 7, pp. 385–404.

388. Ibid., pp. 392, 389.

389. Ibid., p. 387.

390. Ibid., p. 386.

391. See the discussions in Post, *Kritische Theorie*, pp. 122–25; Lienert, *Theorie und Tradition*, pp. 112–15; and Rudolf Siebert, "Horkheimer's Sociology of Religion," *Telos* (winter 1976–77): 127–44. Horkheimer's movement back to his Jewish religious origins is described by Eva G. Reichmann, "Max Horkheimer the Jew— Critical Theory and Beyond," *Leo Baeck Institute Yearbook* 19 (London, 1974).

392. *GS*, 7, p. 480.

393. Ibid., pp. 402–4.

394. According to Habermas the "unresolved argumentative impasse" in Horkheimer is expressed in his vacillation "between Schopenhauer's negative-metaphysical justification of morality and a return to the faith of his forefathers." See the Habermas critique, "To Seek to Salvage an Unconditional Meaning without God Is a Futile Undertaking: Reflections on a Remark of Max Horkheimer," in Jurgen Habermas, *Justification and Application: Remarks on Discourse Ethics*, tr. by Ciaran Cronin (Cambridge, Mass., M.I.T. Press, 1993), pp. 133–46.

395. *GS*, 7, pp. 464–65.

396. Joseph B. Maier, "Contribution to a Critique of Critical Theory," in Marcks and Tar, *Foundations*, p. 35.

397. Zoltan Tar, *The Frankfurt School: The Critical Theories of Max Horkheimer and Theodor Adorno* (New York, John Wiley and Sons, 1970), p. 9.

398. Jay, *Dialectical Imagination*, pp. 292–96. For a discussion of the "common ground" they shared with the German bourgeoisie, as well as their separation from politics and the "concerns of daily life," see George L. Mosse, "Jewish Emancipation: Between 'Bildung' and Respectability," in Jehuda Reinharz and Walter

Schatzberg, eds., *The Jewish Response to German Culture* (London, University Press of New England, 1985), pp. 13–16.

399. Alain Touraine, *Critique of Modernity*, tr. by David Macey (Oxford, Blackwell, 1995), pp. 153–63.

Chapter 4: Leszek Kolakowski

1. See "Zur Zukunft der Kritischen Theorie." Gespräch mit Claus Grossner, Max Horkheimer, *Gesammelte Schriften*, 7, ed. by Gunzelin Schmid Noerr (Frankfurt A.M., S. Fischer, 1985), p. 425.

2. For details, see Gesine Schwan, *Leszek Kolakowski, Eine Marxistischen Philosophie der Freiheit* (Stuttgart, W. Kohlhammer, 1971), p. 9.

3. Biographical details are drawn from Christian Heidrich, *Leszek Kolakowski, Zwischen Skepsis und Mystik* (Frankfurt A.M., Neue Kritik, 1995); and Leopold Labedz, "Introduction" to Leszek Kolakowski, *Marxism and Beyond*, tr. by Jane Zielonko Peel (London, Paladin, 1969).

4. Labedz, "Introduction," p. 11. Later, Kolakowski recalled time spent in Warsaw where he witnessed the destruction of the Jewish ghetto as well as efforts to hide Jews. See his essay "Volkermord und Ideologie," *Merkur* (Mar. 1979): 217.

5. For philosophical developments in Poland during the late nineteenth and early twentieth centuries, see Z. A. Jordan, "Marxistischer Revisionismus in Polen. Hintergrund, Wurzeln und Hauptströmungen," *Marxismus-Studien*, V, ed. by Iring Fetscher (Tübingen, J. C. B. Mohr, 1968), 85–129; and Z. A. Jordan, "The Philosophical Background of Revisionism in Poland," in W. J. Stankiewicz, *Polish Thought since World War II* (New York, Free Press, 1964), pp. 250–89. Kolakowski discussed his philosophical training in a radio interview in 1979. See Alfred Mensak, ed., *Siegfried Lenz Gespräche mit Manes Sperber und Leszek Kolakowski* (Hamburg, Hoffmann und Campe, 1980), pp. 83–126.

6. Schwan, *Kolakowski*, p. 38.

7. Quoted by Labedz, "Introduction," p. 13.

8. Heidrich, *Kolakowski*, p. 59.

9. See the discussions in Schwan, *Kolakowski*, pp. 29–30; and Heidrich, *Kolakowski*, pp. 40–45, 62–64.

10. His critique of the Catholic church and its philosophy is summed up in Schwan, *Kolakowski*, pp. 33–37; and Heidrich, *Kolakowski*, pp. 65–75.

11. Heidrich, *Kolakowski*, p. 79.

12. Quoted by Helmut Wagner, "Die Moralische Revolte des Leszek Kolakowski," *Osteuropa* (Sept. 1961): 632.

13. Schneidermann, *The Warsaw Heresy* (New York, Horizon Press, 1959), p. 224.

14. The meeting is discussed in Heidrich, *Kolakowski*, pp. 89–93; and Jordan, "Philosophical Background," p. 267.

15. For an account of the growth of internal dissent, see Richard Hiscocks, *Poland: Bridge for the Abyss* (London, Oxford University Press, 1993), pp. 174–81.

16. See Ben Fowkes, *The Rise and Fall of Communism in Eastern Europe* (New York, St. Martin's Press, 1993), pp. 91–96.

17. Reprinted in Edmund Stillman, ed., *Bitter Harvest: The Intellectual Revolt behind the Iron Curtain* (New York, Praeger, 1959), pp. 47–50.

18. See Konrad Syrop, *Spring in October: The Story of the Polish Revolution, 1956* (New York, Frederick Praeger, 1957), and "The October [1956] Upheaval in Retrospect," in Tadeusz N. Cieplak, ed., *Poland since 1956* (New York, Twayne, 1972), pp. 1–44.

19. The essay is included in Kolakowski, *Marxism and Beyond*, pp. 176–90.

20. Ibid., pp. 178–80.

21. Ibid., pp. 180–81.

22. Ibid., p. 182.

23. Ibid., p. 183.

24. Ibid., pp. 185–87.

25. Ibid., p. 188.

26. Ibid., p. 190.

27. Included in Leszek Kolakowski, *Der Mensch ohne Alternative. Von der Möglichkeit und Unmöglichkeit Marxist zu Sein* (München, R. Piper, 1960), pp. 163–80.

28. Ibid., p. 165.

29. Ibid., pp. 173–74.

30. Ibid., p. 174.

31. Ibid., p. 179.

32. Included in Kolakowski, *Marxism and Beyond*, pp. 191–205.

33. Ibid., pp. 192–94.

34. Ibid., pp. 192–93.

35. Ibid., pp. 197–98.

36. Ibid., p. 204.

37. Ibid., p. 203.

38. Ibid., pp. 203–5.

39. The development of revisionism in Poland is discussed in Jordan, "Philosophical Background," pp. 250–89, and "Marxistischer Revisionism," pp. 85–129. See also George L. Kline, "Leszek Kolakowski and the Revision of Marxism," in Kline, *European Philosophy Today* (Chicago, Quadrangle Books, 1965), pp. 117–63.

40. See Nicholas Bethell, *Gomulka: His Poland, His Communism* (New York, Holt, Rinehart, and Winston, 1969), pp. 229–42; and Syrop, *Spring in October*, pp. 188–95. For a report on Gomulka's speech to the Central Committee, shortly after his negotiations with the Soviet leaders, see Hiscocks, *Poland*, pp. 215–21.

41. See Adam Ciolkosz, "The Rise and Fall of 'Modern Revisionism' in Poland," in Cieplak, *Poland since 1956*, pp. 25–26.

42. Hiscocks, *Poland*, p. 262.

43. "World View and Daily Life" is included in Kolakowski, *Mensch ohne Alternative*, pp. 191–215; "Responsibility and History" can be found in Kolakowski, *Marxism and Beyond*, pp. 105–75.

44. Schneidermann, *Warsaw Heresy*, p. 225.

45. Kolakowski, "World View," p. 196.

46. Ibid., p. 207.
47. Ibid., p. 191.
48. Ibid., p. 209.
49. Ibid., p. 191.
50. Ibid., p. 196.
51. Ibid., p. 194.
52. Ibid., p. 195.
53. Ibid., p. 199.
54. Ibid., p. 210.
55. Ibid., p. 205.
56. Ibid., p. 196.
57. Ibid., pp. 210–14.
58. Ibid., pp. 204–6.
59. Ibid., pp. 209.
60. Ibid., pp. 214–15.
61. Kolakowski, "Responsibility and History," p. 107.
62. Ibid., p. 108.
63. Ibid., p. 119.
64. Ibid., pp. 114, 125.
65. Ibid., pp. 136–38.
66. Ibid., p. 135.
67. Ibid., p. 141.
68. Ibid., pp. 143–44.
69. Ibid., p. 155.
70. Ibid., p. 160.
71. Ibid., p. 157.
72. Ibid., p. 164.
73. Ibid., pp. 167, 174.
74. See Harald Lauren, "Die Gedenkenwelt Leszek Kolakowski's," *Der Remter* 1 (1961): 47–56.
75. Schaff's role is discussed in Jordan, "Philosophical Background," pp. 251–56, 269–75; and Schneidermann, *Warsaw Heresy*, pp. 239–41. Gomulka, according to Lauren, "found in Schaff one who could represent his retreat" from the October Revolution. See Lauren, "Die Gedankenwelt Leszek Kolakowski," p. 48.
76. Quoted in Schneidermann, *Warsaw Heresy*, pp. 236–37.
77. See Ciepiak, *Poland since 1956*, pp. 26–28; and K. A. Jelenski, "A Window on the Future: The Story of Po Prostu," *Encounter* (Dec. 1957): 45–48.
78. The role of the clubs is discussed in Schneidermann, *Warsaw Heresy*, pp. 229–30. For an account of the most prominent of the clubs, see Witold Jedlicki, "The Crooked Circle Club," in Ciepiak, *Poland since 1956*, pp. 120–29. See also Witold Wirpsza, "Ein Kuntsler-Philosophie," *Europäische Idéen* 33 (1977): 21–23, where another club is discussed.
79. Schneidermann, *Warsaw Heresy*, pp. 230–32.
80. Ibid., pp. 233–36.
81. Spinoza's influence on Kolakowski is discussed in Heidrich, *Kolakowski*, pp.

104–8. See also Kolakowski's essay "The Two Eyes of Spinoza," in Marjorie Grene, ed., *Spinoza: A Collection of Critical Essays* (New York, Doubleday, 1973), pp. 279–94; and Mensak, *Siegfried Lenz Gespräche*, p. 97.

82. Included in Kolakowski, *Marxism and Beyond*, pp. 228–37.

83. Ibid., pp. 231–33.

84. Ibid., pp. 234–35.

85. Ibid., pp. 236–37.

86. Included in Kolakowski, *Marxism and Beyond*, pp. 59–87.

87. Ibid., p. 63.

88. Ibid., p. 67.

89. Ibid., p. 79.

90. Ibid., pp. 80–82.

91. Ibid., pp. 73–74.

92. Ibid., p. 83.

93. Leszek Kolakowski, *Main Currents of Marxism*, III, "The Breakdown," tr. from Polish by P. S. Falla (New York, Oxford University Press, 1981), pp. 461–66. Kolakowski is viewed as a "permanent revisionist" by Alexander Schwan, "Leszek Kolakowski's Philosophie des permanenten Revisionismus," in Franz Martin Schmolz, ed., *Christ zwischen Kirche* (Salzburg, C. M. Beck, 1969), pp. 51–52.

94. "Rationalism as an Ideology" is included in Leszek Kolakowski, *Traktat Über die Sterblichkeit der Vernunft*, tr. from Polish by Peter Lachmann (München, R. Piper, 1967), pp. 206–67. "The Priest and the Jester" can be found in Kolakowski, *Marxism and Beyond*, pp. 31–58.

95. "Rationalism as an Ideology," p. 229. A few years later Kolakowski would develop his critique of positivism more fully. See Leszek Kolakowski, *"The Alienation of Reason: A History of Positivist Thought,"* tr. by Norbert Guterman (Garden City, N.Y., Doubleday, 1968). See esp. pp. 198–206.

96. "Rationalism as an Ideology," p. 224.

97. Ibid., p. 233.

98. Ibid., pp. 252–56.

99. Ibid., pp. 257–63. Kolakowski is included, along with Adam Schaff and Roger Garaudy, in a study of contemporary Marxist efforts to develop a new anthropology. The study concentrates on Garaudy, however, and misses the distinctive features of Kolakowski's thought. See Michael Rustemeyer, *Anthropogische Element in Gegenwartigen Marxismus. Roger Garaudy, Leszek Kolakowski, Adam Schaff*. Inaugural Dissertation zur Erlangung des Docktorgrades der Philosophische Fakultät der Ludwig-Maxmillian Universität zu München (1979).

100. "Rationalism as an Ideology," pp. 252–54.

101. Ibid., pp. 264–67.

102. "Priest and Jester," p. 32.

103. Ibid., p. 44, 46.

104. Ibid., p. 47.

105. Ibid., p. 51.

106. Ibid., pp. 54–55.

107. See Sidney Hook's review of *Toward a Marxist Humanism* in the *New York Times Book Review* (Sept. 1, 1968).

108. See Leszek Kolakowski, *Tales from the Kingdom of Lailonia and The Key to Heaven*, tr. from Polish by Agnieszka Kolakowska (Chicago, University of Chicago Press, 1989). The work is discussed by Francois Bondi, "Kolakowski." Grundmuster und Exempel," *Europäische Idéen* 33 (1977): 12–17.

109. "The Hump," *Tales*, pp. 10–18.

110. "Priest and the Jester," p. 31.

111. Included in the collection of his writings published in *TriQuarterly* (fall 1971).

112. Ibid., pp. 153–56.

113. Ibid., pp. 164–67.

114. Ibid., pp. 171–74.

115. Ibid., p. 175.

116. Ibid., p. 178.

117. Ibid., pp. 178–81.

118. The essay "Cogito, historischer Materialismus, expressive Personlichkeits interpretation" is included in Kolakowski, *Traktat*, pp. 123–52.

119. Ibid., pp. 150–53.

120. Ibid., pp. 156–60.

121. Ibid., pp. 141, 138.

122. Ibid., p. 155.

123. Included in Kolakowski, *Traktat*, pp. 7–32.

124. Ibid., p. 12.

125. Ibid., pp. 12, 26.

126. Ibid., pp. 30–31.

127. "In Praise of Inconsistency," p. 234. See also Schwan, "Leszek Kolakowski's Philosophie des permanenten Revisionismus," pp. 50–52.

128. See Heidrich, *Kolakowski*, pp. 119–20, and the "Foreword" by Leonhard Reinisch to Leszek Kolakowski, *Leben trotz Geschichte, Lesebuch* (München, Deutschen Taschenbuch, 1980), p. 19.

129. Included in Leszek Kolakowski, *Geist und Ungeist Christiicher Traditionen*, ed. by Gerhard M. Martin (Stuttgart, Kohlhammer, 1971), pp. 11–20.

130. Reinisch, "Foreword," p. 11.

131. Kolakowski, "Kleine Thesen de sacro et profano," pp. 17–20.

132. For a discussion of this shift in outlook, see Schwan, *Kolakowski*, pp. 126–41.

133. See his essay "Religiöse Symbole und humanistische Kultur," included in *Geist und Ungeist*, pp. 90–112.

134. Ibid., p. 94.

135. Ibid., pp. 97–101.

136. Ibid., pp. 101–4.

137. Ibid., pp. 106–7.

138. Ibid., p. 109.

139. Ibid., pp. 110–12.

140. See Leszek Kolakowski, "A Stenographic Report of the Devil's Metaphysical Press Conference in Warsaw on the 20th of December, 1963," in *TriQuarterly* (fall 1971): 139–52.

141. Ibid., p. 141.

142. Ibid., p. 145.

143. See Kolakowski, "Die Banalität Pascal," in *Geist und Ungeist*, pp. 58–69. Kolakowski discusses Pascal's understanding of the "two worlds" more fully in his essay "Pascal's Sad Religion," in Kolakowski, *God Owes Us Nothing* (Chicago, University of Chicago Press, 1995). See esp. pp. 145–75.

144. See "Erasmus und sein Gott," *Geist und Ungeist*, pp. 44–57.

145. See "Teilhardismus und manichaisches Christendom," ibid., pp. 70–89.

146. Ibid., pp. 81–82.

147. Ibid., pp. 88–89.

148. The lecture is reprinted in *TriQuarterly* (fall 1971): 65–77.

149. Ibid., pp. 66–68.

150. Ibid., pp. 68–69.

151. Ibid., pp. 73–76.

152. Ibid., p. 77.

153. See "Intellectuals, Hope and Heresy: An Interview with Kolakowski," *Encounter* (Oct. 1971): 44.

154. The book is discussed in Heidrich, *Kolakowski*, pp. 248–60. See also David McLellan, *Marxism and Religion* (New York, Harper and Row, 1987), pp. 139–40.

155. Leszek Kolakowski, *The Presence of Myth*, tr. by Adam Czerniawski (Chicago, University of Chicago Press, 1989).

156. Heidrich, *Kolakowski*, p. 158. For a summary of Kolakowski's views prior to this shift, see Joachim T. Baer, "Leszek Kolakowski's Plea for a Non-mystical World View," *Slavic Review* (Sept. 1969): 475–83. Baer reviews nine essays published between 1959 and 1966.

157. Kolakowski, *Presence of Myth*, p. xi.

158. Ibid., p. 40.

159. Ibid., p. 107.

160. Ibid., p. 16.

161. Ibid., pp. 41–42.

162. Ibid., pp. 48–49.

163. Ibid., p. 95.

164. Ibid., pp. 44–50.

165. Ibid., pp. 74–80.

166. Ibid., pp. 83–94.

167. Ibid., p. 91.

168. Ibid., pp. 96–99.

169. Ibid., pp. 104–5.

170. Ibid., pp. 118–19.

171. Ibid., pp. 120–21.

172. Ibid., p. 131.

173. Ibid., pp. 134–35.

174. Ibid., pp. 106–7.

175. For descriptions of the event, see P. K. Raina, "Poland. Intellectuals vs. the Party: A Report on the Kolakowski Case," *Dissent* (Sept., Oct., 1967): 576–89; Harald Lauen, *Polen nach dem Sturz Gomulkas* (Stuttgart, Seewald, 1972), pp. 59–

60; Karl Hartmann, "Polens Geistiges Leben in der Krise," *Osteuropa* (May–June 1969): 360–61; and Ross Johnson, "Warsaw Politics and Intellectuals," *East Europe* (July 1967): 12–16.

176. For a general account of these years, see Ross Johnson, "Polish Perspectives, Past and Present," *Problems of Communism* (July, Aug., 1971): 59–72.

177. Quoted in Harald Lauen, "Der Intellektuelle Aderlass," *Osteuropa* (Mar. 1969): 198–99.

178. Ibid., pp. 198–202.

179. See Adam Schaff, *Marxism and the Human Individual*, tr. by Jednostka Ludzka (New York, McGraw Hill, 1970). See also Jordan, "Marxistischen Revisionismus," pp. 124–28.

180. See Milovan Djilas, "Beyond Dogma," *Survey* (winter 1971): 184–88; and Milovan Djilas, *Fall of the New Class*, tr. by John Loud (New York, Knopf, 1998), pp. 257–63. For a comparison of the two dissenters, see Gunter Bartsch, "Djilas und Kolakowski," *Osteuropa* (May 1965): 289–95, and (June 1965): 385–92.

181. *Socialist Register*, Ralph Miliband and John Saville, eds. (London, Merlin Press, 1973), pp. 1–95.

182. Ibid., p. 1.

183. Ibid., p. 5.

184. Thompson refers to "Intellectuals, Hope and Heresy," *Encounter* (Oct. 1971): 42–48; Leszek Kolakowski, "Intellectuals against Intellect," *Daedalus* (summer 1972): 1–14; and Leszek Kolakowski, "The Myth of Human Self-Identity," in *The Socialist Idea: A Reappraisal*, ed. by Leszek Kolakowski and Stuart Hampshire (New York, Basic Books, 1974), pp. 18–35.

185. Thompson, "Open Letter," in Miliband and Saville, eds., *Socialist Register*, pp. 14–16.

186. Ibid., p. 33.

187. Ibid., p. 87.

188. Ibid., pp. 61–63.

189. Ibid., p. 89.

190. Ibid., pp. 34, 93.

191. Leszek Kolakowski, "My Correct Views on Everything," *Socialist Register* (1974): 1–20.

192. Ibid., pp. 14–16.

193. Ibid., pp. 18–20.

194. Ibid.

195. The article first appeared in *Kultura*, a journal published in Paris by Polish exiles. It is reprinted in *Survey* (summer 1971): 37–52.

196. See Lauen, *Polen nach dem Sturz*, pp. 7–36.

197. "Hope and Hopelessness," p. 51.

198. Ibid., p. 37.

199. Ibid., p. 44.

200. Ibid., p. 43.

201. Ibid., p. 42.

202. Ibid., p. 50.

203. Ibid., p. 52.

204. David Ost, *Solidarity and the Politics of Anti-Political, Opposition and Reform in Poland since 1968* (Philadelphia, Temple University Press, 1990), p. 58. See also Jan Jozef Lipski, *K.O.R. A History of the Worker's Defense Committee in Poland,* tr. by Olga Amsterdamska and Gene Moore (Berkeley, University of California Press, 1985), pp. 15–16; Michael H. Bernard, *The Origins of Democratization in Poland* (New York, Columbia University Press, 1993), pp. 8, 90–92; and Timothy Garton Ash, *The Polish Revolution* (London, Jonathan Cape, 1983), pp. 22–23.

205. Leszek Kolakowski, "Die gestrandete Linke," *Merkur* (July 1971): 612–22.

206. Ibid., pp. 620–22.

207. Ibid., p. 619.

208. Ibid., p. 622.

209. Leszek Kolakowski, "Vom sinn der Tradition," *Merkur* (Dec. 1969): 1085–92.

210. Ibid., p. 1085.

211. Ibid., p. 1089.

212. Ibid., p. 1090.

213. Ibid., p. 1091.

214. Ibid., p. 1092.

215. Included in Leszek Kolakowski, *Modernity on Endless Trial* (Chicago, University of Chicago Press, 1990), pp. 63–74.

216. Ibid., pp. 67–70.

217. Ibid., pp. 70–71.

218. Ibid., pp. 72–73.

219. Included in *Modernity*, pp. 75–85.

220. Ibid., pp. 78–79.

221. Ibid., p. 81.

222. Ibid., p. 84.

223. Ibid., pp. 84–85.

224. "On the So-Called Crisis of Christianity," in *Modernity*, pp. 86–87.

225. Ibid., pp. 92–93.

226. Reprinted in *Modernity*, pp. 225–27.

227. Leszek Kolakowski, "Preface" to *Main Currents of Marxism*, I, p. v.

228. See the reviews by James Miller, *Telos* (winter 1980–81): 190–96; and Martin Jay, *American Historical Review* 9 (Feb. 1980): 81–83. See also the review essay by Michael W. Fischer, "Die Analyse Eines Zerfalls," *Zeitschrift für Politik* (Mar. 1981): 65–70. For criticisms of Kolakowski's treatment of Marxism, see Ossip Flechtheim, *Vom Marx bis Kolakowski. Sozialismus oder Untergang in der Barbarei?* (Köln, Europäische Verlagsanstalt, 1978), pp. 229–44; and Waclaw Majbaum and Alexandre Zukrowska, "Leszek Kolakowski's Misinterpretation of Marxism," *Dialectics and Humanism* (autumn 1980): 107–18, and (winter 1981): 149–60.

229. Kolakowski, *Main Currents*, I, "The Founders," p. 1.

230. Ibid., pp. 9–12.

231. Ibid., pp. 12–23.

232. Ibid., p. 24.

233. Ibid., pp. 39–41.

234. Ibid., pp. 44–50.

235. Ibid., p. 74.

236. Ibid., p. 77.

237. Ibid., pp. 130–31, 141.

238. Ibid., p. 181.

239. Ibid., pp. 314–16.

240. Ibid., p. 325.

241. Ibid., p. 375.

242. Ibid., p. 348.

243. Ibid., p. 361.

244. Ibid., p. 363.

245. Ibid., pp. 369–73.

246. Ibid., p. 403.

247. Ibid., pp. 408–16.

248. Kolakowski, *Main Currents*, II, "The Golden Age."

249. See the chapter "The Dialectics of Nature," in volume I, pp. 376–98.

250. *Main Currents*, II, p. 17. Chapters 9, 10, and 11 of this volume are devoted to Polish thinkers.

251. See "Stanislaw Brzozowski: Marxism as Historical Subjectivism," ibid., pp. 215–39.

252. Ibid., p. 222.

253. Ibid., pp. 216.

254. Ibid., pp. 223, 238–39.

255. Ibid., p. 514.

256. Ibid., III, "The Breakdown," p. 91.

257. Ibid., p. 161.

258. See the discussion of Lukács, ibid., pp. 253–307.

259. Ibid., pp. 297–300.

260. Ibid., p. 307.

261. Ibid., p. 415.

262. Ibid., p. 395.

263. Ibid., pp. 460–62.

264. Ibid., p. 465.

265. Ibid., p. 523.

266. Ibid., p. 526.

267. Ibid., II, p. 505, and I, p. 419.

268. Ibid., III, p. 529.

269. Leszek Kolakowski, "Modernity on Endless Trial," in *Modernity*, p. 3.

270. Ibid., pp. 6–7.

271. "Looking for Barbarians," in *Modernity*, pp. 26–30.

272. "The Illusion of Demythologization," ibid., p. 95.

273. "Politics and the Devil," ibid., p. 176.

274. See esp. "Marxism and Human Rights," ibid., p. 209, and "The Idolatry of Politics," ibid., p. 149.

275. "From Truth to Truth," ibid., pp. 122–25, and "Revolution—A Beautiful Sickness," ibid., pp. 221–23.

276. "The Death of Utopia Reconsidered," ibid., pp. 130–38.

277. Ibid., p. 144.
278. "Irrationality in Politics," *Modernity*, p. 200.
279. "The Idolatry of Politics," ibid., p. 152.
280. "'Fabula mundi' and Cleopatra's Nose," ibid., pp. 243–47. See also Kolakowski, *Religion*, pp. 154–56.
281. "Politics and the Devil," *Modernity*, pp. 185–91. See also "The Devil in History: A Conversation with George Urban," *Encounter* (Jan. 1981): 9–26.
282. "Irrationality in Politics," p. 194.
283. "Idolatry of Politics," pp. 155–61, and "Politics and the Devil," pp. 177–79.
284. "The Intellectuals," *Modernity*, pp. 36–42.
285. "Death of Utopia Reconsidered," p. 135.
286. See Leszek Kolakowski, *Husserl and the Search for Certitude* (New Haven, Yale University Press, 1975), esp. pp. 81–85, and Kolakowski, *Metaphysical Horror* (New York, Blackwell, 1988), pp. 29–36.
287. Jaspers is discussed in "The Illusion of Demythologization," *Modernity*, pp. 102–7, and "Philosophical Faith in the Face of Revelation," *Modernity*, pp. 108–19.
288. "Philosophical Faith," pp. 111, 116.
289. Ibid., p. 115.
290. "Modernity on Endless Trial," p. 11.
291. "Looking for the Barbarians," p. 30.
292. "The Illusion of Demythologization," pp. 106–7.
293. "Looking for the Barbarians," pp. 29–30.
294. "Idolatry of Politics," p. 150.
295. "The Illusion of Demythologization," pp. 97–99.
296. "Idolatry of Politics," pp. 152–55.
297. See "Epilogue: Education to Hatred, Education to Dignity," *Modernity*, pp. 258–61.
298. "Irrationality in Politics," p. 203.
299. "Illusion of Demythologization," pp. 88–107.
300. "Why Do We Need Kant?" *Modernity*, pp. 44–54. For his rejection of Kant's argument, see Kolakowski, *Religion*, pp. 189–90.
301. See Kolakowski, *Religion*, esp. chs. 3 and 5. For discussions and criticisms of his view of religion, see the reviews by Charles Davis and John Robertson, *Religious Studies Review* (Apr. 1985): 65–70, and 148–51. See also the critiques by Marion Przelecki and Stanislaw Rainke, *Dialectics and Humanism* (winter 1986): 143–55. For a general discussion of Polish reactions to Kolakowski's thought, see Heidrich, *Kolakowski*, pp. 336–60.
302. Kolakowski, *Religion*, pp. 175–76.
303. "Modernity on Endless Trial," p. 9.
304. See Bondi, "Kolakowski: Grundmuster und Exempel," pp. 13–17.
305. See Jean-Francois Bouthors, "Entretien avec Leszek Kolakowski. Le Danger d'effondrement de la Communauté," *Esprit* (July 1995): 155. For Kolakowski's views of the contemporary religious scene, see Adam Michnik, "Communism, the Church, and Witches: An Interview with Leszek Kolakowski," *Centennial Review* (winter 1993): 13–38.

306. "The Revenge of the Sacred in Secular Culture," *Modernity*, pp. 70–71.

307. See Ronald Beiner's review of *Modernity on Endless Trial* in *History of the Human Sciences*, V, no. 3, pp. 65–70.

Conclusion

1. For the relationship of Marxism to the Promethean myth, see Hans Blumenberg, *The Work of Myth*, tr. by Robert Wallace (Cambridge, Mass., M.I.T. Press, 1985), pp. 584–94.

2. Leszek Kolakowski, *Freedom, Fame, Lying, and Betrayal: Essays on Everyday Life*, tr. by Agnieska Kolakowska (Boulder, Colo., Westview Press, 1999), p. 13.

3. Ibid., pp. 52, 114.

4. Ibid., pp. 37, 17–24.

5. Ibid., pp. 47–49.

6. Ibid., pp. 97, 117, 123.

7. Ibid., pp. 37, 123.

8. Ibid., p. 92.

9. Kolakowski's intellectual development resembles, in a number of ways, that of Alasdair MacIntyre. Both thinkers broke with Stalinism in the mid-1950s and attempted to formulate a humanistic Marxism. Compare, for example, MacIntyre's essay "Notes from the Moral Wilderness," written in 1958, and reprinted in *The MacIntyre Reader*, ed. by Kelvin Knight (Notre Dame, Ind., University of Notre Dame Press, 1998), pp. 31–49, with Kolakowski's essays in the late 1950s. Both went on, after their break with Marxism, to reaffirm much of the European tradition, particularly the "virtues" or moral skills acquired through participation in the practices of a community. Compare MacIntyre's discussion of the virtues in *After Virtue* (Notre Dame, Ind., University of Notre Dame Press, 1981), esp. chs. 14 and 15, with Kolakowski's essay "On Virtue," in *Freedom, Fame, Lying and Betrayal*, pp. 47–52. MacIntyre, to be sure, went much further than Kolakowski in reclaiming the Christian tradition by embracing the Thomistic synthesis of Aristotle and Augustine. For both thinkers, moreover, rational inquiry required the preunderstandings, or the mythical grounding, of a particular tradition. And both traced the modern cultural or epistemological crisis back to the process through which secular reason sought to free itself from a religious foundation and achieve autonomy. Compare Kolakowski's discussion of the rupture between faith and reason in "The Illusion of Demythologization," pp. 95–99, with MacIntyre's account in *Whose Justice? Which Rationality?* (Notre Dame, Ind., University of Notre Dame Press, 1988), chs. 18 and 20. The most striking difference between the two figures has been MacIntyre's pursuit of a coherent world view, while Kolakowski has accepted the unfinished nature, and the inconsistencies, of the human quest for meaning.

10. The distinction between the ideological in its narrow, rational sense, and the "more elemental" mythic is developed by Ben Halpern, "Myth and Ideology in Modern Usage," *History and Theory* 2 (1961): 129–49.

11. For the application of Hans Blumenberg's notion of "reoccupation" to Marxism, see Ernesto Laclau, *New Reflections on the Revolution of Our Time* (London, Verso, 1990), pp. 74–78.

12. For discussions of this outcome, see Karl Dietrich Bracher, *The Age of Ide-*

ologies: A History of Political Thought in the Twentieth Century, tr. by Ewald Osers (London, Weidenfeld and Nicolson, 1984), pp. 3–6, 31–33, 110–11, 125–29.

13. See Ferenc Fehér, "The Status of Hope at the End of the Century," in Michael Crozier and Peter Murphy, eds., *The Left in Search of a Center* (Chicago, University of Illinois Press, 1996), pp. 31–42; and Agnes Heller and Ferenc Fehér, *The Grandeur and Twilight of Radical Universalism* (New Brunswick, N.J., Transaction, 1991), pp. 1–6, 551–68.

14. Which is not to deny the continuing presence, as Kolakowski observed, of mythic elements in Marxism and in any ideology or social theory.

15. A major figure in this effort, the German theologian Johann Metz, has reaffirmed a Christian eschatology, in part, through a direct engagement with the critical theorists. See Johann Baptist Metz, *Faith in History and Society: Toward a Practical Fundamental Theology*, tr. by David Smith (New York, Seabury, 1980). Metz found, in the most visionary member of the Frankfurt School, Ernst Bloch, an "apocalyptic wisdom" that had "long been closed to Christians." Metz accepted much of the Marxist critique of capitalistic society, targeting, in particular, the "exchange principle" as a regulating principle at the expense of all other values. And he argued that the "new middle class man," preoccupied with his own interests, had privatized Christianity and thus robbed it of its authentic concepts of freedom and justice, and its critical social force. Where Marxists, however, had placed responsibility for the alienations and oppressions under capitalism on "alibi subjects," the propertied classes, Metz reinstated Christian notions of general sin and guilt, together with the call for personal conversion. In Christian praxis, the imitation of Christ, Metz identified a new "post-bourgeois subject." To reclaim the Christian eschatological attitude, that of "constant expectation," was to break the "grip of prevailing consciousness" and make it possible to redefine reality and truth. For the above quotations, see pp. 169, 28–29, 44–45, 69–82, 200.

The interaction between the German "political theologians" and the critical theorists has continued in the work of Metz's student Helmut Peukert. In his book *Science, Action and Fundamental Theology, Toward a Theology of Communicative Action*, tr. by James Bohman (Cambridge, Mass., M.I.T. Press, 1984), Peukert accepts Habermas's theory of "communicative action" as a convincing approach to the problems of modern society. But he argues that a close examination of the theory reveals aporias, particularly a failure to justify its normative core—"equality, mutuality and solidarity"—which require, therefore, a "theological foundation." The "eschatological tradition" embodied in Jesus fulfills, according to Peukert, the communicative ideal of Habermas. See esp. pp. 205–27. For a discussion of the moral limitations of Habermas's philosophy as well as his recent "more conciliatory attitude toward religion," see Peter Dews, *The Limits of Disenchantment: Essays in Contemporary Philosophy* (London, Verso, 1995), pp. 9–14, 196–210.

16. See Jacques Derrida, *Specters of Marxism: The State of the Debt, the Work of Mourning, and the New International*, tr. by Peggy Kanuf (New York, Routledge, 1994), esp. pp. 37, 59–60, 166–69. For commentaries by Marxists, see Michael Sprinker, ed., *Ghostly Demarcations* (New York, Verso, 1999). Note esp. the essay by Werner Hamacher, "Lingua Amissa: The Messianism of Commodity Language and Derrida's 'Specters of Marx,'" pp. 168–212.

17. See "The Utopian Prospect" in Frank E. Manuel and Fritzie P. Manuel, *Utopian Thought in the Western World* (Cambridge, Mass., Harvard University Press, 1979), pp. 801–14.

18. For pessimistic views of the state of utopianism, see Krishan Kumar, *Utopia and Anti-Utopia in Modern Times* (New York, Basil Blackwell, 1987), esp. pp. 419–24; and Russell Jacoby, *The End of Utopia: Politics and Culture in an Age of Apathy* (New York, Basic Books, 1999). For a more optimistic view, see Ruth Levitas, *The Concept of Utopia* (Syracuse, Syracuse University Press, 1990), pp. 179–200.

19. See Frederick L. Polak, "Utopia and Cultural Renewal"; and Paul Tillich, "Critique and Justification of Utopia." Both essays can be found in Frank E. Manuel, ed., *Utopias and Utopian Thought* (Boston, Beacon Press, 1967). The Manuels, Polak, Tillich, Jacoby, and our three disenchanted Marxist intellectuals all seem to agree on the need for utopian visions while recognizing their dangers.

Index